# China's Finance and Trade

# China's Finance and Trade

## A POLICY READER

EDITED BY
Gordon Bennett

Routledge
Taylor & Francis Group
LONDON AND NEW YORK

First published 1978 by M.E. Sharpe and THE MACMILLAN PRESS LTD

Reissued 2018 by Routledge
2 Park Square, Milton Park, Abingdon, Oxon OX14 4RN
711 Third Avenue, New York, NY 10017, USA

*Routledge is an imprint of the Taylor & Francis Group, an informa business*



A Library of Congress record exists under LC control number: 77099080

ISBN 13: 978-1-138-04506-4 (hbk)
ISBN 13: 978-1-138-04507-1 (pbk)
ISBN 13: 978-1-315-17215-6 (ebk)

To

My father, James Lippincott Bennett

He was not merely a chip of
the old block, but the old
block itself.

— Edmund Burke

# Contents

# Preface

The two disciplines of political science and economics each have distinctive interests in the Chinese development experience. Thus readers from each discipline should discover appropriately distinctive uses for the documentary excerpts assembled here. Political scientists see in China under Communist rule an unpredictable despotism moved by numerous democratic and progressive impulses. The political chemistry by which the Chinese manage to join these apparently contrary currents they find intriguing. Economists see in contemporary China a case of a developing country that has attacked market forces with a vengeance, but also has created enough public authority to implement a reasonably coherent development program. Chinese efforts to reconcile these apparently contradictory impulses they find just as intriguing.

For students of politics the documents in this collection offer an opportunity to analyze a broad policy area — finance and commerce — in search of specific mechanisms by which dictatorship and popular will are both given expression in political life. The Chinese have divided their administration into six overarching systems, one of which is "finance-trade." Narrowing the scope of investigation to one policy system like finance-trade is a helpful way to break down Chinese politics as a whole into a less complex analytical part. Other ways, of course, include selection of a particular region, institution, decision or period. The relative virtues of "public policy" approaches to comparative analysis are discussed briefly in the Introduction. For students of economics these documents offer an opportunity to match Chinese policy declarations against ongoing traditions of economic theory, most of which regard Chinese-style "command economies" as irrational. The central issue, I suspect, is the degree to which Chinese dedication to "external" criteria beyond material progress invites the "irrational" judgment from critics whose own criteria are more narrowly tied to GNP accounting or to enterprise efficiency in terms of inputs and outputs with prices. President Carter's Secretary of Commerce, Juanita Kreps, announced in October 1977 that her Department would soon commence publication of a "social performance index" for American corporations. This index would reveal corporate performance with respect to such social needs as minority hiring, purchasing from minority-operated companies, environmental controls, product testing, and responsiveness to consumer complaints. This index was being developed in cooperation with the Business Roundtable, a lobby formed in 1974 with a membership of the top executives of the 180 largest American corporations. By pursuing profit motives alone, said Secretary Kreps, corporations were not doing themselves a favor because such behavior only led to costly regulatory schemes; ignoring social needs might actually increase costs and reduce profits.[1] In Chinese policy, unlike the American scene portrayed so vividly by Secretary Kreps, "social needs" criteria appear as basic values of the party in power rather than as tactics adopted by enterprises to avoid costly regulation.

My own interest in the politics of economic policy in China has led me into the finance-trade area largely because it has been slighted. Much more and better literature is available on other sectors — agriculture, small rural industries, industrial management, and labor and work incentives. Reports by recent visitors to China reflect the situation well. Most delegations have given all their attention to agricultural production in communes, "walking on two legs" in choice of techniques, factory organization, and pay scales. Hardly anyone has sought out a branch of the People's Bank, a supply and marketing cooperative, a wholesale market, an import-export corporation, a tax office, or a finance-trade oriented middle school or college for a site visit. By contrast, the PRC's own technical and propaganda publishing outlets give noticeable attention to this system.

Almost all the excerpts have been selected from Chinese Economic Studies, edited since its inception in 1967 by Professor George C. Wang and published by M. E. Sharpe, Inc., formerly International Arts and Sciences Press. Only in a few instances where I thought very significant material for this volume had not appeared in Chinese Economic Studies have I drawn upon other sources. Since Chinese policy literature tends to be very repetitive, I have decided to include here only unique, substantive passages. The repetitiveness is an interesting phenomenon in its own right as a device for inculcating important political norms, but for present purposes I have endeavored to avoid most of it.

My first acknowledgment must be to Professor Wang who made all the initial selections for the journal and supervised their translation. Then I would like to single out the energies of my editor at M. E. Sharpe, Douglas Merwin. Himself a scholar of classical China, Doug is responsible for initiating the China Book Project. He has offered me constant criticism and encouragement throughout the design and execution of this work. Finally I have words of loving gratitude for my wife, Carol. Not only did she lend a substantive hand in her capacity as economist, she also suggested many editorial improvements in her capacity as renaissance woman. Nonetheless, stubborn responsibility for what remains is mine alone.

Note

1. The New York Times, October 20, 1977. On the Business Roundtable, see "When Executives Lobby, Congress Listens," Christian Science Monitor, October 7, 1977.

# Introduction

## A Case for "Public Policy" Approaches to China's Finance and Trade

The purpose I hope to advance in compiling these documentary excerpts on Chinese financial and commercial issues is to encourage application of "public policy" approaches to the study of Chinese politics. They have gained much currency in political science in recent years, and they promise some distinctive contributions. Their emphasis has been upon explaining substantive policy outcomes instead of explaining institutional arrangements, such as elite civilian-military relations, or political behaviors, such as campaign contributions. The analytical advantages of focusing on just one "policy subsystem" such as welfare, defense, or urban transit are several. First, for the policy area chosen, the analyst is more likely to see how various parts of a political system — culture and ideology, public opinion and constituency pressures, interest groups, representative bodies, administrative and regulatory agencies, courts, political parties, executive leadership and others — interact. Second, one is likely to be more sensitive to unique actors in the policy subsystem (professional scientists in the case of science policy, or parents in the case of education policy). In American politics, for example, we find that politicians often are willing to defer to doctors on medical matters, but rarely are they willing to leave war to the generals. Third, one is better able to appreciate unique technical characteristics of different policy areas. With respect to the arts, for example, legislatures may do as they will, boldly creating or heartlessly eliminating entire programs. With respect to government intervention in the economy, to the contrary, legislatures are not so free. Even a small change in banking regulations may set undesired repercussions in motion throughout the economy. Finally, one is more likely to look beyond single moments of decision to bring into view as well implementation and evaluation of policy. In short, as public studies accumulate, the gain to political theory should be our capacity to specify "policy area" or "subsystem" as a variable in more refined explanations of "the policy process."

The new focus on policy studies has left some political scientists less than enthusiastic. Their misgivings seem rooted in the fear that political science might decline as a scientific discipline if it is expanded beyond its present boundaries onto the turf of other traditional disciplines. Moreover the aspirations of many behaviorists and others to achieve a "value free science" might suffer a severe setback as political scientists achieve visibility advising normatively what they think policy should be. As one prominent researcher has framed the problem: "What is likely to be the net gain or loss from more study of policy contents for the theoretical sophistication and empirical validity of political science's special body of knowledge?" His answer:

> In sum, our professional skills and utility depend upon the scientific quality of our special body of knowledge. Hence, our primary obligation as scholars and teachers is to improve that knowledge. If frequent trips to Washington or the statehouse or city hall keep most of our best and most creative minds from that nuclear task, both political science and the students and policy-makers who hope to profit from it will be much the poorer.[1]

This Comtian position has been assailed from Left reaches of the discipline as being responsible for the failure of political science to study "in a radically critical spirit, either the great crises of the day or the inherent weaknesses of the American political system."[2] It also has been assailed from a phenomenological perspective as bringing the danger that reality will be carved into such fine analytical categories that the meaning of the whole is lost.

Another prominent political scientist sees a gap between "the sciences" and "the policy complex" which he feels might be narrowed in three ways: alternation of academics between university positions and governmental administrative positions; regular seminars or conferences between social scientists and administrators that go beyond the normal consultant role; and multidisciplinary teams working collectively on policy problems.[3] And recently, multidisciplinary programs have been achieving a new legitimacy within universities themselves. Personally I believe it is not risky to predict that public policy approaches are here to stay. They should result in useful new findings and contribute a significant new literature.

After the legitimacy of any policy approach is accepted, however, one key problem still remains. How much technical understanding of the substance of policy do political scientists need to apply their approach effectively? And how do they attain it? The problem may not be a serious one in some areas. Analysts of housing policy, for example, should not find it difficult to master the essentials of building trades unionism, mortgage markets, or the impact of prefabricated dwellings upon the construction industry's cost structure. But analysts of energy policy face much more formidable technical obstacles related to questions of the size and distribution of oil and natural gas reserves, exploration and extraction costs, the effect of government policies on the operation of the international oil cartel, manufacturers' and utilities' flexibility in substituting coal for liquid or gaseous fuels, and the technology and costs of developing solar collection or nuclear fission as alternative energy sources. Where required technical knowledge is low, as in the case of housing issues, political scientists probably can self-educate themselves sufficiently within a reasonable portion of the time set aside for a research project. Where required technical knowledge is high, however, as in the case of energy issues, either they must plan to devote considerable time to relevant economic and engineering courses or they must plan to work as part of a research team that includes active colleagues from those other disciplines. If political analysts' technical comprehension falls short, the danger is they may be prone to misinterpret a policy outcome as the result of the exercise of power rather than as the result of some logical necessity having no relation to political competition. Or they may be prone to misinterpret the failure of an issue to arise in the first place as the result of behind-the-scenes maneuvering by a power elite instead of as a technical inevitability.[4]

My selection of excerpts from Chinese financial and commercial policy documents of the 1960s and 1970s is intended as a first step toward incorporating these two substantive areas into the public policy literature on China. Other than chapters in the comprehensive book by Audrey Donnithorne and a small number of monographs by other economists such as Dwight Perkins and Nicholas Lardy, the finance-trade sector so far has commanded relatively little attention.[5] Useful parallel analyses of other policy areas include (but are scarcely exhausted by) the studies of agricultural organization by Parris Chang and Richard Baum, of industrial management by Stephen Andors, of work incentives by Carl Riskin and Charles Hoffmann, of welfare by Joyce Kallgren, of medical care by David Lampton, of education by Susan Shirk, of the transfer of educated young people from cities to farms by Thomas Bernstein, of national minorities by June Dreyer, of military affairs by Harvey Nelson, and of foreign policy by John Gittings and Allen Whiting.[6] Most of these are not cast in the "public policy" mold explicitly but the essence is there in reality, and the next step simply is to bring it to the surface. Since this step yet remains to be taken, I will confine my own discussion below to eleven dimensions of public policy that are sometimes reflected in Chinese documents. No such list can ever be complete since thorough examination of a policy area may cross-cut almost every other interpretive question guiding political research. But at very least all eleven dimensions can be applied to some degree to evaluate contemporary Chinese economic documents. For several reasons, perhaps because pertinent documentary passages fail to contain information of sufficient richness, or perhaps because the investigation is focused on a single problem, one might reasonably choose to work with only a few dimensions, or with even just one.

## Analytical Dimensions of Public Policy

1. Content. What is the substance of the policy? How has it changed over time? Which points are central and which points peripheral? Which points have uniform content mandated and which points contain only general guidelines, allowing content to vary among implementing localities and units? Which points are explicit in the documentation, and which must be inferred by investigators?

Where investigators must infer content from outside sources, what specifics appear in the massive publicity given to "advanced producers," "models," "pacesetters," or other progressive experiences? What historical antecedents occur that might offer clues to the thinking of current policy-makers? What contents are negatively deducible from the unacceptable paths specified in charges against "capitalist-roaders," "revisionists," or "ultra-Leftists"? Does the policy area have logical alternatives such that failing to take one path necessitates taking the other one(s)?

2. Source. Who seems to have proposed the new policy? Who has taken visible steps to promote it? Who stands to benefit the most? Who stands to benefit the least, or even to suffer loss? Is the proposal part of a long-run design? Is there evidence of research and planning behind it? Or is it a quick-fix solution to an immediately pressing problem? At about what point in time was the proposal included on the "agenda" for public action? Who helped bring that about?

3. Constituency. Is the policy's constituency (groups and institutions who benefit from it) organized or coordinated or represented in any sense? Might any sort of "interest group" operate? Are other "interests" evident who appear to oppose the policy? Is special pleading ever legitimate? That is, at the different stages of study, debate, decision, implementation and evaluation of the policy, do any forms of self-serving adversary behavior appear to be tolerated? Correspondingly, what forms of organization or coalition, and what tactics of advocacy, by interested parties are clearly proscribed? Within authoritative bodies, and most importantly within the Chinese Communist Party, which interests are represented best?

4. Gratification. Does the policy distribute tangible goods or benefits (economic inducements) such as new investment and construction, higher income, greater availability of consumer goods, more educational opportunity, or better medical care? Or does it provide mainly symbolic gratification (social or psychological inducements) such as heightened self-esteem, recognition of parochial loyalties and sensibilities (regional, ethnic minority, professional, etc.) as legitimate, higher status (perhaps in group terms), publicity as a progressive experience for others to emulate, political security, hope for the future, or heightened feelings of national pride? Does the policy only address people's material wants or does it go beyond that, through use of appropriate ideological metaphors and cultural symbols, to appeal to people's nonmaterial aspirations as well?

5. Benefit. Is the nature of the benefit such that, quite apart from purely political desires of the government or ruling party to exercise control, intervention by public authority can be justified on the ground of improving efficient allocation in optimal quantities and at optimal prices? Four properties cover most cases where efficient allocation through private markets is quite impossible. (1) Collective consumption. If a good must be supplied to everyone to be supplied at all (national defense, flouridation of drinking water, airport) then the market cannot allocate. When provision of a collective good relies upon voluntary contributions, many "free riders" do not shoulder their share of the cost burden, as happens with public broadcasting in the United States (KMFA in Austin estimates that 10 percent of their listeners contribute). (2) Externalities. If some costs are unpaid by either the producer or the consumer in a transaction, then the market cannot allocate optimally. Each cell in the table below gives an instance of each of four basic types of externality:

| | Action by Producer | Action by Consumer |
|---|---|---|
| Social benefit enjoyed by the public (people not directly involved in the transaction) | Investment (brings jobs, trade for local merchants, higher tax base, philanthropy, etc.) | Vaccination |
| Social cost suffered by the public | Pollution | Smoking |

For example, were smokers required to pay the social costs of their habit — costs such as provision of ashtrays, provision of separate smoking areas in public places, removal of cigarette burns, and extinguishing fires started by smoldering butts — then the cost per pack would be several times the present cost, and far fewer packs would be sold. Thus the present price, which takes no account of these social costs, allocates far too many cigarettes. (3) Natural monopoly. If the entry cost is extremely high, and/or marginal cost is low or declining (phone company, highway bridge), then the market cannot keep prices low because no competition will appear. (4) High collection cost. If the cost of collecting payment from each customer is high relative to the value of the good (city streets, police patrols), then the market will allocate only at much higher cost than if the good were supplied publicly.

If a policy will affect the supply of benefits sharing any (or several) of these four properties, then some form of public intervention must substitute for market forces if efficient allocation is to be approximated.

6. Linkage. Is the policy tied to other policies in patterned ways? Does it appear to be treated as part of a package? Does support for the policy tend to parallel support for other policies? Might the policy question be a specific instance of a more general choice? Have "two lines" been articulated on the issue? Do connections drawn between the policy question and the "two lines" appear real or contrived? What theoretical issues in the tradition of Marxism-Leninism-Mao Tsetung Thought does the policy raise? Does it seem to have become involved with factional competition or other raw power struggle?

7. Arena. One imaginative contribution recently is Michel Oksenberg's proposal that we separate different political "arenas" for purposes of analysis.

> In essence, Chinese politics involves the relations among and the activities within five types of policymaking arenas: (1) the domain under Mao's direct control; (2) the policy-specifying bodies (the Party Center, the Military Affairs Commission, the State Council) under the direct control of Mao's chief associates; (3) the highly institutionalized bureaucracies (Party, government, army, mass organizations); (4) the ad hoc campaign arenas; and (5) local communities (communes, factories, urban neighborhoods, schools,

and other "basic units"). Each type of arena is distinguished by its institutions, its values, its power game, its communications network, and its direct linkages to various sectors of society.[7]

For analysis of a public policy, then, one might wish to try and identify the arena(s) in and among which controversies surrounding the policy are resolved.

8. International Dimensions. How are the content of the policy, as well as supporting or opposing arguments, influenced by relevant experiences abroad? Do Chinese policy-makers only take cognizance of experience in other socialist countries? Are their sources of information adequate?

9. Latitude for Public Initiative. To what extent are present authorities bound by past decisions? By financial limitations? By other constraints? What range of choice actually is open to policy-makers? Is this question itself a bone of contention?

10. Administration. Who is responsible for implementation of the policy? Do supporters of amendments or forces of resistance make themselves felt at this stage? How? With what results? How active do supporters of the policy continue to be?

11. Evaluation. How is the policy's effectiveness evaluated? Do the evaluations become part of further politics?

## Public Policy and Comparative Politics

Once studies addressing these questions accumulate, making possible the introduction of "policy area" or "subsystem" as a variable into analyses of policy processes in single countries, then meaningful cross-national comparisons of public policy-making can be written that include this variable. As the state of the art has progressed so far, cross-national policy studies mainly have sought to compare how policy outputs vary under different types of regimes. General examples include Pryor's *Public Expenditures in Capitalist and Communist Nations* and Groth's comparison of nine policy areas under "democracies" and "autocracies."[8] But most researchers have chosen to emphasize only a single policy area in only a few countries. Their findings typically take the form: government A spends a greater proportion of GNP (or per-capita GNP) than government B on output X for reasons $R_1$, $R_2$, $R_3$, ... $R_n$. One problem with these first generation studies is that output X normally is measured in simple aggregate statistical terms without regard to each country's prior performance in the policy area, its performance in other policy areas, or its sensitiveity to the pressures of organized constituencies. Another problem is that $R_n$ always is too large. That is, so many differences between countries A and B exist that the factors responsible for variation in policy area X cannot be isolated.

Findings at a more advanced stage of comparative policy studies, a stage beyond direct analysis of simple aggregate outputs, should take different and more refined forms. After an accumulation of single-country studies, we should be able to determine, for example, whether policy areas with large client publics (such as welfare or education) are debated in more ideological terms than policy areas with relatively small attentive publics (such as defense or basic research). Or perhaps we can determine whether the relationship found holds for some categories of regimes but not others (for example, for postindustrial but not developing regimes, for liberal democratic but not authoritarian ones, or for autonomous but not dependent ones). That is, a joining of research on regime types with research on different policy areas in single countries should yield significant empirical relationships. First, however, must come the spadework of single-country studies.

Notes

1. Austin Ranney, "The Study of Policy Content: A Framework for Choice," in Political Science and Public Policy, ed. by Austin Ranney (Chicago: Markham Publishing Company, 1968), pp. 3 and 20-21. This volume is based on a conference sponsored by The Committee on Governmental and Legal Processes of the Social Science Research Council.

2. Caucus for a New Political Science, Statement of Objectives, quoted in Ranney, Political Science and Public Policy, pp. 18-19n.

3. David B. Truman, "The Social Sciences: Maturity, Relevance, and the Problem of Training," in Ranney, Political Science and Public Policy, p. 284.

4. See Peter Bachrach and Morton S. Baratz, Power and Poverty: Theory and Practice (New York: Oxford University Press, 1970).

5. Audrey Donnithorne, China's Economic System (London: George Allen

and Unwin, 1967), especially chaps. 11 through 17. Dwight H. Perkins, Market Control and Planning in Communist China (Cambridge: Harvard University Press, 1966). Nicholas R. Lardy, "Centralization and Decentralization in China's Fiscal Management," The China Quarterly, No. 61 (March 1975), 33-34.

6. Parris H. Chang, Power and Policy in China (University Park: Pennsylvania State University Press, 1975). Stephen Andors, China's Industrial Revolution: Politics, Planning, and Management, 1949 to the Present (New York: Pantheon Books, 1977). Carl Riskin, "Mao and Motivation: Work Incentive Practices in China," in China's Uninterrupted Revolution from 1840 to the Present, ed. by Victor Nee and James Peck (New York: Pantheon, 1975), pp. 415-461. Charles Hoffmann, The Chinese Worker (Albany: State University of New York Press, 1974). Joyce Kallgren, "Welfare and Chinese Industrial Workers: Post Cultural Revolution Prospects and Problems" (Xerox, 24 pp.). David M. Lampton, Health, Conflict, and the Chinese Political System (Ann Arbor: Michigan Papers in Chinese Studies, No. 18, 1974). Susan Shirk, The High School Experience in China (forthcoming). Thomas P. Bernstein, Up to the Mountains and Down to the Villages: The Transfer of Youth from Urban to Rural China (New Haven: Yale University Press, 1977). June Dreyer, China's Forty Millions (Cambridge: Harvard University Press, 1976). Harvey Nelsen, The Chinese Military System: An Organizational Study of the PLA, 1966-1976 (Boulder: Westview Press, 1977). John Gittings, The World and China, 1922-1972 (New York: Harper and Row, 1974). Allen S. Whiting, The Chinese Calculus of Deterrence: India and Indochina (Ann Arbor: University of Michigan Press, 1975).

7. Michel Oksenberg, "The Chinese Policy Process and the Public Health Issue: An Arena Approach," Studies in Comparative Communism, VII, 4 (Winter 1974), 376-77.

8. Frederic Pryor, Public Expenditures in Capitalist and Communist Nations (Homewood: Richard D. Irwin, 1968). Alexander J. Groth, Comparative Politics: A Distributive Approach (New York: Macmillan, 1971).

PART ONE

# General Economic Line

All policy-making in China is tied closely to ideology. Out of the theoretical tradition of Marxism-Leninism and the concrete practice of the Chinese revolution has been derived the Thought of Mao Tse-tung, described in Chinese statements as a scientific guide to correct action. As expressed in Mao's widely noted "mass line" style of leadership:

> In all the practical work of our Party, all correct leadership is necessarily from the masses, to the masses. This means: take the ideas of the masses (scattered and unsystematic ideas) and concentrate them (through study turn them into concentrated and systematic ideas), then go to the masses and propagate and explain these ideas until the masses embrace them as their own, hold fast to them and translate them into action, and test the correctness of these ideas in such action. Then once again concentrate ideas from the masses and once again take them to the masses so that the ideas are persevered in and carried through. And so on over and over again in an endless spiral, with the ideas becoming more correct, more vital and richer each time. Such is the Marxist-Leninist theory of knowledge, or methodology....[1]

Amid China's great diversity of nationalities, regions, climates local economies, generations, groups, political factions and intellectual orientations, Mao sought to make possible purposeful and effective governmental action on the basis of ideological consensus. To accomplish this feat he prevailed upon the Central Committee of the Chinese Communist Party to arrive at a hierarchy of correct "lines" (lu-hsien) and "directions" (fang-chen) which implementing localities and units would strive to study and follow. Political debate was to be restricted to the mass line process before legislation. Arguments advanced afterward against the officially adopted lines and directions would be denounced as incorrect "deviations" to the Right or to the Left, and people making such arguments would either be regarded patronizingly as "hoodwinked" members of the masses or actually be attacked as "capitalist-roaders" or "enemies of the people." A primary instrumental value was to "unify our thought" (t'ung-i ssu-hsiang). Consequently, differences over policy questions in China have been elevated rather easily to differences over ideological formulations believed to be favorable to one policy outcome or another.

In May 1958 a "general line for socialist construction ("going all out, aiming high and achieving greater, faster, better, and more economical results in building socialism") succeeded the previous "general line for the period of transition to socialism" ("simultaneous development of socialist revolution and socialist construction") dating from 1952.[2] As of 1977 the "general line" (tsung lu-hsien) for socialist construction was still in effect. More specific economic lines and directions in 1977, early in the era of Chairman Hua Kuo-feng's leadership, are expressed in Hua's report to the Eleventh Party Congress:

> The change in our country's economic situation since the smashing of the "gang of four" proves conclusively that tremendous power can be generated once we grasp the major class struggle to expose and criticize the gang and grasp the revolutionary mass movements to learn from Taching in industry and from Tachai in agriculture. We must combine this struggle and these movements more closely, conduct them in a more deepgoing way, build our country independently and with the initiative in our own hands, through self-reliance, hard struggle, diligence and thrift, be prepared against war and natural disasters, do everything for the people and push the national economy forward. We should work hard for several years and, in pursuance of the original plan, turn one-third of our country's enterprises into Taching-type enterprises and one-third of our counties into Tachai-type counties in the period of the Fifth Five-Year Plan, in accordance with the respective requirements set down....
>
> To push the national economy forward, we must conscientiously carry out the general line ... and the complete set of policies known as walking on two legs, and we must bring the country's entire economy into the orbit of planned, proportionate and high-speed socialist development, take agriculture as the foundation and industry as the leading factor, and achieve

> coordinated growth and an all-round leap forward in agriculture, light industry, heavy industry and other sectors.... We must build an independent and fairly comprehensive industrial and economic system in our country by 1980. By then farming must be basically mechanized, considerable increases in production must be made in agriculture, forestry, animal husbandry, side-line production and fishery, and the collective economy of the people's communes must be further consolidated and developed....
>
> Among the broad masses the communist attitude toward labor should be energetically encouraged through ideological education, while in economic policy the socialist principle of "from each according to his ability, to each according to his work" should be upheld and collective welfare gradually expanded. The livelihood of the people should be improved step by step on the basis of increased production. The life of the Chinese people is far better than before liberation, but the standard of living is still low.[3]

Specific policies, however much they might vary from place to place, are all supposed to conform to these common standards.

The overall performance of the Chinese economy under Communist Party rule has been impressive, even while experiencing dramatic ups and downs. China's GNP has grown at an annual rate of approximately 6 percent in real terms since 1952, by when the Communist Party had consolidated its takeover of government and had begun to collect fairly reliable statistics. The mid-1950s were an up-period, benefiting from the return of domestic peace to the country after decades of war and revolution and from much Soviet financial and technical assistance. A down-period followed during the late 1950s through the mid-1960s as the Soviet Union withdrew its aid, severe weather struck three years in succession, and adjustments had to be made in the ambitious programs of the 1958-59 Great Leap Forward. Some further economic disruption occurred during the opening stages of the Cultural Revolution. Another up-period began in later stages of the Cultural Revolution and has been reinforced by new imports of advanced technology, some of it from the United States after President Nixon's visit in 1972, and by heightened investment in sectors directly supporting agriculture (including small industries in rural areas). Some leading estimates of growth rates broken down by period are presented in Table 1.

Table 1

Estimates of Average Annual Growth Rates in China by Sector and by Period

| | 1952-59 | 1959-66 | 1966-74 | 1952-74 |
|---|---|---|---|---|
| GDP (Eckstein, p. 225) | 10.5% | 1.6% | 6.5% | 6.2% |
| Industrial Production (Eckstein, p. 219) Official Chinese series reconstructed by R. M. Field, N. Lardy and J. P. Emerson (Reassessment, p. 170) | 23.1 | 0.2 | 9.1 | 11.4 |
| R. M. Field estimate (Reassessment, pp. 149-50) | 18.0 | 4.0 | 8.0 | 11.0 |
| Grain Output (Eckstein, p. 210) | 2.2 (1952-57) | 6.0 (1963-67) | <2.0 | 2.0 |

Sources: Alexander Eckstein, China's Economic Revolution (New York: Cambridge University Press, 1977). China: A Reassessment of the Economy, a compendium of papers submitted to the Joint Economic Committee, Congress of the United States, 94th Congress, 1st Session (July 10, 1975).

In comparative terms, according to one estimate, China had achieved by 1975 a GNP of about $237 billion (16 percent of the U.S.'s, and 30 percent of the USSR's). Thus China, with over 20 percent of the world's population, generates about 4 percent of the world's income. Assuming a population then of 850 million, per-capita income in 1975 would have been roughly $280.[4] Looking ahead, a recent United Nations study makes several projections for a region defined as "Asia, Centrally Planned" (China, Korea, Vietnam, and Mongolia). The figures derived in Table 2 are my own calculations for China based on the assumption that 93 percent of aggregate quantities in this region are accounted for by China alone.

Such projections never are intended as firm and confident predictions of the future, only as estimates of what is possible given the record to date. China might do much better than the projected performance, or it might do much worse. Much of what happens depends on the government's policy decisions and on its ability to put those decisions into effect. In economist

Table 2

Chinese Growth Projections through the Year 2000
(All dollar figures are in projected current U.S. dollars)

| | 1970 | 1980 | 1990 | 2000 |
|---|---|---|---|---|
| GDP (billion $) | 121 | 208 | 381 | 751 |
| Population (million) | 728 | 859 | 984 | 1,103 |
| GDP/capita ($) | 166 | 242 | 387 | 680 |
| Calories/person/day | 2,100 | 2,100 | 2,200 | 2,500 |
| Investment level (billion $) | 10 | 27 | 62 | 148 |
| Trade volume (imports plus exports, billion $) | 3 | 6 | 13 | 26 |

Source: Calculated from Wassily Leontief et al., The Future of the World Economy: A United Nations Study (New York: Oxford University Press, 1977), p. 91. The numerical results from which my calculations are made are based on Leontief's "scenario X," which assumes that for the rest of the century for all developing countries, GDP will grow at 7.2 percent, population will grow at 2.3 percent, and GDP/capita will grow at 4.9 percent, and that by the year 2000 the income ratio of developed to developing countries will be 769/100. This scenario is associated with the goals of the International Development Strategy and the changes in the conditions of development envisaged in the Declaration on the Establishment of a New International Economic Order (Leontief, pp. 30-31).

Alexander Eckstein's analysis, public policy choices facing the Chinese leadership have revolved about two basic issues: the rate and character of economic growth; and the role of decentralized decision-making (including markets in allocating resources. To explore these issues further, Eckstein breaks them down into five sets of policy problems:

1. Role of material incentives in allocating resources
   a. Role of prices and wages (as opposed to physical output targets) as allocators
   b. Role of markets in allocating goods, services and factors, most particularly the role of commodity and labor markets in resource allocation
   c. Scope of private plots in agriculture
   d. What wage system should prevail in the economy;
2. Desired rate of investment (which is linked to the incentives problem because more investment requires more savings and less consumption);

3. Desired pattern of investment (which also is linked to the incentives problem because inflationary pressures would build up if incomes rose ahead of consumer goods supply);
4. Role of professionalism and technical know-how in the production process and in economic management (planners, economists and technocrats tend to favor a greater scope for the market mechanism, private plots and population control policies, and generally favor a less political approach to economic policy problems);
5. Population policies.[5]

Countless words have been written in the West about "the Chinese model" as author after author has endeavored to abstract from multitudes of Chinese statements some coherent "strategy" in force during each period of the People's Republic. Some of these reconstructions are quite scholarly, and for some purposes they are very useful. Thinking only in terms of such externally imposed concepts, however, carries the danger of yielding too coherent a picture, as if the leadership in Peking had consciously "rejected" one path to "choose" a logical alternative. In fact, the array of policies followed during any one period seems to emerge out of criticisms of the results obtained from policies of the immediately previous period. Some policy continuities are evident across periods, such as the commitment to total collectivization of grain production. Some swings back and forth are evident from period to period as with incentive systems applied to agricultural production, and with the permissible scope of rural free markets. And some evident trends have unfolded over time, such as the gradual replacement of the strictly Stalinist ideas adopted early in the First Five-Year Plan period (1953-57) with more distinctively "Maoist" or "Chinese" ideas. Leading values that have been substituted include: (1) a greater emphasis on the economic development of rural areas, in which communes, small industries, and a high priority for agriculture figure prominently; (2) a greater encouragement of decentralized development and planning carried out within a context of local self-reliance; (3) a more egalitarian outlook that seeks to reduce economic and social differentials throughout the society; (4) a greater emphasis on nonmaterial and collective work incentives; (5) a greater reliance on mass mobilization behind political themes; and (6) a strategy of economic development through radical experimentation, struggle and leaps rather than through gradual, orderly, familiar methods.[6]

Thus the policies followed by the Hua Kuo-feng/Yeh Chien-ying/Teng Hsiao-p'ing triumverate after 1977 in some ways might resemble the policies of an earlier period – perhaps the "agriculture first strategy" of the early 1960s, or perhaps the more "balanced growth strategy" of the early 1970s. But in other ways they must respond to unique problems of the late 1970s and early 1980s such as longstanding workers' demands for industrial wages to be raised and the need to accommodate expanding foreign trade with the important value of "self-reliance."[7]

## Guide to the Documents in Part One

The "two lines" or "two roads" concept has become nearly universal in Chinese theoretical articles. The correct line, said to be derived from Mao Tse-tung's thought, usually is a fairly coherent set of general policies in effect in China at the time. The other line, of "capitalist road," is said to govern contemporary thinking in the Soviet Union, and it often appears to be more of a catchall for various arguments antagonistic to the correct, proletarian revolutionary path. In Selection 1 the two lines concept is applied broadly to economic policy.

A separate theoretical problem – the relationship between politics and economics – is presented in Selection 2. Subtle differences of phrasing are pregnant with meaning in this debate. The position attributed here to Trotsky justifies building up an advanced industrial economy as rapidly as possible to realize the precondition for having genuinely socialist politics; by this measure China has always lagged behind the Soviet Union. In 1977-78, the opposite deviation has been attributed to the notorious "gang of four" (see Selection 34), who are charged with arguing that politics dominates economics in order to justify their opposition to China's rapid economic modernization. Chairman Mao's correct line, it is argued, lies between Trotsky and the gang of four.[8]

Selections 3 through 7 illustrate attacks on China's most prestigious economist in the early 1960s, Sun Yeh-fang. During the Cultural Revolution Sun's work was cited as symbolic of "capitalist road" economic policies. These selections are elaborations of some of the points from Selection 1.

Selections 8 and 9 are merely two examples of hundreds of articles over the last generation that urge people to conserve fuel and materials, to find uses for waste products, and to improve manufacturing efficiency through technical innovation. The object is to inculcate frugality as a national virtue and thereby to diminish material and financial shortages that stand as obstacles to economic growth.

Selection 10 shows just how politicized statistical work had become by the end of the Cultural Revolution. Sometimes, apparently, when one side in a policy debate saw the weight of statistical evidence shifting in favor of the other side, they would attack their opponents as players of revisionist "number games." This article is a defense against this type of attack.

The refutation in Selection 11 is of the widely held argument that there exists a necessary tradeoff between staple grain crops, on the one hand, and "economic crops" (such as cotton, vegetables, and pigs) that bring in cash, on the other. Both categories of crop can be increased simultaneously, say the authors, if a strong brigade leadership group makes the problem a priority and analyzes it properly.

Selection 12, which was published one year after Chairman Mao's death, outlines the successor regime's overall approach to economic strategy. Chairman Hua's continuing, incomplete efforts to consolidate his new government's authority at the time are evident in the approving quotation of Chairman Mao's commitment to insuring that "both revolution and production would forge ahead simultaneously."

## Notes

1. Extracts from a directive of the Central Committee of the Chinese Communist Party dated June 1, 1943, and originally published anonymously (Chieh-fang jih-pao [ Liberation Daily] , June 4, 1943). This text is attributed to Mao in the current edition of the Selected Works. The translation quoted here is from Stuart R. Schram, The Political Thought of Mao Tse-

tung, revised and enlarged edition (New York: Praeger, 1969), pp. 316-17.

2. John Wilson Lewis, Leadership in Communist China (Ithaca, N.Y.: Cornell University Press, 1963), p. 258.

3. Hua Kuo-feng, "Political Report to the 11th National Congress of the Communist Party of China" (Delivered on August 12 and adopted on August 18, 1977), translated in Peking Review, No. 35 (August 26, 1977), 49-50.

4. Herbert Block, "The Planetary Product in 1975," Special Report No. 33, Bureau of Public Affairs, Office of Media Services, U.S. Department of State (May 1977), p. 6. For a multitude of reasons such estimates for China are extremely crude. I reproduce them here simply to establish rough orders of magnitude in comparative perspective.

5. Alexander Eckstein, China's Economic Revolution (New York: Cambridge University Press, 1977), pp. 42-50.

6. See Arthur G. Ashbrook, Jr., "China: Economic Overview, 1975," in China: A Reassessment of the Economy, A Compendium of Papers Submitted to the Joint Economic Committee, Congress of the United States, 94th Congress, 1st Session (July 10, 1975), pp. 20-51. Robert F. Dernberger and Allen S. Whiting, China's Future: Foreign Policy and Economic Development in the Post-Mao Era (New York: McGraw-Hill, 1977). Eckstein, China's Economic Revolution. John G. Gurley, China's Economy and the Maoist Strategy (New York: Monthly Review Press, 1976).

7. See Nicholas R. Lardy, "Current Chinese Economic Policy Problems" (Xerox), available as part of a Briefing Packet distributed by the China Council, 133 East 58th Street, New York, N.Y. 10022.

8. For example, see Wang Hui-teh, "Why Did Chang Chun-chiao Kick Up a Fuss over the Question of Ownership?" Peking Review, No. 1 (January 6, 1978), 16-19.

## 1. People's Daily Correspondent Describes Two Opposed Lines for Building the Economy (Source 27, pp. 3-10) August 25, 1967

There are two diametrically opposite lines in building up a state after the proletariat has come to power.

One is the Soviet modern revisionist, stressing only the material, machinery and mechanization, and material incentives. It opposes putting proletarian politics in command, ignores class struggle, and attempts to eliminate proletarian dictatorship. This line, if followed, will lead to capitalism, never to socialism. The Soviet Khrushchev renegade clique and its heirs are vociferous advocates of this line. Hand in hand with the Khrushchev of the Soviet Union, the Khrushchev of China energetically promoted this line in our country, attempting to restore capitalism.

Our most respected and beloved great leader, Chairman Mao, resolutely criticized and repudiated the revisionist line and set forth the only correct Marxist-Leninist line. In 1949 he laid down the basic principle for building the socialist economy in his report to the Second Plenary Session of the Central Committee of the Communist Party of China. In the report, having analyzed the then-existing economic structure in China, he formulated the basic policy on how "to elevate the state sector to a dominant position in the economy" and to gradually carry out the socialist transformation of agriculture, handicrafts, and capitalist commerce and industry. In 1958 Chairman Mao further expressed the firm determination and great wisdom of the 700 million Chinese people in the General Line of "making all efforts to strive forward and achieving greater, better, and more economical results in building socialism," and a complete set of policies for the development of socialist construction by "walking on two legs." This ushered in a new phase in the socialist construction of China — that is, the Great Leap Forward Campaign. In 1960 Chairman Mao himself summed up the experience created by advanced enterprises during the Great Leap Forward, counterposed the well-known "charter of the Anshan Iron and Steel Complex" to the Soviet revisionist "charter of the Magnitogorsk Iron and Steel Combine," and laid down five basic principles. These are:

"Insist on putting politics in command; strengthen party leadership; push for mass movement; institute a system under which cadres take part in productive labor and workers take part in management and revise irrational and outdated rules and regulations, and cadres, workers, and technicians work in close cooperation; and energetically carry out the technical revolution. Chairman Mao pointed out in 1963: "Class struggle, struggle for production, and scientific experimentation are three great revolutionary movements in building up a powerful socialist country."

It was this series of Chairman Mao's illuminating directions that points out to us the correct line for building up our country. This line stresses putting proletarian politics in command, carrying through to the end the struggle between the two classes and the two roads, continuously consolidating and strengthening the dictatorship of the proletariat, promoting the revolutionizing of people's thinking, mechanization under the guidance of revolutionization, and the principle of "grasping revolution and stepping up production."

It was under the direction of Chairman Mao's revolutionary line that our great motherland has made remarkable achievements in building socialism, and our socialist economy has constantly been strengthened and expanded, thus insuring forever the safety of our proletariat.

Since the establishment of new China, there has always been a sharp struggle between the two lines on the economic front. The crucial point at issue is whether or not to put proletarian politics in command, to build up the country in accordance with the great thought of Mao Tse-tung. In a word, it is a struggle over the question of whether China should build a socialist or a capitalist economy; whether it should take the socialist or the capitalist road.

Chairman Mao, in leading us to build a socialist state, has always accorded priority to the revolutionizing of the people's ideology. He said: "Political work is the lifeblood of all economic work; the lack of a correct political point of view is like having no soul."

There are countless ways to expand socialist production, but the most important one is to carry out a political and ideological revolution. If this is carried out, then the production of grain, cotton, oil, iron and steel, and coal will all increase. Otherwise, there will be no rise in output. The sole guarantee for the success of our socialist construction lies in disseminating Mao Tse-tung's thought to the masses.

China's Khrushchev has done just the opposite. He opposes putting proletarian politics in command and libels the economic measures employed in our socialist construction as "ultra-economic methods." He claims that he advocates "using economic methods to run the economy." Maliciously pointing a finger, he asked: "Why must we run the economy by administrative rules and not by economic laws?"

Nowhere in the world is there an economy that is independent of a political sphere. Nor can any strata in a class society exist in a political vacuum. If proletarian politics is not in command in any department or field, then bourgeois politics must be in command; if Marxism-Leninism, Mao Tse-tung's thought, is not in command, then revisionism, bourgeois ideology, must be in command. By opposing putting proletarian politics in command, China's Khrushchev seeks to restore capitalism in China.

Let us analyze the meaning of China's Khrushchev's so-called "using economic laws to run the economy." It is nothing but putting profits in command. He openly declared: "A factory must make money. Otherwise, it must close down and stop paying wages to the workers." In other words, in order to make money, one is allowed to ignore the unified state plan and the overall interests, and to engage in all sorts of selfish, speculative activities detrimental to the socialist economy.

This is the same notorious "material incentive." In typical capitalist tune, China's Khrushchev said: "Give a good reward to those who labor honestly"; "If you do not pay them more, there will be no incentive and they will not do a good job for you." He attempted to corrupt the masses by bourgeois egoism, divert the people's attention from politics, enlarge wage-scale differentials, and create a privileged stratum. It is a great insult to the revolutionary workers and a knife that kills people without bloodshed.

This is tantamount to shamelessly glorifying capitalism. China's Khrushchev said brashly: "Capitalist economy is flexible and has great variety"; "We should learn from the experience of capitalism in running enterprises, and especially from monopoly enterprises." He requested that our functionaries "seriously learn" from capitalists, alleging that the latter's "ability in management far surpasses that of our party members." In the eyes of China's Khrushchev, money-crazy capitalists are a hundred times wiser than Communists.

In fact, the so-called "using economic laws to run the economy" means letting the capitalist law of value reign over everything, developing free competition, undermining the socialist economy, and bringing about the restoration of capitalism. Had we acted in accordance with what China's Khrushchev called "economic laws," the capitalists who do not like their present status would indeed be very happy, while the emancipated toiling class would again be enslaved and a group of new bourgeois elements would build their "paradise" on the corpses of millions of laboring people.

The opposition of China's Khrushchev to putting politics in command also manifests itself in his opposition to the large-scale mass movement. The socialist cause is the revolutionary cause of millions of the masses. If we fully arouse and rely on the revolutionary initiative of the broad masses, we can build a socialist economy. Whether or not to launch an energetic mass movement is a crucial issue; whether or not one carries out the principle of putting politics in command — these are the important aspects of the fundamental antagonism between the two lines in economic construction.

Our great leader Chairman Mao always trusts the masses, relies on them, and thoroughly respects their initiative. He has taught us: "Of all things in the world, people are the most precious. Under the leadership of the Communist Party, as long as there are people, every kind of miracle can be performed." And "mass movement is indispensable for any work. Nothing can be achieved without mass movement." It is because we insisted both on putting politics in command and vigorously launching a mass movement that we achieved the momentous Great Leap Forward and advanced rapidly in industry, agriculture, national defense, science, and culture.

China's Khrushchev, taking a reactionary bourgeois standpoint, bitterly hated the revolutionary mass movement and did his utmost to sell the one-man-rule system and the reactionary line of relying on experts. In 1949 he told the functionaries of state-owned enterprises in Tientsin: "You are the state's organizers in the factory" and, in construction, "you should particularly rely on the directors, engineers, and technicians."

In a speech delivered in 1952, he said: "There are many difficulties in industrial construction. China has money, labor force, and machinery (that is, all these can be overcome with the assistance of the Soviet Union and the People's Democracies), but few engineers." He desperately attacked the surging revolutionary mass movement launched in 1958, pouring cold water on people's enthusiasm and ridiculing it as "a moment's impulse brought about by some heresy."

According to China's Khrushchev, in economic construction we can rely on a handful of "experts," "rely on directors, engineers, and technicians" who give orders; the revolutionary masses are only "labor" and "ignorant masses" who only obediently take orders from the top. He and his followers taxed their brains to work out a series of revisionist regulations in order to exercise bourgeois dictatorship over the workers. In so doing he not only dampened the socialist initiative of the masses and obstructed the development of socialist economic construction, but he also placed the cadres of management personnel and technicians in an antagonistic position to the workers. The revisionist turned them into bureaucrats and new bourgeois elements who rode roughshod over the masses, thereby gradually changing the nature of socialist enterprises.

Marxism teaches us that politics is the concentrated manifestation of economics. The degeneration of the structure of the socialist economy will inevitably lead to restoration of capitalist politics. In all these years, the whole set of lines, principles, politics, and measures advocated by China's Khrushchev was aimed at fostering capitalist forces in both town and countryside and at undermining the structure of the socialist economy and transforming the socialist economy back to capitalism. Once the basic structure of the economy has been transformed, our party and state would naturally change accordingly, step by step, until capitalism would be restored.

Thus, the struggle between the lines with respect to economic construction is, in fact, the struggle between two political lines, between two roads and two destinies for China.

Our proletarian political party is one which engages in politics, class struggle, and the dictatorship of the proletariat. If our party refuses to do all these, but concerns itself solely with economic construction, as suggested by China's Khrushchev, would it not become an instrument for organizing economic life, and would it not become an "industrial party" or an "agricultural party" like that of the Soviet revisionist renegade clique?

The political party is the highest form of class organization and a tool for carrying out class struggle. This is basic Marxist knowledge. Is there any political party in the world engaging only in production and construction, and not in class struggle? The so-called "agricultural party" or "industrial party" is nothing but a gimmick to reduce the party to an appendage of economic construction, an appendage of the bourgeoisie, whose only purpose is to make "profit." Such a party's sole objective is to chase after money, and it concerns itself with exploitation and capitalism. Is this not a one hundred percent bourgeois political party?

The experiences of the struggle between the two lines on the economic front have taught us that we should never forget

Chairman Mao's teachings, never forget to put politics in command.

Chairman Mao has taught us: "While we recognize that in the general development of history the material determines the mental and that social being determines social consciousness, we also — and indeed we must — recognize the reaction of mental on material things, of social consciousness on social being, and of the superstructure on the economic framework."

In this period, the most powerful spiritual force is the invincible thought of Mao Tse-tung, and the mightiest army is the people armed with the thought of Mao Tse-tung. In wartime, those who only see the power of materiel and are frightened by one or two new weapons of our enemy will shamelessly surrender; in peacetime, those xenophiles who habitually follow foreigners will be their slaves.

We Chinese Communists firmly believe that the people are the creators of history. Once they have mastered the thought of Mao Tse-tung, they will become wise and courageous and the reservoir of immense strength. The Proletarian Cultural Revolution, led by Chairman Mao personally, serves indeed as a good lesson in how to learn and practice the thought of Mao Tse-tung. It is a great driving force for the development of our production. Through the revolution, the bourgeois reactionary line which China's Khrushchev attempted to impose on us has been thoroughly eliminated.

In the wake of the revolution, there will surely emerge a new surge of socialist construction. The Chinese people has the will and the ability to first catch up with and then surpass the advanced countries in the near future.

## 2. Red Flag Author Argues Politics Is a Concentrated Manifestation of Economics (Source 12, pp. 192-197) June 1969

In this debate, Lenin refuted the various fallacies of Trotsky and Bukharin, and in defining the relationship between politics and economics, he pointed out: "Politics is a concentrated manifestation of economics." This means that the fundamental interests of classes and the relationships between classes are centrally manifested in politics, and once a class loses its political power, it can no longer hold its dominant position in the economic sphere. Lenin had this to point out: "Generally speaking, the most important and 'decisive' class interests can only be satisfied through basic political reforms. For example, the fundamental economic interests of the proletariat can only be satisfied through political revolution, replacing bourgeois dictatorship with proletarian dictatorship." The dictatorship of the proletariat is the most concentrated manifestation of socialist economy and is the fundamental guarantee for the establishment, consolidation, and development of the socialist economy.

Proceeding from the basic viewpoint that politics is a concentrated manifestation of economics, Lenin unambiguously advanced the brilliant idea of politics first. He said: "In relation to economics, politics cannot but take first place. Unless this is affirmed, the most elementary knowledge of Marxism is forgotten." Lenin also pointed out that by advancing the fallacy that politics and economics are equally important, Bukharin was "using eclecticism to replace the dialectical relationship between politics and economics." Lenin rebuffed the fallacies of Trotsky and Bukharin, who opposed giving first place to politics under the pretext of "concern for production." Lenin pointed out: "If a class does not correctly handle a question politically, it cannot maintain its rule and hence neither can it solve its production tasks." Trotsky openly used the concept of viewing the question "economically" to oppose the concept of viewing it politically. It was quite obvious that this was the opportunist outlook. Bukharin's eclecticism was opportunism in disguise. He used his so-called "comprehensive viewpoint" to treat politics and economics on an equal footing. This double-dealing tactic while appearing to be impartial was in fact deceptive. Actually, both Trotsky and Bukharin were opposed not to politics, but to proletarian politics. They wanted bourgeois politics and attempted to lead economic construction down the capitalist road.

Chairman Mao has summed up the historical experiences of

the positive and negative aspects of the proletarian dictatorship and created the great theory of the continuity of revolution under the dictatorship of the proletariat. For the first time, he has clearly pointed out that after a great victory is won in the socialist transformation of the ownership of means of production, there are still classes and class struggle; there is still the struggle between the proletariat and the bourgeoisie, between the socialist road and the capitalist road; there is still the danger of capitalist restoration, and the proletariat must carry on the revolution. Without the proletarian dictatorship, without the continuation of the revolution under the dictatorship of the proletariat, it is not possible to develop socialist production, nor is it possible to carry out socialist construction; the only possible course is to restore capitalism. In the great practice of leading the socialist revolution and socialist construction in China and in the Great Proletarian Cultural Revolution, which he launched and led, Chairman Mao has penetratingly criticized and repudiated the counterrevolutionary revisionist line for restoring capitalism of the renegade, traitor, and scab Liu Shao-ch'i and smashed Liu Shao-ch'i's bourgeois headquarters. This has fundamentally guaranteed that China's economic construction can continue to take big strides forward in the socialist direction.

Proceeding from the realities of the socialist revolution and socialist construction in China, Chairman Mao has creatively answered the questions of what is genuine socialist economic construction and how to carry out socialist economic construction. Chairman Mao has put forward the brilliant idea that in socialist construction, it is necessary to bring proletarian politics to the fore and put politics in command of economy; he has laid down the general line of "building socialism by going all out and aiming high to achieve greater, faster, and better results at lower cost"; he laid down the great strategic principles of "be independent and self-reliant," "be prepared for war, be prepared for natural calamities, and do everything for the people," etc., and a series of proletarian economic policies.

During the Great Proletarian Cultural Revolution, Chairman Mao has put forward the great guiding principle of "grasping revolution and promoting production." As pointed out by Vice

Chairman Lin [Piao] in his political report to the Ninth National Party Congress, the guiding principles of "grasping revolution and promoting production" "have correctly provided answers for the relationship between revolution and production, spirit and matter, the superstructure and the economic foundation, production relations and productive forces." This is to say, we must put revolution in command of production and use revolution to promote and stimulate production. Chairman Mao's brilliant ideas concerning politics in command of economy and revolution in command of production are a beacon lighting the way to consolidating the dictatorship of the proletariat, to guarding against capitalist restoration, and to building socialism; they are a sharp weapon for criticizing and repudiating revisionism.

After the seizure of party and state leadership in the Soviet Union, the Soviet revisionist renegade clique has completely betrayed Lenin's teachings and inherited the mantle of Trotsky by vociferously advertising such reactionary fallacies as "economics is more important than politics," "production should be given first place," etc. They naively exaggerate the decisive role of productive forces, science, and technology, and pronounce such nonsense as the "general line" of building communism is to "establish the material, technical foundation." Do they genuinely want to develop socialist "production"? Not at all. Their advertisement of such counterrevolutionary fallacies is entirely for the purpose of opposing proletarian politics, disintegrating the socialist economic foundation, and restoring the capitalist economy. It is characterized by foreign plunder and domestic exploitation so that it becomes the economic foundation of Soviet revisionist socialist-imperialism and gradually completely restores capitalism. The perverse action of the Soviet revisionist renegade clique has gravely endangered the Soviet economy. Their industrial and agricultural production is beset with difficulties, black markets are rampant, commodity prices soar, and the broad masses of the exploited working people have become more proverty-stricken with each passing day.

Like the Soviet revisionists, the renegade, traitor, and scab Liu Shao-ch'i also advertised such reactionary fallacies as "production first," "technique first," etc. He did this in order to make the revolutionary people of the proletariat forget proletarian politics and "pay attention only to grain, cotton, and oil without drawing a distinction between our friends and our foes." In fact, Liu Shao-ch'i never put production and technique in first place; it was, instead, bourgeois politics and the vain attempt to make the building of socialism in China stray down the evil road of capitalist restoration. Under the smoke screen of "production first" and "technique first," he and others like him held to the superstructure and usurped leadership in many units from the central down to the local administrations. Prior to the Great Proletarian Cultural Revolution, some enterprise units were nominally under socialist ownership, but their actual leadership had been usurped by a handful of renegades, secret agents, and capitalists; or they were still in the hands of the former capitalists, and socialist production was being undermined. If we did not carry the revolution to the superstructure, did not recover the power usurped by the bourgeoisie, and did not smash Liu Shao-ch'i's revisionist line, the socialist economic foundation would inevitably be wrecked, and socialist ownership would gradually degenerate.

In order to put politics in command of the economy and revolution in command of production, it is necessary to correctly handle the relationship between spirit and matter. Chairman Mao has creatively put forward the great concept of turning matter into spirit and spirit into matter. He points out: "It is man's social existence that determines his ideology. Once the broad masses grasp the correct ideology of the advanced class, they will turn into a material force that will change society and the world." According to Chairman Mao's teaching, we must not only carry out material construction, but, what is even more more important, we must revolutionize ideology and revolutionize machinery. The means by which we should carry out socialist economic construction and develop production are entirely different from those adopted by imperialism and modern revisionism. We depend neither on coercion nor on material incentive, but rather rely on bringing proletarian politics to the fore and putting Mao Tse-tung's thought in command. Mao Tse-tung's thought is a spiritual atom bomb of infinite power. Once Mao Tse-tung's thought is grasped by the masses of the people, it will engender eternal revolutionary drive and initiative The launching of the mass movement for the creative study and application of Mao Tse-tung's thought in a profound and sustained manner is a great spiritual force that will drive China forward to develop socialist undertakings in a greater, faster, better, and more economical way.

Khrushchev, Brezhnev, and their group of renegades have completely forsaken the communist revolutionary spirit promoted by Lenin. They have instituted on a large scale in the Soviet Union a "new economic system" with "material incentives" and "profit" as the core, and they have changed human relations into capitalist cash relations based on buying and selling. These are their reactionary measures for restoring capitalism. With the same criminal objective in view, the renegade, traitor, and scab Liu Shao-ch'i has also vociferously advertised "material incentives" and "profit in command" in China's socialist economic construction. He has vainly attempted to corrupt the working masses, the poor and lower-middle peasants, and the revolutionary cadres with "money" and bourgeois counterrevolutionary egoism so as to make them forget class struggle and proletarian dictatorship.

## 3. Revolutionary Mass Criticism Groups Denounce Sun Yeh-fang's* "One Black Program" and "Five Soft Daggers" (Source 18, pp. 258-263) February 24, 1970

Under the cloak of Sun Yeh-fang's "academic theory" a counterrevolutionary economic theory at the service of Liu Shao-ch'i's capitalist restoration is hidden.

After the socialist transformation of the ownership of the means of production had basically been completed, Chairman

*Sun Yeh-fang was head of the Economic Research Institute of the Chinese Academy of Sciences and as such was China's most prominent advocate of giving freer play to market forces. His career was terminated during the Cultural Revolution. — G. B.

Mao personally laid down the general line of "going all out, aiming high, and achieving greater, faster, and better results at lower costs in building socialism." He put forward the policy of "walk on two feet" and the famous five basic principles in the "Constitution of the Anshan Iron and Steel Works": insist on politics in command, strengthen Party leadership, launch mass movements in a big way, implement the three-in-one combination of two participating and one transforming [liang-ts'an i-kao san-chieh-ho], go all out for technological revolution. These brilliant instructions of Chairman Mao show the only correct way to command economics with politics and to lead mechanization with revolutionization in building China.

Liu Shao-ch'i and Sun Yeh-fang frantically opposed the General Line of the Party for building socialism and actively promoted the counterrevolutionary revisionist line of economic construction. Liu Shao-ch'i slanderously said that the method of economic construction pursued by the Party and the country is a "supra-economic method," and he tried his utmost to peddle his "manage the economy with economic methods." Sun Yeh-fang regarded these black statements as "imperial edicts" and said, "there is great insight into this problem. I completely support it. I have always insisted on running the economy with economic means." Their so-called "manage the economy with economic methods" is in fact a counterrevolutionary economic program for capitalist restoration.

In this program, Sun Yeh-fang maliciously produced five murderous soft daggers pointed at the socialist economy and the proletarian dictatorship.

The first dagger: advocating "profits in command." This is the anchor of Sun Yeh-fang's counterrevolutionary economic program.

The renegade, hidden traitor, and scab Liu Shao-ch'i publicly announced: "A factory must make money. If it does not, it should be closed down and the payment of wages stopped." Sun Yeh-fang added a "theoretical" cloak to this statement of his black master's. He said: "Profit is the most important overall indicator in evaluating the performance of enterprises. So long as we keep a firm grip on profits, it is just like leading a bull by its nose; in this way the legs of the bull (other targets) will naturally follow along." For the capitalists the size of profit has always been the sole criterion for evaluating the performance of enterprises. These fallacies of Sun Yeh-fang and his gang are actually capitalist "business strategy."

Socialist enterprises must put proletarian politics in command; implement "develop the economy, guarantee supply," "be prepared for war, be prepared for natural disasters, and do everything for the people," and other great policies; serve China's socialist revolution and socialist construction, and aid world revolution. This is the firm and correct orientation for our socialist enterprises. Liu Shao-ch'i, Sun Yeh-fang, and their gang promoted "profits in command" in a vain attempt to make socialist enterprises change their political orientation in the pursuit of profits, to benefit themselves at the expense of others, to engage in speculation and manipulation, to disrupt socialist planned economy, and to replace the socialist relationship between men with the capitalist money relationship. The more "profits in command" is implemented in enterprises, the farther will they deviate from socialism. Socialist economy will change into capitalist economy. Proletarian positions will become supports for revisionism.

The second dagger: advocating "production first."

Liu Shao-ch'i talked nonsense when he asserted: "The sole purpose of enterprises is to produce." Sun Yeh-fang, too, trumpeted: "Politics must be built around production and through production." He further attacked politics in command as "idealistic" and "detrimental to raising productivity" and he attempted to destroy proletarian politics in command through "production first."

Lenin once severely reprimanded those old opportunists: "Politics cannot but occupy the primary position as compared with economics. Not to affirm this point is to forget the minimal knowledge of Marxism." There are many methods for building socialism. But proletarian politics in command, namely, Mao Tsetung thought in command, is the most important. If this is assured, everything else is assured. Chairman Mao teaches us: "We admit that in the overall historical development, material conditions determine ideologies and social existence determines social concepts. But we also admit and must admit the interaction of material conditions and ideology, the interaction of social consciousness and social existence, and the interaction of the superstructure and the economic base." In the contemporary world the most powerful ideology is Mao Tsetung thought. The mightiest force is the people armed with Mao Tsetung thought. The broad masses are the creators of history. Once they understand Mao Tsetung thought, then they will be the most intelligent, the bravest; then they will possess inexhaustible revolutionary dynamism. The great achievements of China's socialist revolution and socialist construction thoroughly smash Sun Yeh-fang and his gang's fallacies that politics in command is "idealistic" and "detrimental to increasing productivity"!

If we follow Liu Shao-ch'i and Sun Yeh-fang's method and grasp material for material's sake, we can never make good use of materials. Even if we have materials it will eventually fall into the hands of the bourgeoisie. The revolutionary people must always keep vigilance against this soft dagger of "production first."

The third dagger: advocating "material incentives."

Liu Shao-ch'i talked nonsense when he claimed: "There must be material incentives!"; "If wages are not raised, production activism will slack off, and workers will not work well." Sun Yeh-fang, too, said: "Material incentives cannot be all wrong." He tried his utmost to corrode workers with bourgeois egoism. He said: "If everybody does not think of his individual interests and thinks only of the national interests every day, things will get worse." This is to say they wanted to use "material incentives" as the "motive force" to "develop production."

The fallacies of Liu Shao-ch'i and Sun Yeh-fang are the biggest slander against our working class. The working class is the leading class in the revolution. It is forward-looking, selfless, and full of revolutionary thoroughness. "Our hearts are with the 700 million people of the country, with the millions and millions of revolutionary people of the world." "We work not for fame, not for money, but for revolution." This is the thundering reply from our working class.

Lenin pointed out: "To work for money — this is the capitalist morality." In the age of socialism, "material incentives" is a manifestation of counterrevolutionary economism. The promotion — by Liu Shao-ch'i, Sun Yeh-fang, and their gang — of "material incentives" and the institution of rewards, overtime pay, and piece-wage rates in enterprises was a vain attempt to corrode our working class with bourgeois "egoism" and to disgrace our working class with money, fame, material comfort, and other bourgeois garbage. Their vicious intention was to make us forsake the basic proletarian interests so as to "struggle for several big things [wei chi ta chien erh fen-tou]." They wanted the revolutionary masses to "think about money and forget about the proletarian political power," and to "get rewards and change orientation" so as to disrupt socialist production and to disintegrate the socialist economic foundation.

The fourth dagger: advocating "factory management by experts."

Liu Shao-ch'i talked nonsense when he said that construction must "rely on the factory managers, engineers, and technicians." Sun Yeh-fang also promoted the management system in which the chief engineer is in charge of all technical problems and the chief accountant is responsible for all economic problems. The broad working people were merely "labor" and the "mob." In the eyes of Liu and Sun, they would only "take orders." The criminal intent of Liu and Sun was to form a black squad in the field of industrial production so as to let a handful of capitalist-roaders and bourgeois-reactionary technical "experts" usurp the leadership in the central and regional authority and in the production units, in order to establish a bourgeois counterrevolutionary dictatorship.

Whether the proletariat or the bourgeoisie will be in command of the socialist economy rests with the crucial question of who will assume the leadership in the factory — the working class or the experts. What Liu Shao-ch'i, Sun Yeh-fang, and their gang did in promoting the idea of "leaving factory management to the experts" is tantamount to letting the bourgeoisie dictate to the proletariat. Had they had their way, the proletariat and the working people would have lost all their rights.

The fifth dagger: advocating "enterprise autonomy."

Liu Shao-ch'i contended that the Party and the government

should give enterprises a free hand and let business agencies run the enterprises. Sun Yeh-fang, closely following Liu Shao-ch'i's example, attacked the socialist planned economy as "moribund" and as inferior to the "free economy." Sun Yeh-fang maintained that "the state need only watch the value target (profit indicator) and leave the rest of business management to the enterprises." "Within the category of simple reproduction, the responsibility should be entirely delegated to the enterprises." In a word, they vainly attempted to peddle the revisionist "enterprise autonomy."

Chairman Mao teaches us: "Without a high degree of democracy, it is impossible to have a high degree of centralism. And without a high degree of centralism, it is impossible to establish a socialist economy." The deadly effects of "enterprise autonomy" are the disintegration of socialist planned economy, the turning of socialist state ownership into ownership by a small privileged class; the opposition to centralized and unified leadership of the Party and the state, and the yielding to the handful of bourgeois representatives so that they can usurp the leadership of production units and overthrow the proletarian dictatorship.

Sun Yeh-fang espoused the nonsense that socialist planned economy is inferior to capitalist "free economy." His so-called "free economy" is the capitalist economy. The "freedom" he wanted is the "freedom" of the bourgeoisie to exploit the proletariat, and the "freedom" of the bourgeoisie to dictate to the proletariat. Had his methods been used, we would have lost our Party and our country; the bourgeoisie would have once again ridden on our heads, and we would have suffered a second dose of misery.

## 4. Revolutionary Mass Criticism Groups Tie Sun Yeh-fang to Liu Shao-ch'i* (Source 18, pp. 264-266) February 24, 1970

We must thoroughly criticize Liu Shao-ch'i and Sun Yeh-

*Liu Shao-ch'i, before his purge in the Cultural Revolution, was the ranking Communist Party leader below Chairman Mao Tse-tung. — G. B.

fang's "profits in command." In the socialist economy, what commands everything else must be proletarian politics only, never profits. When we criticize "profits in command," we are saying that profits should never be in the commanding position. At the same time, we must also increase production, strictly practice economy, implement economic accounting, and pay attention to increase accumulation. Those attitudes and practices that would do away with economic accounting, negate the need of financial management under socialism, and have nothing to do with cost accounting and profit targets are wrong. At present, some people think that "to engage in cost accounting is to put profits in command," "to engage in economic accounting is not to put politics to the fore." There are also people who claim that "waste is justified" to create a favorable theoretical foundation for extravagance. The net effects are to furnish opportunities for corruption, theft, speculation, and manipulation. These viewpoints are very harmful.

We must thoroughly criticize the ideas of "production first" and "business in command" advocated by Liu Shao-ch'i and Sun Yeh-fang. Material goods should never be more important than people. Production should never be pursued at the expense of class struggle. We must seriously implement Chairman Mao's great policy of "grasping revolution and promoting production." Revolution must always be in the commanding position and production in the subordinate position. At the same time, production should not be allowed to fall off; otherwise, losses would be incurred in the national economy, and the great strategic policy of "Be prepared for war, be prepared for natural disasters, and do everything for the people" would not be properly carried out. In the end, revolution would be adversely affected. It is a great mistake to separate revolution from production and to pit one against the other. At present, some people say, "Production is a hard job, politics is an easy job," "Revolution is safe, production is dangerous." All these result from a lack of a correct understanding of the dialectical relationship between revolution and production. All these are the lingering poisonous influence of the ideas of "production first" and "business in command" advocated by Liu Shao-ch'i and Sun Yeh-fang.

We must thoroughly criticize the ideas of "material incentives" and "rewards in command" advocated by Liu Shao-ch'i and Sun Yeh-fang, and we must forever put proletarian politics to the fore. We must pay close attention to the ideological revolutionization of the people. At the same time, we must care for the lives of the masses and correctly handle the relationship among the state, the production units, and the individual production workers, as well as the problem of distribution. At present, a handful of class enemies are once again stirring up various evil versions of counterrevolutionary economism. We must deal them hard blows.

We must thoroughly criticize the ideas of "letting the experts manage the factory" and "putting technique in command" advocated by Liu Shao-ch'i and Sun Yeh-fang. The working class must hold firmly to their power and should never hand over technical and financial power to bourgeois "experts." At the same time, the Party's policy regarding intellectuals must be seriously carried out. We must pay attention to fully mobilizing the activism of revolutionary technical personnel in the three-in-one-combination small groups for business management and scientific experiments.

We must thoroughly criticize the idea of "enterprise autonomy" advocated by Liu Shao-ch'i and Sun Yeh-fang. The centralized, unified leadership of the Party and the state over the socialist economy is an important guarantee for this country's advance along the socialist road. There should be no independent action, no fragmentation, no polycentric movement, no independent arrangement of production plans, no capital construction outside the assigned plans, and no free trade in fixed capital or barters in any socialist economic ventures.

## 5. Provincial Revolutionary Committee Writing Group Asserts Sun Yeh-fang's "System of Political Economy" Is an Ideological Foundation for Liu Shao-chi's Counterrevolutionary Line (Source 11, pp. 268-269) February 1970

Sun Yeh-fang vainly tried to apply all of Khrushchev's methods to the restoration of a capitalist economy in China. He established a revisionist "system of political economy" to provide an "ideological" foundation for Liu Shao-ch'i's counterrevolutionary revisionist line, to undermine socialist construction, and to overthrow the proletarian dictatorship. At present, in criticizing and repudiating the revisionist economic theory, striking at counterrevolutionary economism and other evil capitalist trends, and eliminating "Liu Shao-ch'i's pernicious influence," Sun Yeh-fang's "economics" provides some very good negative examples. By criticizing and repudiating these negative examples, we should be able to firmly hoist the great red banner of Mao Tsetung thought in each and every sector of the economic field.

## 6. Provincial Revolutionary Committee Writing Group Identifies What Sun Yeh-fang Learned from Efsei Liberman* (Source 11, pp. 269-271) February 1970

There were also international developments that motivated Sun Yeh-fang to advance his "economics." In 1956, when the floodgates of modern revisionism were opened by Khrushchev's renegade clique, Sun Yeh-fang visited the "holy land" on several occasions to "pay homage" and received "supreme enlightenment." He wrote one article after another and made countless speeches; he published what he called "internal research reports" one after another. He shamelessly declared that his "basic views" were inspired by the modern revisionists. In 1962, after Efsei Liberman, a writer in the pay of social imperialism, published his article "Plans, Profits, and Rewards" — a big poisonous weed with "profits in command" as its core — Sun Yeh-fang cried out: "I would rather 'take some risks' and be 'more thoroughgoing than Liberman.' "

*Efsei Liberman was a Soviet economist who favored emphasizing profit targets for enterprises to overcome their tendency to conceal their production possibilities in order to obtain an easy plan. — G. B.

What are the "basic views" that Sun Yeh-fang got from the modern revisionists?

1. He advocated the idea that economic plans should be based on profit. He asserted that "of all the laws, the law of value is primary," that it is necessary to "base plans on the law of value."

2. He contended that profit is the goal. He declared: "I have my doubts about the assertion that 'production in capitalist society is for profit, while production under socialism is not for profit but for the use value.'" He also declared: "Increasing labor productivity and improving technology both aim at making profit."

3. He contended that profit is a driving force. He asserted that profit "is capable of stimulating business management" and that "so long as we keep a firm grip on profits, it is just like leading a bull by its nose; in this way the legs of the bull (other targets) will naturally follow along. Otherwise, we will have to carry the bull by its legs."

4. He advocated the idea that profit is the center. He insisted on "making profits the central target of planning and statistics" and pointed out: "The state need only watch the value target (profit indicator) and leave the rest of business management to the enterprises."

5. He clamored that profit is the only criterion by which to assess the worth of a given enterprise. He asserted that "the amount of profit should be the most sensitive indicator of technical progress and the quality of management of an enterprise." He also added that "the rates of profit on capital and commodity prices are needed in a socialist economy" and that "the average rate of profit on the social capital must be attained by each and every enterprise; those surpassing this rate of profit are advanced enterprises, while those failing to reach this level are lagging behind."

In short, in Sun Yeh-fang's mind the purpose of drafting plans and developing the economy is to make money; building factories and running enterprises are also for making money. Sun Yeh-fang maintained that had all economic activities been governed by profits, enterprises would make progress, technology would improve, and society would advance.

## 7. Provincial Revolutionary Committee Writing Group Asserts Sun Yeh-fang's Program Would Serve the Interests of the "Eight Immortals" (Source 11, pp. 278-279) February 1970

Can the capitalist method of "putting profits in command" "give impetus to enterprise management"? On the contrary, as far as management is concerned things will go from bad to worse. Once we put profits in command we would replace the noble ideal of doing everything for revolution with counter-revolutionary economism, willfully changing the orientation of our enterprises. We would only work hard when we saw that there were large profits, would work less enthusiastically when we saw that there were little profits, and would work not at all when we saw that there were no profits; we would replace communist cooperation among enterprises with the capitalist practices of deception and of hurting others to benefit oneself; we would use "material incentives" to corrupt people's souls, to break down their revolutionary will, and to change the socialist relationship among enterprises into a monetary relationship. In short, the more you promote "putting profits in command," the farther you stray from the socialist orientation. This would cause enterprises to break down, and would turn proletarianism into support of revisionism. Such an objective law of class struggle is independent of man's will.

The countries dominated by modern revisionism are "living examples" of using profits "to give impetus to enterprise management." Here is the free play of individual initiatives Sun Yeh-fang has been longing for. "In crossing the sea, each of the eight immortals displayed its magic power." Working in collusion, the "eight immortals" — the capitalist-roaders, the capitalists, the speculators, the sinister contractors, the new well-to-do peasants, those who have committed the crime of corruption, the swindlers, and the embezzlers — are running wild. From cities to rural areas, from production to marketing, from economic departments to government offices, the capitalist forces are rampant, indulging in speculation, stockpiling, raising commodity prices, and swindling. Working hand in glove, the capitalist-roaders within enterprises and government agencies practice embezzlement and engage in corruption; it has become a common practice among them to divide the loot among themselves. As a result, socialist ownership by the whole people has degenerated into ownership by the privileged class, which is manipulated by a handful of capitalist-roaders and the newly emerged bourgeois elements; the national economy is in a state of wild confusion, and the laboring people are once again falling into the abyss of suffering; the socialist achievements won by the proletariat at the cost of its own blood are being wasted. This is a shocking historical lesson.

## 8. State Planning Commission Writing Group Emphasizes the Importance of Thrift (Source 23, pp. 18-22) February 1971

This year is an important year for the people of our country to continue revolution under the dictatorship of the proletariat, the first year to put into effect the Fourth Five-Year Plan for the Development of the National Economy. The high tide that has risen in industrial and agricultural production will be carried forward even more vigorously, and the preparation for war will be further stepped up.

The rapid development of the national economy leads to a greater demand for commodities — especially for certain raw materials, semiprocessed materials, fuel, and equipment on various fronts. To cope with this situation, we must continue to carry out conscientiously Chairman Mao's revolutionary line and policies, putting politics in command, engaging in all-around planning, rousing the masses, increasing production, and practicing economy.

The great leader Chairman Mao teaches us: "We want to carry out large-scale construction, but our country is still very poor — herein lies a contradiction. One way of resolving this contradiction is to make a sustained effort to practice strict economy in every field" ("On the Correct Handling of

Contradictions Among the People"). In accordance with this teaching of Chairman Mao, we have, since last year, launched on the nation's industrial front a grand mass movement to increase production and practice economy, and have achieved great results. In order to insure the all-around fulfillment and overfulfillment of the national economic plan for 1971 and to carry out successfully the Fourth Five-Year Plan, an important task that confronts us on the industrial front is to study conscientiously and adhere consistently to Chairman Mao's great policy of "practice strict economy and oppose waste," to sum up and popularize the experience that has been gained, and to bring about a new high tide in the mass movement to increase production and practice economy.

## Whether to Practice Strict Economy or to Allow Extravagance and Waste Is a Struggle Between the Two Lines and the Two Kinds of World Outlook

Whether we practice strict economy or follow a path of extravagance and waste has always been an important aspect of the struggle between the two classes, the two roads, and the two lines on China's industrial front, an important matter that bears on building socialism with greater, faster, and better results at lower costs, consolidating the socialist system of ownership and of the proletarian dictatorship, and guarding against the restoration of capitalism.

The great leader Chairman Mao has taught us consistently the need for carrying out the policy of economy. Back in the years of the revolutionary war, Chairman Mao pointed out that it was essential to "save every coin for the war and the cause of revolution and for our economic construction" ("Our Economic Policy"). After the founding of the People's Republic of China, during the period of the First Five-Year Plan, Chairman Mao pointed out further: "To economize is one of the basic principles of socialist economics. China is a large country, but she is still very poor. It will take several decades to make China prosperous. Even then, we will still have to observe the principle of diligence and frugality. But it is in the coming few decades, during the present series of five year plans, that we must particularly advocate diligence and frugality, that we must pay special attention to practicing economy" (introductory note to "Running a Cooperative with Industry and Economy"). Chairman Mao's great teaching has profoundly revealed the objective law of the development of socialist economy and clearly pointed out the direction for sustained development of the movement for practicing economy on China's industrial front. Guided by Chairman Mao's revolutionary line, the broad masses on the industrial front, bringing into play the revolutionary tradition of hard struggle, diligence, frugality, and economy, have waged many battles against extravagance and waste, and have ceaselessly repulsed the rabid attack of the bourgeoisie. Many advanced models in running factories with industry and economy have emerged.

Over a long period of time, renegade, hidden traitor, and scab Liu Shao-ch'i, and Po I-po, his agent in the industrial field, carried out a counterrevolutionary revisionist line based on extravagance and waste. In capital construction and design work, they sought for only things "large, foreign, and comprehensive," and promoted large factory complexes, tall factory buildings, and foreign equipment. Technically, they adhered to the established practice and did not improve old equipment, out-of-date technology, and backward products. In the management of supplies, under the pretext of "budgeting liberally and spending sparingly," they actually practiced "liberal budgeting and liberal spending" and "unlimited enlargement of the goods in stock." In production, they promoted independent operation but not comprehensive utilization. All this led to the heavy waste of raw materials, semiprocessed materials, equipment, and funds, and damaged the economic foundation of socialism. Meanwhile, the practice of extravagance and waste also seriously corrupted our revolutionary ranks, and caused some who lacked firmness in their revolutionary will to forget the glorious tradition of diligence, frugality, and economy and to discard the revolutionary style of hard struggle. This line of Liu Shao-ch'i was entirely for the purpose of dissolving the proletarian dictatorship and restoring capitalism.

During the Great Proletarian Cultural Revolution, the working class of China, holding high the great red banner of Mao

Tse-tung Thought, criticized and repudiated Liu Shao-ch'i's counterrevolutionary revisionist line, thus greatly heightening its consciousness in consistently adhering to Chairman Mao's policy of "self-reliance," "hard struggle," "practice of strict economy," and "opposition to waste." The consciousness of the broad masses was quickly translated into action in increasing production and practicing economy. The entire industrial front took inventories, carried out revolution in design, implemented technical reforms, and obtained abundant results in comprehensive utilization. The repairing of old equipment, the utilization of waste, the processing and reconditioning of items, the practice of economy, and the use of substitutes became the custom of the day. Let us take, for example, revolution in design. According to the statistics of many industrial and communication departments, it was generally possible to scale down the investment for construction by 15 to 25 percent for large and medium-sized projects that had been examined and revised and that saved a large quantity of equipment and material compared with the original projects, and the rate of construction was also accelerated. Technical reform affords another example; according to the incomplete statistics of 1970 for Peking, Shanghai, Tientsin, Liaoning, and other provinces and municipalities, of the 120 improved varieties of newly designed electromechanical products, two-thirds were reduced in weight by more than half – in some cases by 90 percent – compared with the original, backward products. In this way, it was possible for the state to save considerable raw materials, semi-processed materials, equipment, and other material supplies, and to "do more things with less money." This shows that the fundamental question in practicing economy is, as in other kinds of work, a question of line. As long as Chairman Mao's revolutionary line is consistently adhered to, the movement to increase production and practice economy has inexhaustible power, and greater, faster, and better results at lower costs can be achieved in industrial production and construction.

The question of practicing strict economy or permitting extravagance and waste represents a struggle between the two kinds of world outlook. Diligence, frugality, and economy are the virtues of the proletariat and the laboring people, while extravagance and waste are the filth of the bourgeoisie and all exploiting classes.

## 9. Provincial Revolutionary Committee Writing Group Warns Putting Politics in Command Is Not Enough (Source 11, pp. 282-283) February 1970

However, we must never think that to put proletarian politics in command means that we can do without economic work, economic accounting, cost reduction, and increased accumulation. If we think so we will fall victim to the cunning scheme of the class enemies. The profits of enterprises are an important source of revenue for a socialist country. The receipts (profits, taxes, and so on) from the state-owned economy amount to about 90 percent of the budgeted national revenue of our country. If enterprises fail to fulfill the plan by not turning in their profits and taxes on schedule and in full, or if they even create unnecessary losses, national revenue and the planned socialist construction will be affected. In managing enterprises we must give prominence to proletarian politics and mobilize the broad masses of workers to vigorously grasp revolution, energetically promote production, launch the movement of increasing production while practicing economy, and "save every penny for war or the revolutionary cause, and for our economic construction." We must oppose the phenomenon of a lack of seriousness in the management of production and finance, and oppose the incorrect tendency of indifference to state properties and of extravagance and waste under the pretext of "though the meat is rotten, it is still in the pot." We must establish the new socialist practice of "practicing economy is an honor, engaging in waste is a shame." We must properly manage finance for the country in order to boost accumulation as much as possible and to accelerate socialist construction.

## 10. People's Daily Correspondent Refutes the Argument "Statistics Is Useless" (Source 13, pp. 32-38) October 29, 1971

At present, a new upsurge of China's socialist revolution and construction is rising higher, and the assignments of the first year of the Fourth Five-Year Plan are being triumphantly carried out. The new situation creates new demands on the work of statistical planning. Much is still to be done in statistical work with respect to "struggle-criticism-transformation." But some comrades still have muddled ideas, to a certain extent, with respect to statistical work. In some departments and factories, after the revisionist view "Statistics is all powerful" has been criticized, there emerges another, "Statistics is useless." We must give attention to the troubles it stirs up.

One view holds "Statistics is all number games. It does not mean anything." In the past, under the interference of renegade, hidden traitor and scab Liu Shao-ch'i's counter-revolutionary revisionist line, there were indeed people who treated statistical figures as number games. But we must realize that accurate statistical figures are based on facts. They reflect the quality and quantity of objective things and the level people have attained or can attain in their efforts to transform the objective world. We must not treat accurate statistical figures as "number games." Chairman Mao teaches us, "We must not make decisions subjectively without any basis." We must "keep count." "If we do not know how to take note of basic statistics, major percentages, and the quantitative boundaries that define the quality of things, we lose count, and mistakes inevitably will be committed." This applies to Party work, and even more so to economic work. Only through basic statistical analysis of the whole process of national economic activities and of the production construction conditions of each individual region, each individual department, and each individual enterprise, and only when basic figures accurately reflecting the actual conditions are obtained, can production be better organized and all our economic activities be more in line with objective laws so as to achieve greater, faster, and better results at lower costs. If we throw away all statistics and do not take count of anything, then we will drift blindly and blankly, like a fool who can neither handle his work nor grip the essence of a problem. Therefore, whether we should keep statistics or whether we should take count of everything is a principal problem in our economic work. It is the problem of whether we should persist in following the theory of reflection in materialism, or should accept idealist apriorism. There is a great deal in statistics, not "nothing in it."

For a long time, the struggle between Chairman Mao's revolutionary line and Liu Shao-ch'i's counterrevolutionary revisionist line in statistical work has been intense. We all know that Liu Shao-ch'i and company championed "Statistics is all powerful." They saw things rather than people. They laid down a maze of Arabic figures. Many people wasted their time in the blind alleys of triviality. In the Great Proletarian Cultural Revolution, the broad masses of industrial workers and peasants criticized the old statistical work. This is extremely necessary and totally correct. But: "With regard to our work, a completely affirmative or completely negative viewpoint is equally one-sided." We must learn to analyze problems dialectically. We must oppose trivialities in statistical work; we must also oppose nihilism in statistical work. Through mass discussion and practical observation, trivialities and "number games" must be eliminated. Statistical work that is needed for laying down production and construction plans and evaluating their implementation must be seriously and properly conducted. It must be likewise in the accumulation of statistical data for the long-term planning of China's socialist construction. These data will be used when needed. Our socialist construction is a hundred-year project. We must prepare today for tomorrow, consider the abnormal period during the normal period. It is not right to think of only the present without regard of the future.

Therefore, when we engage in the reform of statistical work, we cannot muddle through because of a moment's whim. We must see to it that statistics is beneficial to grasping revolution and promoting production, serving immediate work and long-term needs. Statistical forms must be concise, easily understood, and useful. They must also be flexible and combat-oriented to suit the needs of the Party's varying major tasks. Statistical forms that are out of date must be scrapped and replaced by revised new ones. A certain cotton textile factory in Shanghai examined each of the original 95 production statistical report forms; 54 of them which had the effect of obstructing and oppressing the workers were scrapped, while 41 were found to be reasonable and were retained. Seven forms were introduced to suit new needs. In format the revised report forms were simple, easy to fill out, and useful. For example, in the movement to increase production and practice economy, the workers grasped the major contradiction that obstructs the progress of the movement and established a new system for statistical report. As a result, the workers kept count of the situation, and consciously strengthened production management, raised their standard of operation, and promoted the development of production. Among the statistical items, quite a few were useful for later historical analysis. Thus, both the immediate and future needs were taken care of. After such reforms, specialized statistical workers realized that accurate statistics were necessary for doing a good job in socialist construction and established the idea of doing a good job in statistical work for revolution.

Another view regarding "statistics as useless" is: "Production can be managed even without statistics. It is more important to do a good job in production." This viewpoint is obviously wrong. Whether there is or is not statistics makes a great deal of difference in managing production. An important feature distinguishing socialist production from capitalist production is the fact that under socialism the national economy is developed according to plan. Everything in capitalist production revolves around the extraction of more surplus value. All of social production is chaotic, and the national economy can scarcely be considered to be planned. Socialist production cannot for a minute be divorced from national planning. And plan formulation cannot be divorced from accurate statistics. Planning involves the application of a large amount of statistical data on the actual conditions of the national economy to reveal and analyze the contradictions in economic construction, and to suggest solutions. Therefore, to finish in good time current or historical statistical data on the national economy, to accurately reflect the actual level and speed of development, the interrelationships among its components, and the proportional relations of the national economy is an important basis for establishing planning on a scientific and reliable foundation.

If we do not keep count, we cannot even talk about planned management. Production can never be properly managed. Even if production can be temporarily boosted, is it actually a solid gain? Not really. As it has been well put by the worker comrades: "Production without plans and statistics must be chaotic production!" In such circumstances, class enemies will fish in troubled waters by corruption, theft, and deceit. This is a matter on which we should maintain strict vigilance.

Statistics is an essential tool for inspecting results of plan implementations, for every department, every region and productive unit must earnestly arrange and organize production according to state plans; they must try in every way they can think of to ensure the overall fulfillment of national economic plans. It is necessary, therefore, to reflect through statistics the results of implementing the plans, to enable the leading state agency and the broad masses to take timely actions to eliminate the contradictions that have arisen in the process of executing the plans. Sometimes, it is even necessary to revise the plans according to the situations reflected by the statistics. For instance, in the fourth quarter of last year, an industrial enterprise in Shanghai, in carrying out the combat mission "for fulfillment or overfulfillment of the 1970 national economic plan," adopted by the Ninth Session of the Second Plenum of the Central Committee, discovered in its analysis of the statistical reports regarding production of all related plans that 5 of the 42 plants encountered great difficulties in fulfilling the state plan. According to further analysis, the entire situation and fraternal regions would be adversely affected should the 5 plants fail to meet the targets. Because of this, the cadres went to these plants, where they mobilized the masses by telling them the complete truth. They also organized wide coordination to facilitate the early fulfillment of the state plans in the 5 plants. As a result, the whole company overfulfilled the state plans 25 days ahead of schedule. They said, "Statistical analyses reveal contradictions. Keeping count enables one to have a clear idea of the situation. Mobilizing the masses generates many solutions. All these guarantee the overfulfillment of plans." Examples such as this are numerous. These enterprises are vastly different from those that do not bother to make statistical analyses and adopt the attitude: "We will finish whatever gets finished and drift to wherever we happen to be." How can we say: "Production can be managed just the same, even without statistics"?

Before the Great Proletarian Cultural Revolution, under the pernicious influence of Liu Shao-ch'i's counterrevolutionary revisionist line, statistical work was seriously divorced from proletarian politics, reality, and the masses. Part of statistical work even went the stray path of serving to "control, obstruct, and oppress" and serving "material incentive." But when we level the criticism that revisionist statistics aims at "controlling, obstructing, and oppressing" the broad masses, we should not conclude, because of some people's persuasion, that all statistics "controls, obstructs, and oppresses." If we agree to such a conclusion, we as much as agree to the elimination of socialist statistical work. And the elimination of statistics amounts to elimination of the planned economy. This not only affects the development of socialist production construction, but also weakens the economic base of proletarian dictatorship. Lenin once correctly pointed out: "If there is no overall state statistics and supervision of production and distribution of output, the political power and the freedom of the laboring people cannot be maintained and the restoration of the exploitative capitalist system will be inevitable." This can never be permitted by our proletariat and the revolutionary people!

Does engaging in statistical work mean not trusting the people? This is not true at all. When we make revolution and launch construction, we depend on Marxism-Leninism-Mao Tse-tung thought, Chairman Mao's proletarian revolutionary line, and the command of proletarian politics to mobilize and organize the masses and to fully mobilize mass activism. When we say that statistics is useful, we do not mean that figures determine everything. Indeed, many factors such as people's ideology and activism cannot be wholly reflected by figures. Even material factors must combine with the masses and with reality before they can be reflected in figures. But in doing anything, we must "adopt the best possible plan allowable by the objective conditions." Only by keeping count, by drawing up plans according to Chairman Mao's revolutionary line, specific and general policies, and the actual conditions of the regions, departments, and units concerned can the broad masses have a clear target for struggle. Only by exploiting the superiority of the socialist system and establishing our work on a scientific basis under the guidance of Chairman Mao's revolutionary line can mass activism be fully protected and mobilized and can plans be fulfilled and overfulfilled. Accurate statistics tells people how much has been achieved, what targets have been reached, and what new starts have been made. It also tells people the disparities between what is required and what has been achieved and it furnishes data to help decide where to go and what to do in the next step. If we do not understand all these things and force planning, mass activism will surely be hurt!

Chairman Mao teaches us: "Mass movement is necessary in all work. Mass movement is indispensable." Statistical work is certainly not the sole business of a minority in the leadership and specialized organs. All tasks of our socialist enterprises are carried out by the leadership of the various levels leading the masses under the guidance of Chairman Mao and the Party Central Committee. Therefore, first, our statistical work must be performed with the help of the masses and not by a minority behind closed doors. The basis of statistical work is raw data. Only by mobilizing the masses can this work be properly carried out. Some plants elect workers of a certain shift to be responsible for the processing and publication of the raw data of their own shift. This effectively eliminates the cheating typical of the bourgeoisie and the evil wind of anarchism whereby no record or accounts are kept and no one is in charge. Second, statistics must be used by the masses and serve mass participation in management. This is to say that not only must the leadership of the various levels keep count, the masses must also keep count. We must be good at using statistics and figures to persuade, mobilize, and organize the masses. To make it easier to understand, some plants publicize relevant statistics in the form of charts and diagrams of the various shifts in their combat to complete key activities. The worker master said: "Charts and diagrams illustrate statistical figures best. Once we keep count properly, our determination to complete key activities is heightened." Practice shows that when the leadership and the masses keep count, Chairman Mao's revolutionary line can be better implemented, the initiative in struggle can be better taken, and greater victory in revolution and production can be achieved!

## 11. Provincial Revolutionary Committee Writing Team Argues Land, Labor and Capital Are Insufficient to Explain Economic Development (Source 1, pp. 70-71) April 7, 1971

Some comrades think: "Land, capital funds, and labor are all limited. When it comes to the production of food grains and economic crops, we can grasp one only at the expense of the other. It is difficult to take care of both of them."

This is also a metaphysical viewpoint. Indeed, the development of economic crops contains a contradiction with respect to the use of land, manure, and manpower. But looking at the problems from the viewpoint of development, we find that they have the aspect of mutual promotion and mutual assistance. For instance, Hunghsing Brigade of Tangt'u hsien expanded its rapeseed acreage by over 100 percent over the past few years, and raised the per mou rapeseed yield by over 100 percent as compared with that reaped before the Great Cultural Revolution, as a result of the scientific farming method. The development of rapeseed production not only aids the state by providing large amounts of oil seeds but also promotes the production increase of grains. First, income can be increased by over 10,000 yuan each year, providing a favorable condition for public capital accumulation and for the improvement of the livelihood of commune members. Second, the supply of manure cakes is directly increased by large quantities, sufficient to provide base manure for 1,000 odd mou of late rice. Third, the ripening period of rapeseed is early. When rapeseed is planted, the rice fields can also be planted with double rice crops, and thus three crops a year can be realized. Over the past few years, this brigade has raised its grain output each year, and the per mou yield last year reached 1,360 catties. Therefore, if we combine revolutionary enthusiasm with scientific attitude, carry out unified planning and remain attentive to all aspects, make overall arrangements, and thoroughly implement the "Eight-Character Constitution" for agriculture to make strenuous efforts in scientific farming, then we shall be able to tap potentials for production increases ceaselessly, correctly tackle contradictions between production food grains and economic crops, and enable the two to achieve mutual promotion and mutual development.

Here, the basic question lies in the presence of a revolutionized leadership squad. Kuo-chuang Brigade of Hsiao hsien in the Huai-pei area, an advanced collective in our province in learning from Tachai, provides a good example. Prior to 1965, this brigade had continued to be a backward brigade with low yields of grains and cotton, due to the serious impurity of the leadership squad. Subsequently, during the storm of class struggle, they set up a leadership squad which had great revolutionary enthusiasm and had close association with the masses. They relentlessly grasped the struggle between the two classes and the two lines, resolutely and thoroughly carried out Chairman Mao's revolutionary line, conscientiously implemented Party policies, and fully roused the masses, bringing about drastic changes in both production and revolution. Last year, in spite of the natural disasters of a major hailstorm and continuous rainfall for over 40 days, they raised the per mou yield of grains from 633 catties in 1969 to 1,030 catties, and the per mou yield of the major economic crop of cotton from 124 catties to 185 catties.

## 12. State Planning Commission Charts the Future of the Chinese Economy in the Post-Mao Era (Source 28, pp. 7-14), September 12, 1977

For more than half a century, Chairman Mao led the Chinese

people in successfully overthrowing the reactionary rule of imperialism, feudalism and bureaucrat-capitalism after protracted and extremely bitter and hard struggles, winning complete victory in the new-democratic revolution and founding the People's Republic of China. Following this, Chairman Mao led us, through repeated trials of strength between the proletariat and the bourgeosie, in carrying out the socialist revolution, with each stage deeper than the previous one, in undertaking the task of socialist construction on a large scale, in consolidating the dictatorship of the proletariat, thereby turning China from a poor and backward country into a socialist state with the beginnings of prosperity.

Under Chairman Mao's leadership, we abolished the feudal system of exploitation, confiscated bureaucrat capital, transformed the capitalist and individual economies, and set up an independent, new socialist economy. Industry owned by the whole people and by the collective now accounts for 99.9 percent of China's gross industrial output value. Our industry has grown rapidly and is now able to supply increasing amounts of technical equipment for the various branches of the national economy and for defense construction. Organized in more than 50,000 people's communes, China's several hundred million peasants have been advancing along the broad road of socialism. Our agriculture has given powerful support to socialist construction; it feeds a population which exceeds one-fifth of the world's total although our cultivated acreage accounts for less than 7 percent of the world's total. Rapid advances have also been made in communications and transport, finances and trade, science and technology, culture, education, medicine and health, and other undertakings. We have hydrogen bombs and guided missiles and have launched man-made earth satellites. Our revenue and expenditure are balanced, prices have remained stable, and people's living standards have greatly improved.

All the victories we have won are great victories for Chairman Mao's revolutionary line and Mao Tsetung Thought.

Chairman Mao's theory on socialist construction holds an important place in the comprehensive system of Mao Tsetung Thought. By summing up the experience of economic construction in the revolutionary base areas during China's democratic revolution and the experience of socialist construction since nationwide liberation, and making an incisive study of the positive and negative experience of socialist construction in the Soviet Union and the lessons of capitalist restoration there, Chairman Mao creatively set forth the theory, line, principles and policies for socialist construction and pointed out China's road of building socialism, thus advancing Marxist-Leninist theory on socialist construction to a new stage.

The basic concepts in Chairman Mao's theory on socialist construction are: Persevere in the continued revolution under the dictatorship of the proletariat; and correctly handle the question of classes, class contradictions and class struggle; correctly handle the relationships between the various branches of the national economy; boldly arouse the masses and fully mobilize all positive factors so as to achieve greater, faster, better and more economical results in building socialism. Chairman Mao's concepts have not only guided us to great successes in socialist construction but will remain great guiding principles for us in winning new and still greater victories in the future.

## Grasping Revolution and Promoting Production

Applying the dialectical materialist law of the unity of opposites to study and analyze socialist society, Chairman Mao created the great theory of continuing the revolution under the dictatorship of the proletariat. Using this theory to guide socialist construction, he firmly grasped the principal contradiction, that is, the struggle between the proletariat and the bourgeoisie and between the socialist and capitalist roads, and he used revolution to command production so that both revolution and production would forge ahead simultaneously. This is an important contribution by Chairman Mao to the development of the Marxist theory on socialist construction.

The founding of the People's Republic of China in 1949 marked the beginning of the stage of socialist revolution. With the completion of the agrarian reform throughout the country in 1952, the contradiction between the proletariat and the bourgeoisie and between the socialist and capitalist roads was focused on the issue of ownership. Capitalist ownership and widespread individual ownership seriously hampered the growth of the productive forces. Chairman Mao told us explicitly that, in order to consolidate its political power and carry out socialist construction on a large scale, the proletariat must "destroy capitalist ownership and transform it into socialist ownership by the whole people, destroy individual ownership and transform it into socialist collective ownership" ("Have Firm Faith in the Majority of the People," 1957). Grasping this central issue in resolving the contradiction between the proletariat and the bourgeoisie at the time, Chairman Mao formulated in good time the general line for the period of transition, a line which called for the socialist transformation of agriculture, handicrafts and capitalist industry and commerce simultaneously with socialist industrialization. Chairman Mao closely integrated socialist construction with socialist transformation and combined the socialist transformation of agriculture with that of capitalist industry and commerce with great skill, so that they developed in coordination and promoted each other. In the course of fierce class struggle, Chairman Mao led our Party in rapidly and steadily bringing about such a great change as the transformation of ownership, and created the experience of carrying out socialist transformation and socialist construction simultaneously. During the transformation of ownership, agricultural production increased year by year, industry and commerce expanded steadily, the socialist economy grew from strength to strength, and the First Five-Year Plan (1953-57) for economic construction was crowned with complete success.

A new question arose at that time in our revolution and construction, a question which had not been correctly solved in the international communist movement. It was: After the issue of ownership had been settled in the main, were there still contradictions, classes and class struggle in socialist society and should socialist construction be still carried out in the course of socialist revolution? Chairman Mao pointed out in explicit terms for the first time in the history of the development of Marxism that there is correspondence as well as contradiction between the relations of production and the productive forces and between the superstructure and the economic base even after the socialist transformation of ownership has been completed in the main. Such contradiction remains the fundamental contradiction in socialist society, and class struggle is by no means over. In these circumstances, the productive forces must still develop in the course of constant efforts to resolve the fundamental contradiction and under the impetus given by class struggle. Chairman Mao formulated for our Party the basic line for the historical period of socialism (see Peking Review, No. 2, 1977, p. 11), and armed our Party and people with the theory of continuing the revolution under the dictatorship of the proletariat. This ensures that China's construction always develop in the socialist orientation.

The principle of "grasping revolution, promoting production" advanced by Chairman Mao succinctly answered the question of the relationship between continuing the revolution under the dictatorship of the proletariat and carrying out socialist construction. Chairman Mao pointed out in a talk in 1964 that class struggle, the struggle for production and scientific experiment must be integrated. If people engage only in the struggle for production and scientific experiment but neglect class struggle, they won't be really fired with great enthusiasm and they can't do well in the struggle for production and scientific experiment. Neither will it do to engage only in the struggle for production without making scientific experiment. If people who only wage class struggle without carrying out the struggle for production and scientific experiment claim that they "support the general line," the claim will eventually prove to be false.

What are the main points we should bear in mind and earnestly put into practice today as we restudy Chairman Mao's teachings about grasping revolution and promoting production in the light of the present situation?

1. Chairman Mao said: "Class struggle is the key link and everything else hinges on it." In the historical period of socialism, all our undertakings in the field of construction will have a correct orientation and develop in a sound way only when we persevere in the class struggle waged by the proletariat against the bourgeoisie to ensure the triumph of socialism over capitalism, and when the task of consolidating the dictatorship of the proletariat is carried out to the letter at the grass-roots level.

The struggle between the proletariat and the bourgeoisie at present finds concentrated expression in the struggle waged by our Party against the "gang of four." We must carry this struggle through to the end.

2. The power of leadership must be firmly kept in the hands of genuine Marxists and the broad masses of the working people. This is a crucial point in ensuring the implementation of the correct line and consolidating the socialist political and economic systems. The historical experience of the Great Proletarian Cultural Revolution has proved fully that if the three bourgeois headquarters of Liu Shao-ch'i, Lin Piao and the "gang of four" had not been smashed, if these renegades, enemy agents, new and old counterrevolutionaries and diehard capitalist-roaders had not been exposed and their counterrevolutionary revisionist line thoroughly repudiated, the power of leadership by the proletariat might have been usurped, the dictatorship of the proletariat subverted and the socialist economic base disintegrated. How then can we speak of socialist construction?

3. We must constantly repulse the attacks by urban and rural capitalist forces and defend socialist public ownership. This is one of our major tasks in continuing the revolution under the dictatorship of the proletariat in the realm of the relations of production, and it should be done continuously and persistently for a long time to come. Chairman Mao reminded us time and again that in socialist society classes still exist, the new and old bourgeoisie seize every chance to attack us, illegal capitalist activities such as embezzlement, theft and speculation frequently occur and bourgeois ideology seriously erodes our ranks. He pointed out in 1975: "Lenin said that 'small production engenders capitalism and the bourgeoisie continuously, daily, hourly, spontaneously, and on a mass scale.' They are also engendered among a part of the working class and of the Party membership. Both within the ranks of the proletariat and among the personnel of state and other organs there are people who take to the bourgeois style of life." We must persistently deal blows at the class enemy's restorationist activities in undermining the socialist economy and at the same time pay attention to overcoming capitalist tendencies within the ranks of the people.

4. We must continue to improve the relations among people in work and promote the consolidation of socialist public ownership and the development of the productive forces. Cadres at all levels, leading cadres in particular, should restrict bourgeois right of their own accord and conduct themselves as ordinary workers. They must consult with the masses when matters arise and be concerned with their difficulties. We must uphold the principle of cadre participation in collective productive labor and worker participation in management and apply the "three-in-one combination" of leading cadres, workers and technicians to a wide field of endeavors and keep up and carry forward the revolutionary tradition of unity between cadres and the masses and of sharing weal and woe, as we did in the revolutionary war years. We must criticize in a deep-going way the evil bourgeois tendencies encouraged by the "gang of four" to expand privileges and pursue personal gains.

5. Political work is the lifeblood of all economic work. We must strengthen political and ideological work so as to invigorate the revolutionary spirit of the millions and tens of millions of cadres and workers throughout the industrial sector (and commercial and agricultural sectors as well). The fundamental task in doing political and ideological work is to arm the masses with Marxism-Leninism-Mao Tsetung Thought and strive to bring up a large contingent of workers who are politically conscious, energetic, disciplined, good in their style of work and highly skilled.

6. Transformation in the relations of production and the superstructure is conditioned by the development of the productive forces and must help promote it and not vice versa. Political work should serve the economic base and ensure the accomplishment of economic work. Chairman Mao long ago said: "In the last analysis, the impact, good or bad, great or small, of the policy and the practice of any Chinese political party upon the people depends on whether and how much it helps to develop their productive forces, and on whether it fetters or liberates these forces" (On Coalition Government, 1945). The "gang of four" asserted that "it is all right for production to go down so long as we do a good job in revolution" and "it doesn't matter if no grain is reaped at all." These are utterly reactionary fallacies.

7. Increasing or decreasing production is an important criterion in judging whether a revolution is successful or not. While leading the Chinese people in unfolding a large-scale agricultural cooperative movement, Chairman Mao pointed out: "The main criterion by which every cooperative judges whether it is sound is to see whether its production is rising and by how much" (Editor's Notes from "Socialist Upsurge in China's Countryside," 1955). He also said: "In the Soviet Union and in some East European countries, agricultural collectivization invariably brought about decreases in grain production for a number of years. We have had agricultural cooperation for several years, and we went all out last year, yet, far from falling, our grain production has increased. If another good harvest is reaped this year, there will be no parallel in the history of the agricultural cooperative movement as well as in the history of the international communist movement" (Talks at a Conference of Secretaries of Provincial, Municipal and Autonomous Region Party Committees, 1957). In fact, in the course of the agricultural cooperative movement, agricultural production in China kept rising for years running. Likewise, in every political movement unfolded under his leadership, Chairman Mao again and again taught us to strive for good results in both revolution and production.

8. It is necessary to learn to do economic work well. We must put revolution in command of production, but the former cannot replace the latter. Revolution has its own laws, so does production. We must be well-versed in politics and be proficient in professional work, that is, we must be both red and expert. If we Communists do not concern ourselves with industry and the economy and do not know how to do any other useful work, if we are ignorant of these things and incapable of doing anything except a kind of abstract "revolutionary work," we would be good-for-nothing "revolutionaries."

## The General Line for Building Socialism

Chairman Mao made a profound study of the objective laws governing socialist revolution and construction and put forward the general line of going all out, aiming high and achieving greater, faster, better and more economical results in building socialism and a complete set of principles of "walking on two legs," thus pointing out the correct orientation and road for us to develop our national economy as a whole in a planned way, proportionately and at high speed.

The question of speed in socialist construction is a very important one. It is even more so for our country, which has a backward economy and a large population and faces the threat of aggression and subversion by imperialism and social-imperialism. It is a question of life and death for our country, a state under the dictatorship of the proletariat. Lenin put it this way: "Either perish or overtake and outstrip the advanced countries economically as well" (The Impending Catastrophe and How to Combat It, 1917). After nationwide liberation Chairman Mao more than once called on us to develop socialist construction at high speed and catch up with and surpass the developed capitalist countries economically so that our national economy will advance in the front ranks of the world. In 1956 he made a comparison between China and the United States and urged us to overtake the United States economically in 50 to 60 years.

In the 28 postliberation years, China has outstripped many capitalist countries in the speed of economic development. But, owing to the interference and sabotage by Liu Shao-ch'i, Lin Piao and, in particular, the "gang of four," our socialist construction did not achieve the expected results. With the smashing of the "gang of four" a major obstacle to building socialism has been removed. Under the leadership of the Party Central Committee headed by Chairman Hua, as long as we persevere in doing things in accordance with Chairman Mao's theory, line, principles and policies and in continuing the revolution under the dictatorship of the proletariat and understand and grasp still better the objective laws governing socialist construction, we will certainly be able to expedite socialist construction so that our socialist system will display its superiority still more fully.

In the light of the objective laws governing socialist construction which Chairman Mao made known to us, what then are the relationships which we must make special efforts to handle properly and what are the questions which we must solve well at present in order to quicken the pace of our socialist construction?

(1) Handle properly the relationship between industry and agriculture and the relationship among various trades and branches in industry and agriculture.

The general policy for national economic development put forward by Chairman Mao — "Take agriculture as the foundation and industry as the leading factor" — fully reflects the importance of agriculture and industry in the national economy as a whole and the essential link between these two major economic departments. Agriculture concerns the question of feeding China's population of 800 million; it is the chief supplier of raw materials for light industry and an important source for accumulation by the state. The countryside is an important market for light and heavy industrial products. Unless agriculture develops, the growth of industry and the national economy as a whole is out of the question.

As far as agriculture is concerned, it is imperative to keep to the policy of "taking grain as the key link and ensuring an all-round development." Industry must support agriculture and serve it better. In other words, it must help promote the technical transformation of agriculture with modern equipment. It is necessary to persevere in "taking steel as the key link," build a strong basic industry, and provide the various departments of the national economy and defense construction with advanced techniques and equipment.

Serious attention must be paid to grain and steel production, the fuel and power industries and railway construction, and it is necessary to work out a plan for developing the national economy in the order of agriculture, light industry and heavy industry.

(2) Bring into full play the initiative of both the central and the local authorities and carry out the policy of simultaneously developing the national and local industries, the large, medium-sized and small enterprises and simultaneously using modern and indigenous methods of production. Chairman Mao said: "Our territory is so vast, our population is so large and the conditions are so complex that it is far better to have the ini-

tiative come from both the central and the local authorities than from one source alone" ("On the Ten Major Relationships," 1956). Time and again he instructed us to let the local authorities do more under unified planning by the central authorities, so as to promote the growth of the national economy with greater, faster, better and more economical results.

Concentration of power in the central authorities and distribution of power to the local authorities are a unity of opposites. We should proceed from the actual conditions and handle this contradiction properly so as to facilitate the development of the productive forces. While opposing rigid and all-inclusive control by the central authorities which might stifle local initiative, we must oppose departmentalism and decentralism which only take into consideration the interests of this or that locality or department at the expense of those of the whole nation. Centralization must be exercised wherever necessary. Power must be concentrated in the central authorities with regard to the following: formulation of the principles and policies in developing the national economy, setting major industrial and agricultural production quotas, making investments in capital construction and building key projects, distribution of important materials, the purchase and allocation of major commodities, setting the state budget and issuing currency, fixing the number of workers and staff to be added and their total wages, and the prices of major industrial and agricultural products. In such matters no locality or department is allowed to do as it pleases. The "gang of four," however, attacked centralized, unified leadership, which is indispensable for the state, as "exclusive control by the ministries concerned," adding that such control amounted to "dictatorship of the bourgeoisie." Obviously, it was with malicious intent that they distorted the relationship between the central and the local authorities as one of dictatorship by one class over another.

(3) Persist in working hard and building our country through diligence and thrift and correctly handle the relationship between accumulation and consumption and the relationship between the state, the collective and the individual.

Chairman Mao said in 1957: "We must see to it that all our cadres and all our people constantly bear in mind that ours is a large socialist country but an economically backward and poor one, and that this is a very big contradiction. To make China prosperous and strong needs several decades of hard struggle, which means, among other things, pursuing the policy of building up our country through diligence and thrift, that is, practicing strict economy and fighting waste" ("On the Correct Handling of Contradictions among the People"). Since then, we have made tremendous progress in socialist construction, but the present level of our productive forces is still comparatively low. To speed up construction, we must unswervingly continue to implement the policy of working hard and building our country through diligence and thrift.

Accumulation is the source for expanded reproduction. Only by constantly increasing accumulation can we maintain a high-speed development of socialist economy.

The aim of socialist production is to meet the growing needs of the people. Herein lies the essential difference between socialist and capitalist production. Chairman Mao said: "We must lay emphasis on the development of production, but consideration must be given to both the development of production and the improvement of the people's livelihood" ("Combat Bourgeois Ideas in the Party," 1953). In economic policy, we must uphold the socialist principle of "from each according to his ability, to each according to his work" and gradually expand and improve collective welfare.

(4) Make every effort to introduce advanced techniques, vigorously carry out technical innovations and the technical revolution and raise labor productivity. Chairman Mao always attached importance to the development of science and technology, regarding scientific experiment, class struggle and the struggle for production as the Three Great Revolutionary Movements for building a powerful socialist country. To achieve this, we must take effective measures to train and bring up a mighty contingent of scientists and technicians.

(5) It is imperative to have socialist unified planning and make earnest efforts to achieve an overall balance. Socialist economy is a planned economy. This is a basic characteristic that distinguishes it from the capitalist economy. To build a powerful socialist country, it is imperative to have a strong

and unified central leadership and unified planning and discipline throughout the country; disruption of this indispensable unity is impermissible.

## Independence and Self-Reliance

Taking into consideration the world situation and drawing on the experience of the dictatorship of the proletariat in other countries, Chairman Mao pointed out that in our socialist revolution and construction we must adhere to the strategic principles of maintaining independence and keeping the initiative in our own hands and relying on our own efforts and of being prepared against war, being prepared against natural disasters, and doing everything for the people. These principles provide the most reliable guarantee that our country will be invincible.

China's socialist construction has all along been carried out in the midst of sharp and complicated international class struggle. The two superpowers, the Soviet Union and the United States, are intensifying their contention for world hegemony, and a world war is bound to break out some day. The Soviet revisionists are bent on subjugating China. The struggle against social-imperialist and imperialist aggression and subversion is a grave one that concerns not only the existence of China's socialist system but the world proletarian revolution as a whole. In this struggle, the above-mentioned strategic principles will always be brilliant banners guiding us to victory.

According to the Marxist viewpoint, a socialist country must rely chiefly on its own strength in construction. Only by proceeding from the specific conditions of the countries concerned, relying on the hard work and wisdom of their own people and making the best of all available natural resources can they achieve notable and effective results in building socialism.

Chairman Mao time and again told us that in the course of socialist construction we must build an independent and comprehensive industrial system and national economic system. For a country to be independent it should first of all achieve political independence. But if it is not independent economically and is dependent on other countries for the things it needs, its political independence will not be secure. Therefore, building an independent and comprehensive industrial system and national economic system is not only an economic question but, first and foremost, a political issue. This is a requirement for consolidating the dictatorship of the proletariat and for the struggle to oppose social-imperialist and imperialist aggression, subversion, interference and control. Over the last two decades and more, we have achieved great success in building a comprehensive economic system. In the years to come, we will continue to set up economic systems in the six big regions — northeast China, north China, east China, central-south China, southwest China and northwest China — which are different in their level of development and which will have their own special features, operate independently, cooperate with one another and ensure a fairly balanced growth of agriculture, light industry and heavy industry.

Building an independent and comprehensive economic system does not mean closing our doors to the rest of the world. We must expand our economic, technical and cultural exchanges with other countries on the principles of equality, mutual benefit and supplying each other's needs.

## The Mass Line

Chairman Mao's theory concerning socialist construction is characterized by a very important concept, which is to arouse the masses boldly and launch mass movements under the leadership of the Communist Party. This is our Party's fundamental line in building socialism.

The essence of the general line of going all out, aiming high and achieving greater, faster, better and more economical results in building socialism formulated by Chairman Mao is to attach great importance to the initiative and creativeness of the hundreds of millions of people and to give full scope to their enthusiasm, wisdom and strength. The complete set of policies of "Walking on two legs" advanced by Chairman Mao, namely, the simultaneous development of industry and agriculture, of industries run by the central and local authorities and the building of big industries and medium-sized and small ones and the simultaneous use of modern and indigenous methods, are aimed not only at correctly handling the ratio between the various branches of the national economy but, more important, at bringing into fuller play the positive factors in all fields of endeavor, so that the people in their hundreds of millions can fully devote their energy to socialist construction which in turn will truly become an undertaking of theirs.

Chairman Mao said: "Society's wealth is created by workers, peasants and working intellectuals. Provided they take their destiny into their own hands, provided they have a Marxist-Leninist line and energetically tackle problems instead of evading them, they can overcome any difficulty on earth" (Editor's Notes From "Socialist Upsurge in China's Countryside," 1955). Practice in socialist construction over the past 20 years and more fully testifies to the correctness of this thesis of Chairman Mao's.

The theory, line, principles and methods Chairman Mao advanced for launching mass movements in socialist construction have enormously enriched and developed the basic Marxist principle that the people are the makers of history.

We must rely on the working class and the poor and lower-middle peasants wholeheartedly, have greater faith in the masses, rely on them more fully and respect their pioneering efforts.

We must keep to the line of "from the masses and back to the masses" and conscientiously follow this line in all our work. When we decide on the principles and policies, draw up plans, establish rules and regulations and deal with problems, we must listen to the opinions of the masses and be good at gathering their correct opinions and carrying them through so as to turn them into conscious actions by the masses.

We must do well in combining soaring revolutionary spirit with a strict scientific approach and keep to the fine tradition and style of work of seeking truth from facts.

We must go deep into reality, make investigation and study, be adept in discovering and summing up the advanced experience of the masses and conscientiously popularize it. Meanwhile, we must show concern for the well-being of the masses.

We must strengthen Party leadership, uphold the principle of democratic centralism and do a good job of combining full democracy with centralized, unified leadership. In those enterprises and localities where the Party's mass line is correctly implemented and big efforts are made to launch mass movements, the people's political consciousness has invariably been enhanced and production has made rapid headway.

At present, our socialist revolution and construction have entered a new period of development. The revolutionary mass movements In industry, learn from Taching and In agriculture, learn from Tachai initiated by Chairman Mao are surging ahead. The socialist revolutionary emulation campaign is gaining momentum in all parts of the country and on all fronts. The people throughout the country are now working hard to build China into a great, powerful and modern socialist country. And in all this, Chairman Mao's great theory is the guide to our march forward.

PART TWO

# Planning and Markets

"Distribution is inescapable," writes a leading expert on development. "The Western economist has always been fascinated with how swiftly, efficiently, and with how little direction free markets can perform this function."[1] In the economic history of Western Europe the "commercial revolution" preceded the "industrial revolution" and in several ways seems partly responsible for it. Markets spread beyond face-to-face contacts between buyer and seller where all goods were traded physically on the spot; consequently important changes in the structure of economic transactions occurred. Negotiated prices declined in favor of list prices. The caveat emptor tradition "let the buyer beware" declined in favor of the principle of sellers' responsibility for the quality of their merchandise. Standard weights and measures replaced local ones, and buyers increasingly insisted on standard grades (such that ungraded food grains mixed with stones and mice, for example, could no longer find markets). Entrepreneurial talent developed as markets expanded. And eventually capital accumulated that was available for investment in manufacturing. Correspondingly, large-scale manufacturing was possible only if outlets existed for expanded production. When technological inventions were made, the economy had to be ready to exploit the new ideas. Based upon this Western European experience, a strong case has been advanced that commercial modernization must precede industrial modernization.

Sometimes Japan is held up as a counter-example, an instance in which rapid industrialization proceeded without a prior stage of commercialization, especially in international trade. Also, not every premodern society which developed a commercial network later experienced a period of rapid industrialization. Yet the overall relationship is strong, and China gives confirmation. Chinese commercial development before the Communist period was very limited, and industrialization had barely begun.

One leading student of rural social structure in modern China, anthropologist William Skinner, elaborates hierarchies of marketing areas as a basic concept for his discussion of commercial "modernization."[2] A "standard market" begins the flow of farm produce and handicrafts upward into the higher reaches of the marketing system, and ends the downward flow of imported items destined for peasant consumption. An "intermediate market" usually services six standard markets and also meets periodically (such as on the second, fifth, and eighth days of a ten-day cycle). Skinner finds, significantly, that most rural trade in Republican China was restricted to intermediate market areas which contained populations of 350-1,000 or more households. A small share of agricultural products flowed out of intermediate market areas, but often even standard market areas were almost self-sufficient. Either increasing density of households on the land, or increasing household productivity and participation in the marketing process, would induce traditional commercial systems to develop in both size and complexity — increases in total volume of trade carried on in the town, in the number of marketing hours per week, in the proportion of permanent to mobile firms, and in the degree and scope of economic specialization — but alone all this still would be limited to what Skinner terms "false" modernization. To have "true" modernization a modern freight system — by river steamer, railway, or all-weather road — had to grow up within a market area; only then would the area be extended and household self-sufficiency contract, and only then would traditional markets die off. Where narrow dirt roads connected villages and town "more goods were carried in more carts to more shops in more markets more frequently convened — but there was no systemic change." Skinner concludes there was "pitifully little" true modernization in Republican China. He estimates that by 1949 only 10 percent of China's intermediate marketing systems had been converted to truly modern trading systems and the correspondingly few traditional markets died in the twentieth century. Of 63,000 rural traditional markets which existed prior to the beginnings of modernization in the 1890s (including standard, intermediate and central markets, but excluding those in local and regional cities), no fewer than 57,600 survived through 1949.

The Communists who took power in Peking in 1949 were deeply suspicious of markets as core institutions of despised capitalism. Ideology led them to favor immediate nationalization of modern sectors of the economy, steady collectivization of less developed sectors, and substitution of comprehensive state planning for market mechanisms in all allocation. That is, they were inclined to follow the lead of the Soviet Union under Stalin.

Development economists outside the Marxist tradition occupy some shared ground with advocates of market restriction. Hla Myint writes that short sharp rises in prices can be effective in cutting down demand, but may not be the best way of stimulating long-term supply. Thus the market mechanism may simply lead to windfall profits which do not affect supply.

> In the short run, the market mechanism deals with a shortage of a particular commodity or factor of production by raising its price sharply enough to cut down demand and equate it to the given supply. In the long run, it deals with a shortage by raising the price of the scarce commodity high enough to induce the increase in its supply. Now, although the price of the scarce commodity rises in both cases, the ways in which it may be raised to solve the short-run and the long-run problems are different. . . . What is likely to be more effective for stimulating the long-term supply is a somewhat smaller rise in the price, but maintained steadily over a period of time.[4]

In many cases government intervention may be necessary to "distort" natural market prices for the purpose of bringing about desired long-term increases in supply, and in the process for dealing with groups in the private sector whose short-run sacrifices are demanded for overall long-run growth. Charles

Kindleberger concurs: "the price system works well at the margin, but is not competent to produce the structural changes which development calls for. Once a society has some amount of activity in every line, the price system can redirect resources from one to another through small changes. It is much harder to use prices to start new industries."[5]

The ideal of comprehensive state planning and price control has met predictable difficulties in contemporary China, with the result that the commercial system emerging in the 1960s and 1970s has retained planning as the allocator of priority goods (such as energy, key raw materials, capital goods, military equipment, important Chinese exports, goods transferred among provinces, staple food products, and cotton), but admits a role for markets and prices in allocating other goods. Practical difficulties include lack of input-output tables specifying mutual transfers of products between each pair among dozens of sectors; insufficient computer facilities for making millions of allocating decisions (in manufacturing alone China has approximately 5,000 medium and large-scale industrial enterprises); instability of agricultural production (because output varies greatly with the weather); tendency for black markets to crop up whenever state list prices become too unrealistic; and trade-offs between administrative advantages of economic decentralization (advantages especially attractive considering China's vast size) and the consequent loss of control by central planners. Hence most market activity is evident in local rural trade. Black markets operate outside the law, although sometimes with tacit official approval. Periodic markets which meet every fifth day or so, commonly called "rural trade fairs," are perfectly legal, though they regularly come under attack for exemplifying undesirable capitalist tendencies in rural life. Stores and procurement stations run by supply and marketing cooperatives located either in rural production brigades or in commune towns officially represent "collective" commerce; for all practical purposes, though, the rural cooperative system now is a regular agency of the Ministry of Commerce. Sometimes conflict between private and socialist commerce in China takes the form of competition between supply and marketing cooperatives and rural trade fairs, with the former usually trying to encroach upon the scope of the latter. Usually they are successful only if local farmers feel cooperative prices are competitive.

Above the rural collective level are various state-owned commercial enterprises such as the Shanghai General Department Store and foreign trade enterprises such as the China National Native Produce and Animal By-Products Import and Export Corporation. All state-owned commercial enterprises belong to a specific administrative level — county, province or center.

After the question of the proper role for "capitalistic" rural markets and market prices, the leading debate in the domestic commerce area has been over decentralization and local autonomy. These two broad questions are related since both market allocation and local autonomy represent challenges to full control by central planners. But the rationale for decentralization is different than that for markets, and decentralization, especially in the guise of "self-reliance," is more acceptable ideologically. Economists have identified two types of insularity in the Chinese economy which naturally encourage decentralization. Referring specifically to the 1950s, Dwight Perkins notes how the combined effect of variable sales taxes and state control of commerce was the isolation of major sectors such as agriculture, industry, and the urban consumers' goods market. This means that during that period these sectors depended very little upon one another. Only after 1961 has a more energetic policy of increasing supplies of industrial inputs to farmers been followed.[6] Audrey Donnithorne characterizes China's economy and society as "cellular," meaning that many regions are self-sufficient to a large degree, and that local enterprises mainly are subject to leadership from local Party committees. She too points to the inevitability of change.

> While we stress the cellular nature of the present-day Chinese economy, a word of warning is necessary. As the economy becomes modernized, the tendency will be for its cellular nature to evolve into more complex systems of relationships. Even now the economy is less cellular than in the past, as exemplified in particular by the countrywide operations of the People's Bank, and also by the changes taking place in the more modernized parts of the country.[7]

Nevertheless, during the 1960s and 1970s, the period of the

Figure 1

Basic Organization of Commerce, 1970s

| Level | Party (CCP) | Administration | |
|---|---|---|---|
| Center | Central Committee Finance-Trade Work Department (FTWD) | State Council Finance-Trade Office (FTO) | |
| | Ministry Party Committees | Ministry of Commerce | |
| | | All-China Supply and Marketing General Cooperative | |
| | | Ministry of Food | |
| | | Ministry of Foreign Trade | |
| | | Export Corporations | |
| Province | Provincial Committee FTWD | Revolutionary Committee FTO | |
| | Department Party Committees | Department of Commerce | |
| | | Supply and Marketing Cooperative (SMC) | |
| | | Department of Food | |
| | | Urban | Rural |
| City or district (<u>ti-ch'ü</u>) | Municipal (or District) Committee FTWD | Municipal Revolutionary Committee FTO | District Administration FTO |
| | Division and Enterprise Party Committees | Division of Commerce | Division of Commerce |
| | | | SMC |
| | | Division of Food | Division of Food |

| | | | |
|---|---|---|---|
| | | Department stores and specialty shops variously managed by special product companies of appropriate administrative agencies (e.g., a provincial Department of Public Health might form a pharmaceutical company to operate a chain of drug stores) | |
| Town or County | Municipal (or County) Committee FTWD<br><br>Bureau and Enterprise Party Committees | Same as city | County Revolutionary Committee FTO<br><br>Bureau of Commerce<br><br>SMC<br><br>Bureau of Food |
| Local Levels | Party committee members with special responsibility for finance and trade<br><br>Enterprise Party committees or branches | Food markets<br><br>Specialty shops<br><br>Urban districts, neighborhoods and streets may organize collective enterprises | <u>Commune</u><br><br>SMC general store, specialty shops, and procurement stations (for grain, oil bearing crops, vegetables and other sideliners)<br><br>Rural "trade fairs" (periodic markets)<br><br><u>Production brigade or large team</u><br><br>SMC branch store, and/or procurement points |

documentary excerpts included in this collection, repeated manifestations of a regional cellular structure have appeared — high proportions of department store goods produced in the store's same province, the claim that certain categories of motor vehicles are manufactured in all 29 provinces and province-level units, concentrated efforts to grow more rice in the North and wheat in the South, efforts to extract usable coal from dispersed new mines, the Center's practice of disapproving province-determined prices only if price differentials between neighboring provinces might lead to undesirable price competition, and others.

Perhaps the principal bottleneck in the process of modernizing domestic commerce in China is the relatively primitive level of interior transportation and the resulting high cost of inter-regional shipping. Some grain is imported into coastal cities from Canada, Australia, or elsewhere overseas largely because it is cheaper than grain transported from China's own breadbasket in the Red Basin of Szechwan. In the mid-1960s, experiments with "economic regions" designed to transcend the rigidities of trading solely within administrative boundaries generally proceeded from distribution cost considerations based on market proximity to rail transportation.[8] The ideal, it would seem, is to preserve political control of commerce by denying markets a legitimate role while at the same time striving to achieve cost-effective distribution through appropriate decentralization.

## Guide to the Documents in Part Two

Some differences between the "two lines" in socialist commercial policy are outlined in Selection 13. Several political dimensions of this struggle between the two roads in commerce are laid out in Selection 14. And a subtle theoretical point is the topic of Selection 15: here the authors acknowledge that commercial work does not at all play a passive role; it will stimulate production when it is carried out well, and it will impede output when it falters. Nonetheless, they argue, this argument differs in important respects from the fallacy "circulation determines production." Selection 16 focuses on the specific question of the proper scope for free markets in socialist rural commerce. Selection 17 elaborates other capitalist-roader policies in rural commerce.

Selection 18 draws a line between multiple undertakings, economic crops, and household sideline production, all of which are good, on the one hand, and giving up farming to engage in speculative and profiteering activities, all of which typify "spontaneous capitalist influence," on the other. In Selection 19 Chairman Mao identifies the individual sector of China's rural economy as a "petty commodity economy." What Mao means by this, in class terms, is explained in Selection 20. In current Chinese thought, "capitalist" influence and even capitalist restoration are considered real dangers even though "99.9 percent of the nation's trade is now handled through socialist commerce, and this is the dominant factor in commodity distribution."[9] Selection 21 details some characteristics of a so-called petty commodity economy.

Selection 22 touches on the crucial issue of whether income should be siphoned off from agriculture to create a pool of investment for industry, or whether farm income should be retained to increase producitivity in agriculture itself. By charging that Liu Shao-ch'i "squeezed" the peasants, the writers are saying that he tilted too far toward the former alternative. Though no precise figure is obtainable, it is almost certainly the case as of the mid-1970s that a net drain of resources away from agriculture still exists but continues to grow smaller.[10]

A number of issues arise from efforts to institute economic planning in a country like China which has a dominant agricultural sector; a few of them are raised in the next article. Selection 23 spells out why desirable planning can occur only under a system of public ownership. Selection 24 lists a necessary set of enterprise planning targets, only one of which is profit rate. Selection 25 introduces a dialectical argument about abstract, constantly changing equilibria in order to stress the point that state economic plans must seek a balance among sectors while at the same time they must upset past balances to achieve growth. Selection 26 gives important specifics for individual enterprises to consider in drawing up their own plans. The concluding paragraph here underscores the main difficulty with economic planning for enterprises, especially without the help of large computers: "In practice, however, it is far more diversified and complicated."

A classic issue in planning pits the argument that enterprise managers should be controlled tightly, even though sometimes they may not be able to fulfill their targets due to external supply bottlenecks, against the argument that enterprise managers should be given complete responsibility coupled with wide flexibility, even though this might mean that they would often resort to illegal channels to get hold of needed inputs (and, if successful, create new bottlenecks elsewhere). In Selections 27 through 29 two concepts commonly employed to support the latter argument — the "law of value," and the "rate of profit" as the most sensitive indicator of enterprise success — are downgraded, and the charge is made that too much emphasis on these concepts would cause the whole system of socialist ownership to "immediately disintegrate."

The reason such dire consequences might flow from seemingly so small a source is made clear in Selection 30. A "tiny counterrevolutionary bourgeoisie" survives in socialist China and cleverly uses arguments that sound less dangerous than they really are to undermine the final victory of socialism. They attack on the finance-trade front because "it has multifarious connections with all aspects of society."

As a result of experiencing political struggles prompted by such articles as these, some leaders of rural production teams and brigades, and some personnel of commercial units, grew fearful of speaking out on trade problems. Selection 31 encourages them to study hard to attain a more refined political understanding that will enable them to actively promote commodity production in the service of socialist construction without crossing the fine line beyond which such development is "the soil engendering capitalism."

Selection 32 is a very politicized attack on rural periodic markets, the so-called "free markets" where farm families earn cash income by selling products from their own small private plots or household enterprises. The model "socialist big fair" (Ha-erh-t'ao she-hui chu-i ta chi) described in this article has not lasted. On November 16, 1977, People's Daily published a scathing criticism of it by the Theory Group of the

Agriculture Office of the Liaoning Province Revolutionary Committee. This Theory Group writes that the Ha-erh-t'ao fair was a creation of the gang of four and their "sworn follower" in Liaoning (see Selection 34) and a violation of the Party's rural policies. Specifically, they point out, "In China's countryside today, the level of productivity of the collective economy is not high . . . about a quarter of the present agricultural subsidiary products purchased by commercial departments are provided by household sideline undertakings." Allowing farm families to earn some income through household sidelines "helps to arouse the peasants' enthusiasm for socialism."[11]

The final two selections contrast in theoretical terms the politicization of commercial issues before and after the late 1976 fall of the gang of four.

Notes

1. Charles P. Kindleberger, Economic Development, 2nd ed. (New York: McGraw-Hill, 1965), p. 166.

2. G. William Skinner, "Marketing and Social Structure in Rural China," The Journal of Asian Studies: Part I, XXIV, 1 (November 1964), 3-43; Part II, XXIV, 2 (February 1965), 195-227; Part III, XXIV, 3 (May 1965), 363-399.

3. Joan Robinson, "A British Economist on Chinese Communes," Eastern Horizon, III (May 1964), 7. Quoted in Skinner, "Marketing and Social Structure," Part III, 398.

4. Hla Myint, The Economics of the Developing Countries (New York: Praeger, 1965), p. 171.

5. Kindleberger, Economic Development, p. 194.

6. Dwight H. Perkins, Market Control and Planning in Communist China (Cambridge: Harvard University Press, 1966), pp. 9-20 and 202-203.

7. Audrey Donnithorne, China's Economic System (London: George Allen and Unwin, 1967), p. 507. Audrey Donnithorne, "China's Cellular Economy: Some Economic Trends Since the Cultural Revolution," The China Quarterly, 52 (October/December 1972), 605-619.

8. John Wilson Lewis, "Commerce, Education, and Political Development in Tangshan, 1965-69," in The City in Communist China, ed. by John Wilson Lewis (Stanford: Stanford University Press, 1971), pp. 156-62.

9. New China News Agency, December 15, 1977; Daily Report, 1, 242 (December 16, 1977), p. E8.

10. Dwight H. Perkins, "Constraints Influencing China's Agricultural Performance," U.S. Congress, Joint Economic Committee, China: A Reassessment of the Economy, 94th Congress, 1st Session, 1975, p. 364.

11. "The Party's Rural Policies Brook No Interference: In Refutation of Several Fallacies about 'Big Fairs' Concocted by the Sworn Follower of the 'Gang of Four' in Liaoning," People's Daily, November 16, 1977, p. 2.

## 13. Ministry of Commerce Writing Group Refutes Four Main Issues in the Two-Line Struggle in Commerce (Source 16, pp. 66-67) November 6, 1970

Since the founding of People's Republic of China, the struggle between the two classes, the two roads, and the two lines has been intense. The struggle has revolved around four main issues.

"Develop the economy and insure supplies," or "circulation determines production" and "profits in command."

Support agriculture, support the collective economy, consolidate the worker-peasant alliance, or exploit the peasants and sabotage the worker-peasant alliance.

Wholeheartedly serve the workers, peasants, and soldiers, or serve the bourgeois minority.

Strengthen Party leadership, insist on politics in command, carry out mass supervision, or abolish Party leadership, carry out "single line leadership," "regulations in command," "business first," and "management by the bourgeoisie."

## 14. Ministry of Commerce Writing Group Contrasts Correct Line for Leading Commerce with Liu Shao-ch'i's Line (Source 16, pp. 78-81) November 6, 1970

To run socialist commerce well, we must mainly rely on

Party leadership, politics in command, and mass supervision. These are Chairman Mao's earnest teachings and the basic guarantees that the leadership in commerce will be firmly controlled by the proletariat and that socialist commerce will never change its nature.

The renegade, hidden traitor, and scab Liu Shao-ch'i openly opposed Party leadership and advocated "single line leadership" and "regulations in command." He urged, "Don't be afraid of local Party committees," "the local authorities have no power to interfere"; he opposed proletarian politics in command and promoted "business first"; he opposed mass supervision and promoted "factory management by experts." His intention was to allow the bourgeoisie to control the commercial leadership and change socialist commerce into capitalist commerce.

"The Chinese Communist Party is the leadership core of the whole Chinese people. Without this core, socialist enterprises will never succeed." Under Party leadership, and with Mao Tsetung thought as the commander, socialist commerce follows the unified goals and policies of the Party Central Committee and the unified plans of the state. At present, special attention must be paid to strengthening the leadership in commerce by the Party committees and revolutionary committees of various levels, and to further promoting local activism. Only by doing these can socialist commerce correctly handle the relationship between industry and commerce and between agriculture and commerce, strengthen its relationship with the masses, and better play its role in socialist revolution and socialist construction. Liu Shao-ch'i replaced Party leadership with "single line leadership" and "regulations in command." It was an usurpation of commercial leadership. This is the crux of the matter.

Politics is the commander, the soul. "Political work is the lifeline of all economic work." Socialist commerce must resolutely adhere to proletarian dictatorship in command and firmly grasp class struggle in order to consolidate the proletarian leadership. At present the struggle to discredit the counter-revolutionary elements, to oppose corruption and theft, speculation and market manipulation, to oppose extravagance and waste is a struggle to consolidate the leadership of the proletariat. Liu Shao-ch'i advocated "business first" in order to make commercial workers forget class struggle and proletarian dictatorship and become muddleheaded persons absorbed in their daily routine, never bothering about politics. In real life, any business is subjected to certain politics. If it is not proletarian politics in command, it is bourgeois politics in command. The so-called "business first" is in fact bourgeois politics in command. Socialist commerce serves proletarian politics and not a simple business organization. Socialist commercial workers are proletarian fighters and not capitalist buyers and sellers. If politics is not put to the fore, the bourgeois stink cannot be suppressed, and we may get lost in the storm of class struggle.

Commercial work involves the handling of money and goods and is in constant touch with all sorts of people. All sorts of ideologies are reflected over the service counters. Over the three-feet high counter there is class struggle. We must put proletarian politics strongly to the fore, grasp the "One Blow and Three Antis [i-ta san-fan]" movement, use Mao Tsetung thought to educate commercial workers, conscientiously readjust and build up the commercial ranks and the leadership groups of various levels, do a good job in ideological revolutionization — especially among the leadership groups — make sure that commercial leadership is firmly in the hands of the proletariat, and implement the basic mission of consolidating proletarian dictatorship at various basic levels.

"The basic principle of a communist party is to rely directly on the broad revolutionary masses." Commercial work must rely wholeheartedly on the working class and the poor and lower-middle peasants, and conscientiously accept mass supervision. In the struggle-criticism-transformation period of the Great Proletarian Cultural Revolution, the poor and lower-middle peasants managed rural commerce, and the worker and peasant masses supervised urban commerce. This is a revolution in the commercial front. This revolution thoroughly smashed Liu Shao-ch'i's fine dream of "factory management by experts."

It is an excellent thing that the worker and peasant masses supervise and manage urban and rural commerce! The worker and peasant masses supervise and manage commerce, grasp the fundamentals, use Mao Tsetung thought to command everything, grasp class struggle, raise the consciousness of the commercial working personnel about class struggle and the struggle between the two lines, grasp the direction of service, and wholeheartedly serve the workers, peasants and soldiers; they grasp policy and ideological education, guarantee the thorough implementation of the Party's goals and policies, and have a significant effect on improving commercial work.

The supervision and management of commerce by the worker and peasant masses is a concrete application of Chairman Mao's mass line in commercial work and is an important part of struggle-criticism-transformation on the commercial front. It must be broadly developed. Those units that have already started must summarize their experience, persist in their effort, and raise their level of achievement.

Let us closely unite around the Party Central Committee headed by Chairman Mao and his deputy, Vice Chairman Lin, resolutely respond to the call of the Second Plenary Session of the Ninth Party Central Committee, and raise still higher the great red banner of Mao Tsetung thought so that commercial work will advance victoriously along the socialist road.

## 15. Ministry of Commerce Writing Group Refutes Liu Shao-ch'i's Fallacy "Circulation Determines Production" (Source 16, pp. 67-70) November 6, 1970

The renegade, hidden traitor, and scab Liu Shao-ch'i consistently opposed the great direction of "develop the economy and insure supplies" and blatantly promoted the fallacy "circulation determines production" in a vain attempt to sabotage socialist construction.

Marxism-Leninism-Mao Tsetung thought tells us: Production is the foundation; there is no circulation without production. Only after production has been developed can the circulation of commodities be expanded and the market prosper. "Once efforts have been made with respect to the former, the latter becomes easy." Divorced from production, commerce becomes a fountain without water, a plant without roots. "We must oppose the erroneous viewpoint of one-sided emphasis on finance and commerce at the expense of agricultural and industrial production." Only when the general direction of "develop the economy and insure supplies" is thoroughly and earnestly carried out can commercial work improve. This means starting from production through massive support to agricultural and industrial production to the promotion of the continual development of production. Liu Shao-ch'i championed the fallacy "circulation determines production." He simply started from circulation with the market as the focus in a vain attempt to use the law of value and the supply-demand relationship to adjust and regulate production. He wanted the commercial units to dominate the production units. With a "cleaver" on the one hand and a "whip" on the other, excess production was "chopped out." The market thus dominated production and construction, disrupting the socialist planned economy.

Liu Shao-ch'i was a pure and simple "profit enthusiast." His so-called "circulation determines production" was simply his justification for profits. Under the capitalist system the sole purpose of commercial operation is the pursuit of maximum profits. In that system the market supply-demand relationship is a profit indicator. Variations in the conditions of supply and demand and the size of profits determine the direction of capital. Marx accurately pointed out: "The mission of bourgeois society is to make money"; "to produce surplus value and to get rich by making money is the absolute law of this form of production." Our socialist economy is a planned economy. Our principle is planning first, pricing second. Socialist commerce does not aim to make profits, but to develop production and insure supplies. What Liu Shao-ch'i wanted was to model socialist commerce after capitalist commerce. "Do whatever brings the highest profits." If we "do whatever brings the highest profits," it means that we run many lucrative operations, but only a few low-profit operations, and no zero-profit operations. Thus supplies are disrupted. It means that products are of uneven quality, and measurements are of a downward bias so that the interests of the masses are undermined. It means the goading of production units to blindly pursue profits, to deviate from the national plans. It leads to corruption and to theft and disruptions by speculators and manipulators, which undermines the foundation of socialism. In short, if Liu Shao-ch'i's "profits in command" were carried out, socialist commerce would surely be transformed into capitalist commerce.

"Profits in command" must be thoroughly criticized. But this does not mean that socialist commerce can do away with profits. Commercial units must follow Chairman Mao's great teaching to "run shops with diligence and economy," put proletarian politics to the fore, improve business management, expand circulation of goods, strengthen economic accounting, lower expenses, reduce wear and tear, and obtain reasonable profits to provide capital accumulation for socialist construction. The viewpoint that profits, cost accounting, and economic accounting are not necessary is erroneous.

The fallacy "circulation determines production" is bankrupt. But its residual poison has not been completely purged. Some of our comrades harbor a simple commercial viewpoint. They distribute goods in a mechanical way and try to balance in a passive way. They worry about gluts as much as about scarcity and carelessly allow production units to engage in shock labor to increase production at one time and reduce or stop production at another in response to temporary over or under supply. This is a manifestation of the poison left behind by "circulation determines production." These comrades do not understand that the state of imbalance is permanent and absolute, while the state of balance is temporary and relative. Gluts and deficiencies of certain products in the market are reflections of the law of contradictions in the supply-demand relationship. In a socialist country with 700 million people like ours, production must be developed on a large scale. We must start from production and regulate the state of balance with a positive attitude. We must be promoters of progress and make proper overall arrangements for the market so that the urban and the rural areas, times of peace and times of war, bumper harvests and poor harvests, the state, the collective, and the individual are taken into account. We must never start from circulation and regulate the state of balance passively. We must never be promoters of retrogression. When the supply of certain products temporarily falls short, production should be stepped up and distribution should be regulated. When there is temporary over-supply of certain products, purchases should be stepped up, sales expanded, and inventories expanded. Only when it is absolutely necessary should production be suitably adjusted through plans. Of course, our opposition to the "simple business viewpoint" does not mean that commerce plays only a passive role compared with industrial and agricultural production. When our commercial work is carried out well, it will stimulate production; when our commercial work falters, it will impede output. We must do our commercial work well and fully explore the special property of the commercial agency, that is, its broad contact with many other related departments. We must take the initiative to pass on to the production departments information on the people's opinions and demands so that we can work together with the production agencies in coordinating our plans for production, purchasing, and marketing, so that we can assist each other and depend on each other. It is erroneous to think or assume in our actions that commercial work can not affect production or stimulate output; it is equally erroneous to think or assume in our actions that the trade agency will purchase whatever is produced or procure whatever is available, regardless of its demand and its use value.

## 16. Ministry of Commerce Writing Group Criticizes Liu Shao-ch'i for Advocating Free Markets (Source 16, pp. 74-75) November 6, 1970

Chairman Mao teaches us: "If socialism does not take the rural front, capitalism surely will." The struggle between the proletariat and the bourgeoisie over the question of market is mainly the competition for the peasants. This struggle is closely related with the struggle between the two roads in the whole rural area. The Party Central Committee, headed by Chairman

Mao, while pushing ahead the socialist transformation of agriculture, put into effect the unified purchasing and marketing of food grains, cotton, and oil. The economic ties between the bourgeoisie and the peasants in commodity circulation were thus severed, and the socialist urban-rural economic ties were established. This facilitated the socialist transformation of agriculture and of capitalist industry and commerce and the consolidation and development of the rural collective economy. The consolidation and development of the collective economy in turn laid down a reliable basis for the consolidation and expansion of the socialist planned market. Liu Shao-ch'i's design to develop capitalism in the rural areas was aimed at the occupation of the rural market by capitalism. In the early period of the People's Republic of China, he wildly advocated "freedom in trade" in a vain attempt to pave the road for the development of a rich peasant economy. In the temporary difficult periods of the national economy, he once again fanned up the black wind of greatly developing the capitalist free market in a vain attempt to prepare conditions for the sabotage of the collective economy of the people's communes and the restoration of capitalism. Liu Shao-ch'i's so-called "free trade" and "free markets" are purely and simply slogans representing the interests of the bourgeoisie and the rich peasants. They were designed to develop the "freedom" of capitalism. Just as Lenin pointed out, "To engage in free trade is to restore capitalism."

## 17. Ministry of Commerce Writing Group Describes How Liu Shao-ch'i Promoted Capitalism in Rural Commerce (Source 16, pp. 75-78) November 6, 1970

"Whom to serve is a basic question, a question of principle." To serve the workers, peasants, and soldiers, or to serve the bourgeois minority: this is the watershed between socialist commerce and capitalist commerce.

The renegade, hidden traitor, and scab Liu Shao-ch'i made a big fanfare over "to serve the whole people" in a vain attempt to transform the nature of socialist commerce.

"To serve the whole people" — what a beautiful statement! Where is the commerce that "serves the whole people" in this world? In a class society, commerce belongs to and serves certain classes. There has never been a commerce independent of class, or to put it another way, there can never be any service that is independent of class. The masses of workers, peasants, and soldiers are the creators of history, the masters of our times, and the main forces of socialist revolution and socialist construction. Socialist commerce must serve the workers, peasants, and soldiers. The direction of resolutely serving the workers, peasants, and soldiers is the political direction of resolutely upholding socialist commercial work. If it were otherwise, socialist commerce would be transformed into capitalist commerce. Liu Shao-ch'i's "to serve the whole people" negates the class nature of socialist commerce. When the cloak of "to serve the whole people" is stripped off, the true form of serving the minority of the bourgeoisie is exposed.

Socialist commerce wholeheartedly serves the people. It is first and foremost a new brand of commerce that serves the workers, peasants, and soldiers. The variety of products carried, the variety of services rendered, the method of purchasing and marketing, office hours, network and location, trading procedures and systems all take into account the needs and convenience of the workers, peasants, and soldiers.

Liu Shao-ch'i tried his best to promote bourgeois "variety" and wanted socialist commerce to handle messy feudalist, capitalist, and revisionist commodities to satisfy the needs of bourgeois officials, madams, masters, and misses. When these intentions were thwarted, he unashamedly slandered socialist commerce as being "inferior to capitalist commerce in terms of variety." Do the workers, peasants, and soldiers require this "variety"? We not only do not need it but also must resolutely reject it. We must be determined not to permit goods poisoned with feudalism, capitalism and revisionism to enter the socialist market and to corrode the soul of the masses. We must actively handle economical, simple, durable goods and goods of a variety acceptable to the workers, peasants, and soldiers. The worker-peasant-soldier orientation and the emphasis on popularity do not mean a deterioration in the quality and quantity of services. We oppose bourgeois "variety," but champion proletarian multiplicity.

Liu Shao-ch'i also had his say about his attitude toward service. He mouthed such nonsense as "the bourgeois treatment of customers is better than the service in our state-run shops," and hailed the bourgeois service attitude as "a good thing." What "good thing"! The bourgeois service attitude is to bow, to flatter, and to judge by one's attire. These conceal the legal cheatings of bourgeois commerce. We cannot accept the bourgeois way. Nor can we turn socialist commerce into an establishment that looks down upon the workers, peasants, and soldiers. The service attitude of socialist commerce should be one of "extreme responsibility in one's job and extreme cordiality to the comrades and the people" and wholehearted service to the workers, peasants, and soldiers.

Whether the service attitude is good or the quality and quantity of services is high is not a general question of service. It is a political question bearing on the worker-peasant alliance and the relationship between the Party and the people. Those ideas that are contemptuous of commercial work regard "commercial work as waiting on people, as inferior, and as unpromising." Those measures are not designed for the convenience of the workers, peasants, and soldiers, but for their own convenience. Those measures that reduce the variety and range of service and shorten business hours at will, and those unfriendly and condescending attitudes toward the workers, peasants, and soldiers are all erroneous. We must realize that commercial work is glorious revolutionary work. The labor of commercial workers is necessary labor required by society. Without their labor, production cannot be transformed into consumption (including consumption for production and consumption for living). We must realize that division of labor exists in every society; so does growth and decay. The same is true in socialism. Only the people we serve are different. We should render better service, better quality, and better quantity.

The most fundamental requirement in serving the workers, peasants, and soldiers is to change one's stand, attitude, and sentiment, or, to put it another way, simply to transform one's world outlook.

To transform one's world outlook, one must creatively study and apply Mao Tsetung thought in a conscientious way, resolutely follow Chairman Mao's brilliant "May 7" road, toil shoulder to shoulder with the workers, peasants, and soldiers, participate in collective production labor, seriously grasp the question of class feelings, and thoroughly transform one's stand. The change in one's feelings is an indication of the transformation from one class to another. Only when a deep feeling for the workers, peasants, and soldiers is developed can one's attitude toward them be corrected, can one think as they think and worry about what they worry about. In the Three Great Revolutionary Movements of class struggle, production struggle, and scientific experimentation, workers in socialist commerce must study the "Three Constantly Read Articles" and Chairman Mao's works on philosophy; destroy private interests and foster public interests; transform their world outlook; establish the idea of wholeheartedly serving the workers, peasants, and soldiers; be messengers of Mao Tsetung thought, fighters in class struggle, and errand boys in the service of people.

## 18. Provincial Revolutionary Committee Writing Team Analyzes the Danger of Spontaneous Capitalism When Diversifying Rural Economies (Source 1, pp. 71-73) April 7, 1971

Still, some other comrades held that it is safe to grasp grains but dangerous to grasp economic crops. They are afraid that the development of economic crops will promote the growth of spontaneous capitalism.

We must realize that the counterrevolutionary revisionist lines of "three privates and one guarantee" and "four freedoms" and calls to give up farming to take up commerce pushed in the rural areas by renegade, hidden traitor, and scab Liu Shao-ch'i and his agents still exert widespread and pernicious influence. In developing economic crops, the struggle between the two classes and the two lines is still very acute and complex. We shall certainly be diverted to the sidetrack of capitalism if we do not give prominence to proletarian politics, if we do not hold the idea of developing economic crops for revolution, and if we disregard the interests of the state and take "money as the key link." On this point we must exercise high vigilance. However, there is no necessary inner connection between the development of economic crops and capitalism. Whether it will promote the growth of capitalism or not depends on the pivotal question of what line is to be carried out.

That spontaneous capitalist influence is in objective existence is a necessary reflection of class struggle during this historical period of socialism. Spontaneous capitalist influence will still be able to attack us, if we fail to exercise vigilance even though we may grasp only grain production without taking up economic crops. Fear is not a proper attitude for materialists. Historical experiences tell us that in developing the production of economic crops, we must relentlessly grasp the struggle between the two classes and the two lines. We must "ceaselessly spread the socialist ideology and criticize capitalist tendencies" among the broad cadres and masses, strengthen education in ideology and political line, continuously, penetratingly, and persistently unfold revolutionary mass criticism and repudiation, and thoroughly eliminate the "Liu poison." We must persistently carry out Chairman Mao's revolutionary line, conscientiously implement the Party's policies, and expel rightist and "leftist" interferences. In growing economic crops, it is necessary to take food grains as the key link and achieve all-around development. It is necessary to meet the needs of the state, include them in the state plan, and oppose "free growing." In the sphere of marketing, it is necessary to fulfill state procurement tasks, oppose free buying and selling, and forbid speculative activities and profiteering. In the sphere of income distribution, it is necessary to resolutely comply with the principle of paying simultaneous attention to the interests of the state, the collective, and the individual, increase public accumulation, give aid to grain production, and appropriately and gradually raise the individual incomes of commune members. It is necessary to ensure that food grain rations to the commune members of the economic crop growing areas will not be lower than the level of the nearby grain production areas. Commune members should be permitted to engage in a small amount of household sideline production, under the condition that the development of the collective economy has been ensured and has gained an overwhelming superiority. It is necessary to draw a clear line of demarcation between multiple undertakings, appropriate household sideline production, and speculative and profiteering activities and the practice of giving up farming to take up commerce. The result of these methods and the development of economic crops not only will not promote the growth of spontaneous capitalist influence but will certainly promote the consolidation and development of the collective economy of people's communes, and enable them to become more forceful in resisting and smashing spontaneous capitalist influence.

It is necessary to firmly strengthen leadership in order to correctly and thoroughly carry out the principle of "taking food grains as the key link and achieving all-around development," and to actively develop economic crops with plans. It is necessary to conscientiously conduct investigation and research of land, labor force, capital funds, and other natural conditions of our own areas and our own units, carry out overall planning and rational arrangement with measures to suit local conditions, at the same time that the masses are mobilized to unfold a struggle between the two classes and the two lines in the rural areas. It is necessary to pay attention to developing the contributing role of the industrial and commercial sectors and to promoting the development of economic crops from various sides. It is necessary to sum up experience conscientiously, grasp typical models well, and strengthen concrete leadership.

## 19. Economist Asserts China's Individual Peasant Economy Is Basically a Petty Commodity Economy (Source 24, p. 3) August 1965

In 1953, Comrade Mao Tse-tung pointed out: "Concerning the

rural front, if it is not occupied by socialism, it is bound to be occupied by capitalism." This is an inevitable conclusion to be derived on the basis of the law of political and economic development.

China's individual peasant economy is basically a petty commodity economy.

## 20. Economist Analyzes Classes in a Rural Petty Commodity Economy (Source 24, p. 9) August 1965

The transformation of the individual economy of peasants from natural economy into petty commodity economy is based upon the premise that there has been a class split among the peasants themselves.

In the production of petty commodities, the labor of individual peasants becomes a part of the total labor of society; the market, as a social force, turns into a master that determines their destiny. In the meantime, it has become impossible for them, as petty commodity producers, merely to exchange their products among peasant families or with handicraftsmen. Because of the contradictions between petty producers and the big market, they can only subsist on commerce. Because the production unit in a petty agrarian economy is small, and because agricultural production is subject to seasonal fluctuation, whenever the peasant has surplus grain he will market it; whenever his consumption outruns his production, or when natural calamities or social disorder break out, he will have to borrow. Thus, social classes will inevitably emerge in the country. Lenin, in analyzing the emergence of social classes in the countryside in Russia toward the close of the 19th century said: "In order to prove that petty economy is bound to be excluded by large-scale economy, it is not enough to say that the latter reaps higher profit (and the products are cheaper); one should also establish the fact that monetary economy (which is also commodity economy) is superior to natural economy. This is because where there is natural economy, products are for the consumption of the producers and do not enter the market, with the result that cheaper products will not encounter more expensive ones on the market, and thus it will be impossible to exclude them."

## 21. Economist Analyzes Growth of Speculation and Usury after Land Reform (Source 24, pp. 10-14) August 1965

As producers of petty commodities, it is impossible for individual peasants to maintain a position of stability for a long period of time.

Since land reform, China's rural villages have undergone several years of production development. The peasants soon realized that the mode of production characterized by petty agrarian economy has shackled the development of production forces, and some began to think of returning to the old capitalist road. In 1951, the Northeastern Bureau of the Central Committee of the Chinese Communist Party reported in its rural investigation: "The basic problem is not whether the peasants dare to expand their production but the painful question of how to expand production under current conditions. For example, in Hsiao-pao village of Feng-Ch'eng, five farming families wanted to buy rubber-wheeled carts, but, because of the lack of manpower and of their reluctance to join with others, they could not afford to buy them; there are four families that wanted to hire labor, but it was unavailable; in Chao-chou's Fa-chan Village, peasant Chang Ju-fu said: 'We should not rely on farming only, but should think of some other means to make money.' "

During the interval between the land reform and the realization of agricultural cooperativization, because of a certain degree of equalization in land and other means of production, coupled with the development of agricultural production, a considerable number of poor peasants were promoted to middle peasants. According to investigations of 14,334 peasant families

Table 2

| | At conclusion of land reform | End of 1954 |
|---|---|---|
| Poor hired peasants | 57.1 | 29.0 |
| Middle peasants | 35.8 | 62.2 |
| Rich peasants | 3.6 | 2.1 |
| Landlords | 2.6 | 2.5 |
| Others | 0.9 | — |

Note: In 1954, peasant families that joined cooperatives accounted for 4.2% of the total.

in 21 provinces during 1954, since the conclusion of land reform and up to the end of 1954, changes have occurred in the composition of rural classes as shown in Table 2.

During this period, the number of poor hired peasants dropped from 57.1% to 29%; the number of rich peasants dropped from 3.6% to 2.1%; while the number of middle peasants rose from 35.8% to 62.2%. Nonetheless, this was by no means a phenomenon of stability. As a matter of fact, even at that time the individual agrarian economy already showed a tendency toward forming two extreme social classes. In areas where the agricultural mutual-aid and cooperative movement was more advanced, this tendency was more restrained; but where the movement was not so well developed, the tendency became more striking.

Division of rural classes before the agricultural cooperativization campaign was manifested first of all in the growing activities of commercial speculations and usury.

According to statistics for several provinces in the Central South region, since 1953 some 12% to 18% of all farming families had engaged in commercial activities. In Chu-i hsiang in the first ch'u of Feng-chieh hsien, Szechwan, during the autumn harvest in 1953, some 330 peasant families left their farms to do business. When sesame was being marketed, some peasants bought 80,000 chin in 20 days, which they processed and then sold to cooperatives at high prices when the supply was low. These rich peasants usually colluded with capitalist businessmen, merchants, and petty peddlers to engage in speculative activities, cornering the market in order to make excessive profits.

Usury is the twin brother of commercial capital. In China's rural villages, commodity and monetary economy was relatively underdeveloped. When disasters struck, either natural or social, and the peasants would be urgently in need of money, they had to pay high interest to borrow from rich peasants and merchants. During the period of the Democratic Revolution, the law forbade usurious exploitations. Nevertheless, since the land reform, because the state banks and credit cooperatives were still unable to satisfy fully the peasant need of loans, usurywas not completely eliminated. Engels said: "When a small peasant fell into hardships, and when the service of the usurer would seem to him to be a relatively small peril, it would always be possible for the usurers to find the means to suck the peasant's blood without incurring the sanctions of law against usurious practices."

Based on investigations in 16 hsiang in the four provinces of Hupeh, Hunan, Kiangsi, and Kwangtung, approximately 10% of the farming population granted loans, or an increase of 100% as compared with 1952. Middle peasants were the most numerous among creditor families (especially the prosperous middle peasants).

In the 16 hsiang in Hupeh, Hunan, Kiangsi, and Kwangtung provinces, about 70% of the middle peasants granted loans either in money or in kind. Among them, one-third of the families and one-third of the amount of grain granted were attributed to the affluent middle peasants. It was the poor peasants who received the loans. In 10 hsiang in Hupeh, Hunan, and Kiangsi, one-third of the poor peasant debtor families borrowed some 64.85% of the total amount of loaned grain; in Kwangtung, the debtor families among poor peasants accounted for one-half of the total, or 40% of the total debtor families and the total amount of grain borrowed.

Although practically all the loan relationships in rural villages were of the nature of mutual assistance among the masses, there was also a portion that consisted of "usury" for excessive profit, which was practiced in times of natural disasters. According to investigations in seven villages in Hsing hsien, Shansi, in 1952, among some 2,486 families, 20 made out usurious loans amounting to 2,680,000 Jen-min-pi (in the old currency) and 199 tan of grains. Usurious families accounted for 0.8% of the total. The interest rate per month was generally about 5%, the highest being 10%. The creditors were generally middle peasants (some of the loans were incurred before liberation). These loans were made to 62 families, among whom 79% were poor peasants, and 24.2% middle peasants. Judging from the usages of loans, middle peasants incurred loans largely to meet the expenses of weddings and funerals as well as to cope with natural disasters, while poor peasants used them to relieve hardships of livelihood. In 1952, the Han-t'an committee of the Chinese Communist Party also stated in an investigation report on the division of rural classes: "In the last two years, usury has steadily developed in rural villages and become ever more diversified, such as the practices of 'leasing out livestock,' or grain, or cotton. For instance, in the five villages in Ch'eng-an's Tao-tung-pao, there were altogether 922 families, among which 91 'leased out cotton' and livestock, or about 10% of the total. The practice of 'leasing out livestock' and/or cotton usually is to lend livestock either in late autumn or before wheat harvest, and then the borrower would pay it back after the wheat harvest or after autumn, at about 50% interest. In Ch'eng-an, Lin-chang, and Wei-hsien, 'leasing of livestock' has become a common practice."

Commercial speculation and usurious activities form a bridge that leads the peasant individual economy to capitalism. A peasant must become a merchant and amass a small amount of wealth before he can be a rich peasant and capitalist. On the other hand, the activities of business speculation and usury are bound to cause some of the peasants to become impoverished and bankrupt, until they lose their means of production and can only sell their own labor. For instance, in Jung-tang village, Lung-men hsiang, Ch'ang-lo hsien, Fukien, "from the time of the autumn harvest in 1952 to the time before spring plowing in 1953, among 31 families of peasants who sold their land, 13 families did it because of the payment of usurious loans, and 43% of the land was sold to 12 middle peasant families."

## 22. Ministry of Commerce Writing Group Charges Liu Shao-ch'i Advocated "Squeezing" the Peasant Sector (Source 16, pp. 71-73) November 6, 1970

The renegade, hidden traitor, and scab Liu Shao-ch'i pushed reactionary policies to exploit peasants. He maliciously ordered the commercial departments to "strangle the peasants," to "squeeze the peasants" in a vain attempt to disintegrate the collective economy and sabotage the worker-peasant alliance.

The peasants are the mainstay of the industrial market. The main purpose of socialist commercial production and exchange is the consolidation of the worker-peasant alliance. The economic alliance of the workers and the peasants is realized chiefly through the commercial link. The struggle between the proletariat and the bourgeoisie over the market question is mainly a struggle for the peasants. That is to say, the question of the domestic market is in fact the question of the peasants.

Chairman Mao clearly points out: "The peasants are the mainstay of China's industrial market. They and only they can supply foods and raw materials and absorb industrial products in large quantities." Agriculture is the base of the national economy and is also the base of the domestic market. The development of industry and the prosperity of the market cannot be divorced from that base. Without a well-developed agriculture, the abundant raw materials for industry and the large market for industrial products would not be available, and a large amount of development funds could not be accumulated. Of course, "without industry there is no secure national defense, no welfare for the people, and no prosperity for the country." The modernization of agriculture and the massive development of agricultural production must be supported by a strong industry. But, in the final analysis, the scale and the speed of development for industry and other enterprises are determined mainly by the quantity of commercial foodstuffs and industrial raw materials supplied by agriculture. The achievements since the establishment of the People's Republic of China prove that whenever there are bumper harvests our industry develops faster and the market is more prosperous. This is a law.

The main purpose of socialist commercial production and exchange is to consolidate the worker-peasant alliance. At present, the people's communes in the rural areas of China are still collective economies based on three-level ownership, with the production team as the basis. The exchange of goods is the only acceptable form of economic relation between agriculture and industry as far as the peasants today are concerned. And it is the chief form of economic integration between socialist ownership by the whole people and collective ownership. For the peasants there can only be exchange and not exploitation. This is the basic viewpoint of Mao Tsetung thought. The state needs for farm and sideline products, with the exception of a nominal agricultural tax, are largely obtained through exchange. Lenin said: "To exchange the peasant's produce for large scale ("socialist") produced industrial products is the economic fact of socialism and the basis of socialism." Socialist commerce consistently implements policies for the stabilization of prices, the policy of selling in large quantities at lower profits for industrial products, and the policy of trading at equal values or close to equal values in the exchange of industrial and farm products to gradually narrow the disparity [ in prices between industrial and farm products] ; it correctly handles the relationship between the state, the collective, and the individual. It has mobilized the socialist activism of the broad peasants, stimulated the urban and rural economies, and consolidated the socialist base.

## 23. Economist Argues That Capitalist Planning Is Unscientific, Unreliable, and Wasteful (Source 15, pp. 69-70) July 1964

Under the capitalist system, social production is anarchistic.

So far as each capitalist is concerned, "he does not exactly know what society wants. This is true of the quality, the variety, and the quantity." Thus, the capitalist can only formulate his plan according to his subjective speculation of market conditions. This kind of planning, without scientific foundation, is unreliable and subject naturally to frequent fluctuations in market conditions, which often cause substantial waste of the manpower, materials, and capital of the enterprise.

The socialist enterprise planning is carried out under centralized leadership and unified planning of the state. The plan sets forth the social needs, determines the things to be produced; thus, the product markets are guaranteed. The unified plan of the state also fixes the supply of raw materials, intermediate inputs as well as manpower, and fuels which are necessary to carry out the production; thus the supply of materials is secured. The socialist enterprise, in the process of formulating its operation plan, must begin, under the state supervision, with practical, thorough, and detailed investigation, and must correctly calculate its own production capacity, market potential, demands for raw materials, inputs, fuel, manpower, etc. Then it must carry out repeated experiments to reach general equilibrium. This sort of planning, based on a scientific foundation, is reliable and capable of correctly directing production and of efficiently utilizing all manpower, materials, and capital.

## 24. Economist Lists Necessary Socialist Planning Targets (Source 15, p. 71) July 1964

The planned goals handed down by the state to the enterprises include only the important indexes to be achieved, namely, the variety, quality, and quantity of output, the rate of production, cost and profit rate, etc. Each enterprise must also independently formulate its plan in conformity with the goal fixed by the state, its complete unified plan of production, technology, and finance, incorporating into it all production activities of individuals as well as groups within the enterprise, and all internal functions such as production, technology, and finance. Thus, the production management of an enterprise could be organized according to the requirements of the state unified plan and the overall fulfillment and overfulfillment of the state plan fully ensured. Conversely, if the enterprise fails to formulate its plan in accordance with the goals fixed by the state, or if the formulated plan is incomplete in the sense that it does not incorporate every internal task in the enterprise, then the production management of the enterprise could not function harmoniously and the fixed goals of the state could not be successfully accomplished.

## 25. Economist Analyzes Socialist Planning as Continuous Preparations to Handle Disequilibria (Source 15, pp. 74-75) July 1964

On the one hand, expansion of production requires the maintenance of a relative equilibrium and of certain ratios among various units in the enterprise; on the other, it inevitably creates many disequilibria. This is a contradiction. The purpose of socialist enterprise planning is to deal with such contradiction consciously and correctly and to make efforts continually and actively to bring relative equilibrium to absolute disequilibrium and to bring unity to opposites, thus stimulating production. Lenin said: "In effect, the attribute of planning is to maintain equilibrium consciously and constantly." Comrade Mao Tse-tung also said: "Every year our country must draw up a national economic plan so as to determine the ratio of accumulation to consumption. This is necessary because equilibrium must be maintained between production and consumption. The so-called equilibrium is a transitory phase of a contradiction. A year later, the equilibrium, viewed from the process of development as a whole, will once again generate contradiction, thus turning equilibrium into disequilibrium and unity into opposites, which in turn calls for new equilibrium and unity in the second year. Such is the superiority of our planned economy. In fact, every month and every quarter, equilibrium and unity are broken up, and adjustments, partial or sectorial, are called into action. Sometimes, contradictions emerge and equilibria are upset because subjective wishes are at variance with objective reality. This is when a mistake is committed. The constant emergence of contradictions and the constant solution of such contradictions constitute the law of dialectical materialism." As Comrade Mao so lucidly illustrated here, the development of the state economy will produce disequilibria every year, every quarter, or even every month. The purpose of planning is to make proper arrangements to handle such contradictions in order to reach new equilibrium.

## 26. Economist Outlines Four Main Equilibria Socialist Planning Should Strive to Achieve (Source 15, pp. 75-79) July 1964

To accomplish the task of planning and administration of socialist enterprises, the first prerequisite is to draw up a good plan. What plans do socialist enterprises need?

There are three types of plans, classified by the period of time involved, namely: long-term, annual, and operational. These plans are interrelated and interdependent. The long-term plan is made up of several annual plans, while the annual plan is made up of several operational plans. To look at it from the opposite side, the annual plan is a means to realize the long-term plan, and the operational plan is a means to materialize the annual plan. Only when a good long-term plan is available can a good annual plan be worked out; only when a good annual plan is available can an operational plan be drawn up. Or only when a good operational plan is available can an annual plan be successfully fulfilled; only when a good annual plan is available can a long-term plan be carried out.

As objective conditions change, these plans may be revised within limits through proper procedure, so as to adjust to the changing conditions. Otherwise, the plans may deviate from objective reality and may fail to serve as a production indicator. This does not necessarily mean, however, that one can neglect the factual relationships among the three types of plans. If the annual plan is drawn up independently of the long-term plan, or the operational plan independently of the annual plan, it is tantamount to no plan at all. In that case, the plans would lose their function as indicators of the direction of production.

Among all industrial enterprise plans, the most important one is the annual plan for technology and finance, which comprises all activities with regard to production, technology, and funds of all the units in the enterprise. It serves as a general guide for all productive activities of all the workers and personnel in the enterprise during the plan period.

The content of the annual plan for technology and finance varies from industrial enterprise to industrial enterprise. As a rule, it consists of: (1) production plan, (2) supplementary production plan, (3) equipment maintenance plan, (4) labor and wage plan, (5) material supply plan, (6) transportation and shipment plan, (7) cost accounting plan, (8) finance plan, and (9) technology control and organization management plan. In addition, those enterprises which carry on pilot experiments of new products should draw up a new-product experimentation plan, and those which are engaging in capital construction should make a capital construction plan.

On the one hand, each of the various subplans should have its specific content with regard to its respective objectives and activities in the enterprise; on the other hand, these subplans should also have close coordination according to their intimate relations, because the planning of one enterprise will affect that of another, and vice versa. Since these plans are interrelated and yet interrestrained, together they form an organic entity with the production plan placed in the center. The indices in the industrial enterprise plan for technology and finance are made up of a series of production coefficients drawn from the various subplans. When drafting the plans, we must be fully aware of the interrelations among the units, so as to make them interrelated, interdependent, and interconnected.

To do a good planning job, the industrial enterprise must carry out a great deal of preparatory work. First, it must do well at political and ideological work and thoroughly implement the general party line on how to make all efforts to forge forward and on how to build socialism faster, better, and more economically; it must faithfully follow the party's directives and policies. Meanwhile, it must conduct intensive investigations and understand and grasp the situation in the enterprise; it must rely on the broad masses and fully exploit their enthusiasm and initiative; it must rigorously analyze the enterprise's past activities and find its strong points and shortcomings; it must inspect the economic quotas for various production technology and collect data for further research; and it must study the constructive suggestions for improvement of production and technological innovations brought up by the masses, and weigh the possibilities of adopting such suggestions and their possible effects.

The process of drafting an industrial enterprise plan is, in effect, one of repetitious forward and backward synthesis, of horizontal and vertical integration, and of constantly reaching out for equilibrium. As previously mentioned, in the process of developing industrial production, disequilibria frequently pop up. Since such disequilibria take many forms, the equilibrium work in the enterprise plan must have a correspondingly great variety. In general, the equilibrium work includes the following:

First, it is the equilibrium between the production objective and the supplies of equipment, manpower resources, raw materials, inputs, and fuel.

All these are important elements in enterprise operation. There exist certain ratios between these factors of production and the objectives of production which the enterprise seeks to accomplish. In the process of expanding production, contradictions between the production objectives and the factors of production frequently occur; contradictions also develop among the factors of production. The main purpose of planning is to handle these contradictions correctly, that is, to reach equilibrium between production objectives and the factors of production such as machinery and equipment, manpower resources, raw materials, inputs, and fuel. It must also seek equilibrium among the factors of production.

Second, it is the equilibrium among all internal functions and operations of an enterprise.

The departments and production units in an enterprise must also maintain certain ratios. Yet, in the process of development, leads and lags are inevitable; contradictions and disequilibria always pop up. The objective of industrial enterprise planning is to handle these contradictions in the pursuit of the equilibria between basic production and supplementary production, among the operation departments in the basic production, among the related shops in supplementary production, as well as the equilibrium between production and its preparation, etc.

Third, it is the equilibrium among the indicators.

Production in industrial enterprises under socialism must meet the demands for better, faster, and more economical output. In practice, contradictions may also occur among the indicators, resulting in disequilibrium. For instance, when the quantity index is set too high, the quality of the product would certainly be impaired; when emphasis is put only on increasing the variety of product and on improving quality, little attention is paid to increasing production and reducing costs; or when the cost reduction index is set too high, quality improvement would be relatively ignored; and so forth. The enterprise planning must also correctly handle these contradictions so as to meet fully and simultaneously demands for quality, quantity, as well as economy.

Fourth, it is the equilibrium between the production of the planning year and the year after.

This is also called the equilibrium between the annual plan and the long-term plan. Modern enterprise production has a high degree of continuity. Close relationships exist between development of production of the planning year and that of the following year, or even several years after. For example, if the production level of the planning year is fixed too low, it will affect the level of production for the following year; if the production goal for the planning year is set so high as to delay the repair and maintenance of machinery and equipment, or to preempt raw materials, inputs, and fuel, then it will affect the normal production of the following year, or even several years after. Hence, in formulating the annual plan, the enterprise must carefully and correctly handle, in compliance with the requirements of the long-term plan, the relationships of production equilibrium between the planning year and the following year or years.

The foregoing explanation deals with only several important aspects of equilibria in enterprise planning. In practice, however, it is far more diversified and complicated.

## 27. Provincial Revolutionary Committee Writing Group Criticizes Sun Yeh-fang's View That "Plans Should Be Based on the Law of Value" (Source 11, pp. 272-273) February 1970

According to what he called his "basic views" on plans, "profits should be regarded as the center of plans and statistics," and "plans should be based on the law of value." What does this mean? It means that in drawing up plans, the state and enterprises should proceed from "value" and "profits." In a word, it is necessary to proceed from making money; it is also what Liu Shao-ch'i said: "Do whatever is profitable." The state should draw up a big plan to make money, while enterprises should work out small plans to make money.

According to Marxism-Leninism-Mao Tsetung thought, politics is the concentrated manifestation of economics, and plans are subordinate to politics. There are socialist plans and revisionist plans. The basic distinctions between them rest on their political basis and on which political class they serve.

## 28. Provincial Revolutionary Committee Writing Group Puts the "Law of Value" in Perspective (Source 11, pp. 274-276) February 1970

As far as the state is concerned, if "our plans are based on the law of value," it is impossible for unprofitable national-defense industries to develop; it is impossible to establish heavy and inland industries; it is also impossible for regions, provinces, and municipalities to built industrial systems under different conditions proceeding from the viewpoint of war preparedness; it is impossible for the support of agriculture to develop those industries of low production value that make little profit in the short run; it is impossible for the state to run and develop certain categories of daily necessities that must be subsidized within a certain period of time; and, in accordance with the proletarian spirit of internationalism, it is impossible to produce products needed for the struggle of the revolutionary people of the world. In short, Sun Yeh-fang wanted us to abandon the great task of building a strong socialist state and to deviate from the victorious path pointed out by Chairman Mao. Such a revisionist "plan" is exactly what is needed by Liu Shao-ch'i to restore capitalism and to lead us back onto the old, semi-feudal and semicolonial road—it is a plan that will lead to the destruction of our Party and our state.

Commodities and the law of value do exist in a socialist society. We use the law of value as a tool in planning work and economic accounting. But we resolutely oppose making the law of value the basis for regulating production and for planning. The modern revisionists have a characteristic in common in their restoration of capitalism in the economic field; they try their utmost to exaggerate the theoretical value of the law of value and to promote the use of this law to regulate and control all social production. In this way, economic construction is shifted from the socialist path of putting proletarian politics in command to the capitalist path of putting "profits in command."

"The rule of value is in fact another point of view of the General Line." "Of all the laws, the law of value comes first." These absurdities advanced by Sun Yeh-fang are used to justify the "basing of our plans on the law of value" and to justify the use of the law of value to regulate all social production. This is a most shameful and most vicious distortion of the Party's General Line for socialist construction.

Basing our plan on the law of value and planning in accordance with the General Line constitute two lines of construction that are diametrically opposed to each other. The Party's General Line for socialist construction, personally formulated by Chairman Mao, is the Marxist-Leninist line for arousing the enthusiasm of hundreds of millions of people for building socialism. It serves as the revolutionary line for competing with imperialism and socialist imperialism in terms of time and speed of development, and it constitutes the means for the proletariat to thoroughly defeat the bourgeoisie and all class enemies. "Of all important things, Chairman Mao's revolutionary line must come first." This is the conclusion reached by the broad revolutionary masses from their historical experience. Sun Yeh-fang's absurdities have fully exposed his reactionary hostility toward great Mao Tsetung thought and have exposed his ugly attempts to lead socialist construction into the counterrevolutionary revisionist orbit.

Sun Yeh-fang attacked our country's socialist plan, which is subordinate to proletarian politics, by saying that the plan "is overcontrolled and has no flexibility." Pleading for the enterprises, he demanded power from the state by clamoring that "the state need only watch the value target (profit indicator)" of enterprises, "leave the rest of business management to the enterprise," and in other respects "let it make its own operational decisions."

What do these "other respects" include? First of all, they mean the abolition of the political orientation by which enterprises are controlled by the proletarian state. As for what kind of products can be produced by an enterprise and the way to handle these, the state should leave the enterprise alone. Moreover, the enterprise can engage in "free transactions of fixed capital." It is obvious that he wanted enterprises to depart from the state's centralized and unified leadership and proclaim independence.

Sun Yeh-fang wanted the state to "grasp only the profit target" in regard to enterprises. This would completely turn the socialist relationship of enterprises, which are subordinate to the proletarian state, into a cold, capitalist relationship of monetary transactions, and the whole system of socialist ownership by the people would immediately disintegrate. Anarchism in competition and production would become rampant and harmful, and the socialist planned economy would become a capitalist free economy. Sun Yeh-fang has been thinking day and night to bring about such a change. By clamoring that the planned system "is inferior to the free economy" Sun Yeh-fang himself has exposed his own evil intention.

## 29. Provincial Revolutionary Committee Writing Group Criticizes Overemphasis on Profits (Source 11, p. 278) February 1970

Sun Yeh-fang said: "The amount of profit should be the most sensitive indicator of the technical progress and the quality of management of an enterprise." He said that "profits can give impetus to business management." This is an out-and-out capitalist view on running enterprises.

## 30. Red Flag Author Exposes Class Enemies' Tactics on the Finance-Trade Front (Source 19, pp. 203-210) September 1969

Our great leader, Chairman Mao, has taught us: "We have won a great victory. But the defeated class will continue to struggle. Those people are still there and that class still exists. Therefore, we cannot talk about final victory yet, not even after several decades. We must not lower our vigilance." Our Vice Chairman, Lin Piao, has pointed out in his political report to the Ninth Party Congress: "There will be further adversity in the class struggle. We must never forget class struggle and never forget the dictatorship of the proletariat."

At present, the financial and trade front, like all other fronts, has gone through acute struggles between the two classes, the two roads, and the two lines, and it has achieved a very great success under the guidance of the latest directives from Chairman Mao. Under these favorable conditions, however, some of our comrades have slackened in class struggle, failed to see clearly the acute and complex class struggle on the finance and trade front, and relaxed their vigilance against the class enemy's attack on socialism in the economic field. Hence, whether or not we can hold high the banner of revolutionary mass criticism, firmly grasp class struggle in the economic field, and repulse the attack of the bourgeoisie depends on whether struggle-criticism-transformation can be developed in depth on the finance and trade front.

"This is about all we can do in the struggle-criticism-transformation on the financial and trade front." This view is inconsistent with the actual condition of the movement on this front.

Although much has been achieved in the struggle-criticism-transformation on this front, the poison left by the counterrevolutionary revisionist line of that renegade, traitor, and scab Liu Shao-ch'i is widespread and has not yet been completely wiped out. The work of purification of the class ranks, Party rectification, and Party building is still stupendous. The small handful of corrupt elements, speculators, and reactionary capitalists have been badly hurt by the storm of the Proletarian Cultural Revolution, but they have not yet been completely liquidated. The capitalist influence still stirs up trouble in certain weak links and sabotages the socialist economy in a vain attempt to dissolve socialist ownership and rock the economic foundation of proletarian dictatorship.

The attack that the small handful of class enemies mounts against us in the economic field is very treacherous. Some of them steal, rob, speculate, deceive, disrupt the market, and sabotage production. Others try in every way possible to sneak into corrode our cadres and recruit new agents. Still others try their best to peddle reactionary anarchism, loosen labor discipline, and fish in troubled water. Some even spread fallacies such as "your shoes are bound to get wet if you stand on the river bank all the time"; or "it is a time-honored truth that the pavilion that is close by the waterfront will see the reflection of the moon first." They even use small benefits and favors to drag the weak-minded into wrongdoing so as to cover up their own corruption, thefts, speculation, and swindling.

With class struggle as intense as it is in the economic field, how could one say that we have done about all we can in the struggle-criticism-transformation on the financial and trade front?

We must soberly observe that the small handful of class enemies are taking advantage of the relaxed attitude manifested by some in our revolutionary ranks in an attempt to obscure the acute struggle between the two classes, the two roads, and the two lines on the financial and trade front, thus disarming us ideologically and making us give up our struggle against them.

Chairman Mao has taught us: "Throughout the transition period, class contradictions exist, the struggle between the proletariat and the bourgeoisie exists, and the struggle between the two roads of socialism and capitalism exists. To forget this basic theory and practice that our party has followed over the past ten and more years will lead one astray." The principal contradiction currently facing the struggle-criticism-transformation on the financial and trade front is still the contradiction between the proletariat and the bourgeoisie, between the two roads of socialism and capitalism. If we fail to grasp this main contradiction, struggle-criticism-transformation cannot be conducted in depth and the Great Proletarian Cultural Revolution on the finance and trade front cannot be carried through to the end.

"Why is the question of man a fundamental question, a question of principle?" To serve the exploiting class or to serve the working people manifests the struggle between the two classes, the two roads, and the two lines; it also manifests the direction and road the enterprises are taking. Only when the struggle between the two classes, the two roads, and the lines is firmly grasped, when the leadership of the finance and trade front firmly rests in the hands of the true Marxists, and when socialist ownership is consolidated, can there be any fundamental guarantee that proletarian politics and the interests of the workers, the peasants, and the soldiers will be served and that the general line of "developing the economy and insuring supplies" will be carried out.

One question that should be solved in struggle-criticism-transformation concerns the service attitude, or the work attitude and work style of the business personnel. This is not a question of whether or not "we have done the best we can." If the service attitude is not good, it will be impossible to really serve the workers, the peasants, and the soldiers. However, the service attitude has its class character. The question of service attitude cannot be completely solved unless proletarian politics is brought to the fore, the attack by the bourgeoisie in the economic field is repulsed, and the struggle between the two classes, the two roads, and the two lines is firmly grasped. Education in class struggle must be conducted with all seriousness, and the reactionary habit of serving the bourgeoisie and looking down on the working people must be criticized so that a strong revolutionary sense of responsibility and a good work style of wholeheartedly serving the people can be established.

"Economic problems are not political problems. To concentrate on minute economic problems may overlook the general and overall direction." This is a mistaken idea that negates the political struggle existing in the economic field.

Corruption, theft, speculation, and swindling are definitely not just "economic problems," but important political problems related to the consolidation of the economic base of proletarian dictatorship.

Those who are engaged in corruption, theft, speculation, and swindle expropriate social wealth created by the labor of the working class and the poor and lower-middle peasants. They are reactionary in politics; they accumulate wealth through criminal means; they are decadent in life; they are outright bourgeois elements. Is it not in line with the general and broad direction to attack them?

The criminal activities of those engaged in corruption, theft, speculation, and swindling are by no means isolated incidents. The financial and trade front is the link between production and consumption, between the city and the countryside, and between industry and agriculture. It has multifarious connections with all aspects of society. This small handful of class enemies frequently act in collusion with each other. They form a tiny counterrevolutionary bourgeois force to undermine the socialist foundation. To attack them represents a struggle for triumph of the proletariat over the bourgeoisie, socialism over capitalism. Is this not in line with the general and broad direction?

Among the bourgeois elements engaged in corruption, theft, speculation, and swindle are those who were originally counter-revolutionaries and bad elements, and they are the targets in the purification of the class ranks. For the restoration of capitalism, they try every way possible to change the character of proletarian political power through a change in the socialist character of enterprises. Is it not in line with the general direction to attack them so that the leadership can firmly rest in the hands of the Marxists?

Chairman Mao has taught us, "Economy is the base and politics is the concentrated manifestation of economy." All class struggle is political struggle. To smash the attack of the bourgeoisie in the economics field is precisely a political struggle to defend socialism and to consolidate proletarian dictatorship. Some of our comrades, however, do not carry out struggle in the economics field and give up the proletarian leadership. As a matter of fact, to repulse the bourgeoise attack in the economics field is one of the conditions for the deepening of the revolutionary mass criticism on the financial and trade front, for the continual purification of the class ranks, and for Party rectification and Party building; it is also part of the content of the reform of irrational regulations and systems. Simultaneously, in conjunction with our efforts to continue the several kinds of work described above, it will be entirely in line with the general direction for us to carry out this struggle, which will help do a thorough job in struggle, criticism, and socialist transformation.

What merits our attention is that currently a small handful of class enemies are trying hard to spread fallacies such as "to tackle economic problems is to point the spearhead downward," in order to confuse people, throw our ranks into disarray, and obscure the general direction of struggle. Our comrades must remain sober so that they will not be misled by the smokescreens set up by the class enemy.

"All economic problems are the people's internal contradictions. [To solve these contradictions] reform and reeducation are sufficient; there is no need to mobilize the masses to mount an attack." This way of thinking is also wrong.

An overwhelming majority of economic problems do fall within the scope of the people's internal contradictions. But a few of them are antagonisms between ourselves and the enemy. "All social forces and social organizations that resist and are hostile to the socialist revolution and sabotage the socialist construction are the enemy of the people." The small handful of people who have committed acts of corruption, theft, speculation, and swindling are the enemy of the people.

The reason why we wage a class struggle on the economic front is precisely for the purpose of drawing a distiction between and correctly handling the two types of contradiction: namely, the people's internal contradiction, on the one hand, and the antagonism between us and our enemy, on the other. The purpose is to unite all forces that can be united – including those who did commit series errors, but are not beyond redemption – to isolate a small handful of die-hard class enemies, to drive the incorrigible class enemies into a dead-end corner and deal them a fatal blow.

"No enemy will fall unless you strike him down." If we fail to see this point clearly and do not actually lead the masses to launch a struggle against the enemy, he may slip away.

For those who have economic problems in general, we must provide direct education insistently, seriously, meticulously, and patiently so that they may heighten their consciousness, reform their ideology, and relieve their worries so as to unite with us against our common enemy. As for the small handful of class enemies, we must fully mobilize and rely on the masses to expose them and knock them down. Educating the masses and attacking the enemy require "mobilization of the masses." In our struggle against the enemy, we must resolutely carry out the principle consistently advocated by Chairman Mao: "Make use of contradictions, win over the majority, oppose the minority, and knock them down one by one." It is necessary "to stress evidence and investigation and research; forced confessions must be strictly forbidden." Chairman Mao's policy of "leniency toward those who confess, severe punishment toward those who resist," and "giving them a way out" must be followed.

To do a good job of direct education, it is essential to carry out penetrating mass revolutionary criticism. We must, armed with Mao Tse-tung's thought, relentlessly criticize the counterrevolutionary revisionist line of the renegade, traitor, and scab Liu Shao-ch'i in the light of the characteristics of the financial and trade front. We must discredit his "theory of the extinction of class struggle" and his whole lot of counterrevolutionary revisionist "black goods," such as "exploitation has its merits," "the merging of the public and the private," "profit in command," "material incentives," "business above all," and "relying on the capitalists to run shops."

Such fallacies as "your shoes are bound to get wet if you stand on the river bank all the time" or "the pavilion that is close by the waterfront will see the moon reflection first," which are spread by a small handful of class enemies on the financial and trade front, are simply the rubbish from Liu Shao-ch'i's garbage dump and are rehashed reactionary philosophy of the exploiting class, who believe that "God will condemn those who do not help themselves." This handful of people even blatantly declare that economic problems are only "occupational maladies" of those on the financial and trade front. What "occupational maladies"? What an insult to the broad masses of revolutionaries on the financial and trade front! The broad masses of cadres and workers on this front dearly love Chairman Mao and socialism. Nurtured by Mao Tse-tung's thought are many progressive persons who stay "spotlessly clean though living in busy streets" and who selflessly and wholeheartedly serve the broad worker, peasant, and soldier masses. These comrades "stand on the river bank all the time, but their shoes never get wet." They see through the plot of the class enemy and carry out an acute struggle, showing noble qualities of revolutionaries.

Chairman Mao has taught us: "At no time and no place shall a Communist Party member put his own interests first. He must submit his own interests to those of the nation and the people. For this reason, egoism, slow-down strikes, corruption and decadence, exhibitionism, etc., are most despicable, while selflessness and diligence are truly respectable." Through revolutionary mass criticism, we must struggle against the small handful of class enemies and realize that "corruption and waste are a big crime," and it is shameful even to profit oneself a penny at the expense of the public. Through revolutionary mass criticism, we must heighten the class consciousness of the masses and their consciousness for the struggle between the two lines so that they can distinguish what is Chairman Mao's proletarian revolutionary line and what is Liu Shao-ch'i's counterrevolutionary revisionist line, what is the road of socialism and what is the road of capitalism. We must make them see that class struggle in the economic field is protracted, stupendous, and complex so that they can independently carry this struggle through to the end. In the course of the struggle, we must take one further step to make the revolutionization of the thinking of the ranks and the revolutionization of the organizations on the financial and trade front realities; and at the same time we must, through the reform of irrational regulations and systems, set forth new regulations and systems for the socialist enterprises.

To repulse the attack of the bourgeoisie in the economic field, to block the path of capitalism, to solve the problem of ownership and the problem of leadership on the financial and trade front, and to consolidate proletarian dictatorship — such is our fundamental purpose for carrying out the current struggle. We must hold higher the great banner of Mao Tse-tung's thought, seriously implement the various proletarian policies set forth by Chairman Mao, and keep ourselves on guard against the small handful of class enemies who are exploiting bourgeois factionalism and anarchist thinking in order to throw the class ranks into disarray and confuse the general direction of struggle. We must fight for new and still greater victories on the financial and trade front in struggle, criticism, and socialist transformation. Let the invincible Mao Tse-tung's thought prevail forever over the socialist economy.

## 31. People's Daily Correspondent Urges Commercial Departments to Promote Development of a Diversified Rural Economy (Source 14, pp. 245-246) August 22, 1975

Guided by Chairman Mao's revolutionary line, China has

reaped good harvests in agriculture for thirteen years in succession, and there has also been very great development in forestry, animal husbandry, side-occupations, fisheries, and other undertakings. Under the leadership of Party committees at various levels, the rural commercial departments have made great achievements in helping the communes and production teams vigorously develop grain production and a diversified economy. Under the present excellent situation, how vigorously to develop grain production as well as to work for the upswing of the diversified economy is an important problem for the rural commercial departments.

Some of the comrades think that the greater part of the diversified economy involves commodity production, and as the commodity system is the soil engendering capitalism, they are afraid that the promotion of a diversified economy would give rise to capitalism. Therefore they dare not boldly grasp such work. This understanding is one-sided. It should be perceived that even under socialist conditions, the commodity system is still the soil that gives rise to capitalism and the bourgeoisie. However, we should also see that because the system of ownership has changed in our country, commodity production under the socialist system is mainly carried out in accordance with the demand of the planned economy of the state to serve socialist construction. In the meantime, the commodities of our country are not too much or rich enough, and it is necessary to develop commodity production on a large scale. Therefore, we can never mix up the development of a diversified economy and the development of commodity production with the tendency toward capitalism.

The facts show that under the condition of the dictatorship of the proletariat in our country, as long as we seriously implement Chairman Mao's revolutionary line and the Party's policies, comply with the unified plans of the state, make overall planning, strengthen the leadership, and constantly criticize the revisionist line and the tendency toward capitalism, commodity production can serve the cause of the socialist construction very well. Some areas and some units have shown the tendency toward capitalism in the process of organizing the production and circulation of commodities not because they have developed commodity production or promoted the diversified economy, but because they have run counter to Chairman Mao's revolutionary line and the Party's policies. This lesson deserves to be borne in mind.

In order to better implement the general policy of "developing the economy to safeguard supply," the rural commercial departments in all places must, through the functions and role of commercial work, vigorously support the socialist collective economy, develop commodity production and energetically promote a diversified economy so as to enable the rural people's commune to produce more grain, cotton, oil-bearing material, pigs, poultry, eggs, and other agricultural produce and byproducts.

"Policy and tactics are the life of the Party." In order to promote the development of the diversified economy, the commercial department must seriously carry out the existing policies of the Party in the countryside. The correct handling of the relations between the collective economy and the family side-occupations of the commune members is an important aspect in the correct implementation of policies. First, it is necessary to devote our main energy toward vigorously supporting the socialist collective economy. The collective should be actively helped to carry out properly whatever it has the conditions to undertake. When the collective is still not in a position to carry it out for the time being, we should actively create conditions to make this possible. Under the condition of guaranteeing the development of the collective economy of the people's commune with absolute superiority, it is also necessary to permit and encourage the commune members to take up proper family side-occupations.

Family side-occupations of commune members are essential supplements to the socialist collective economy and are in conformity with the level of development of productive forces at the present stage and the degree of awareness of the masses. At present, a given proportion of the diversified economy is made up of family side-occupations of the commune members. As a considerable part of the pigs, poultry and eggs, minor medicinal herbs, and piecemeal and scattered native produce and animal products is derived from the family side-occupations of the commune members, such side-occupations are definitely not unimportant things. Some people think that in order to develop collective ownership, it is necessary to reduce ownership by the individual. They even restrict at random the raising of pigs, sheep, chickens, and ducks by commune members and forbid the taking up of proper family side-occupations. This way of thinking and doing things is not in conformity with Party policies.

The experiences of many areas show that the rural commercial departments can do much to help develop the diversified economy in communes and production teams. The broad masses of staff members and workers of the commercial departments, by actively participating in and organizing production, helping the communes and production teams make proper planning, supplying the means of production, adjusting the seedlings, ushering in advanced techniques, exchanging experiences, and purchasing and marketing products, have effectively promoted the planned development of diversified economy with very good results. At present, in the course of studying the theory of the dictatorship of the proletariat, the rural commercial departments in all places seriously sum up experiences in conjunction with reality, properly conduct investigations and studies, energetically promote the progress of the diversified economy, and unremittingly make new contributions toward strengthening socialist economic construction and consolidating the dictatorship of the proletariat.

## 32. New China News Agency Correspondent Reports on New-style Rural Periodic Market Where Private Transactions Are Minimized (Source 22, pp. 61-65) May 9, 1976

Last year, just when the arch unrepentant capitalist-roader within the Party Teng Hsiao-p'ing was vigorously whipping up the Right-deviation wind to reverse verdicts, the Party committee of Ha-erh-t'ao Commune, Chang-wu hsien, Liaoning Province, through taking class struggle as the key link, adhering to the Party's basic line and closely relying upon the poor and lower-middle peasants, transformed the old rural trade fair and created a new type of fair — the socialist big fair. This gave an effective boost to the movement to learn from Tachai in agriculture. The socialist position in the countryside was thus further consolidated.

## Contradictions Calling for an Urgent Solution

Ha-erh-t'ao Commune is situated near the border between Liaoning and Kirin provinces. It has poor soil and an arid climate. In the past, grain output was very low. In the winter of 1974, spurred by the movement to criticize Lin Piao and Confucius, this commune whipped up a new upsurge in "learning from Tachai in agriculture." The broad masses of cadres and people broke the habit of "allowing land to lie fallow in winter" and energetically participated in farmland capital construction. However, after a period of time, attendance gradually diminished. When the Spring Festival drew near, there were still fewer people at work on farmland capital construction. Where did the people go? After an investigation, the commune Party committee discovered that the force of old habit had attracted the people to the trade fair.

The trade fair in Ha-erh-t'ao had a history of many years. On the fifth, tenth, fifteenth, twentieth, twenty-fifth, and thirtieth days of the month, people from the neighboring areas and even from as far as several tens of li away converged on the trade fair, numbering from 4,000 or 5,000 at the most to 2,000 or 3,000 at the least. A few profiteers made use of the fair to corner the market, play tricks, and carry out capitalist activities. Such a fair held a great attraction for some rich peasants who had not rid themselves of their private-ownership mentality. Under the influence of this kind of fair, the collective economy of this commune was weakened, the movement to learn from Tachai failed to get off the ground, and agricultural production long remained in a backward stage.

The Party committee of Ha-erh-t'ao Commune investigated the conditions of the rural fair and made clear the relations between the two-road struggle and trade fair in the countryside.

It felt that if such a fair was not subjected to restrictions and transformation, capitalism would make a breach through this fair and run wild, and more and more people would deviate from the socialist orbit. How should the rural trade fair be transformed? There were two ways: One was to follow the previous practice of closing it down by way of an administrative order or to exercise general control over it. As a result, it could neither be closed nor controlled properly. Another way was to establish the "socialist big fair" in light of the situation where a small number of private plots and family side-occupations were still retained at the present in the countryside. Efforts should be made to take class struggle as the key link, deepen education in the Party's basic line, arouse the masses to sell to the state the agricultural produce and by-products instead of bringing them to the trade fair. At the same time, the supply and sales departments should be organized to break with the usual practice and expand their scopes of buying and selling, and the exchange of commodities should be actively organized among the masses, so as to occupy the rural commercial position in a planned manner. The commune Party committee made a study of the matter and decided to adopt the latter measure to transform the existing trade fair.

## Fair of a New Type Appears

In the process of establishing the socialist big fair, Ha-erh-t'ao Commune first organized the cadres and the masses to vigorously run political night schools, to learn the fundamental experience of Tachai, and to unfold penetrating criticism against capitalist tendencies existing in the rural trade fair. Meanwhile, conscientious ideological education was conducted to further raise the socialist consciousness of the masses. After spending a period of time on study, criticism and ideological education, many commune members on their own initiative offered to sell to the state private agricultural produce and by-products intended for the fair, so as to support socialist construction. The commune Party committee decided to take advantage of this favorable situation to organize a socialist big fair.

On New Year's day 1975, this fair of a new type made its debut in Ha-erh-t'ao Commune. That day, the masses of commune members of various brigades, led by the cadres, carried on their shoulders their own agricultural produce and by-products and, beating gongs and drums and holding red banners, came from all directions and converged on the streets of Ha-erh-t'ao to take part in the socialist big fair. They sold to the supply and marketing cooperative their surplus agricultural produce and by-products. Then they headed for the stalls of the supply and marketing cooperative to buy various kinds of farm implements and other daily necessities they needed. The brisk bourgeois practice of shouting prices and driving bargains was swept away at one stroke.

At this fair, the spare-time cultural and art propaganda teams of the commune and various brigades also presented various cultural and art programs and propagandized new men, new deeds, and new practices. The masses could participate in the fair and, at the same time, receive socialist education.

At such a fair, there were also various support-agricultural activities organized by factories in the city. What people witnessed here was a vivid scene of the worker-peasant alliance and the exchange between town and country. What they heard were the principles of socialist revolution and the advanced deeds in learning from Tachai, grasping revolution, and promoting production. They said elatedly, "The more we attend the socialist big fair the greater the hatred we develop toward capitalism and the closer our hearts draw toward socialism. The socialist big fair is just fine."

Such a fair is a socialist new thing emerging in the struggle between the two roads, and its appearance holds down the capitalist influence. With the support of the broad masses of poor and lower-middle peasants, this kind of socialist big fair is run better and better. Now, apart from the periodical comprehensive big fairs, big fairs for the exchange of one chosen kind of commodities are run in light of agricultural seasons and the people's needs. Such exchange fairs are supplements to the comprehensive big fair. At a specified time and locality and within certain limits, they strictly stick to prearranged prices. With regard to agricultural produce and by-products, such as piglets, ducklings, chickens, seedlings, etc., which they find it inconvenient to handle for the present, the supply and marketing cooperative organizes exchange among the individuals and between one collective and another so as to meet each other's needs. Thus, 128 kinds of agricultural produce and by-products under the nine categories of commodities including pigs and fowl, fabricated straw goods, firewood, weeds, etc., which were freely traded in the past are put in the socialist orbit. The predominance of socialism is established in the rural trade fair. Apart from the buying and selling of ordinary agricultural produce and by-products, the commune also takes advantage of the big fair to organize various brigades to sell to the state grain, pigs, and other products under the unified purchase and sales program and under the planned purchase scheme. Actually, this kind of socialist big fair has become the main form of economic exchange activity in the countryside.

## Another Leap Forward in Understanding

Not long after the socialist big fair was established, Chairman Mao's important instruction on the question of theory was published.

"Our country at present practices a commodity system, and the wage system is unequal too, there being the eight-grade wage system, etc. These can only be restricted under the dictatorship of the proletariat." "Lenin said, 'Small production engenders capitalism and the bourgeoisie continuously, daily, hourly, spontaneously, and on a mass scale." The cadres and the masses of Ha-erh-t'ao Commune studied these teachings of Chairman Mao's, applied the theory of the dictatorship of the proletariat in summing up and analyzing the practice of running the socialist big fair, and saw the direction of advance more clearly. They realized that to run the socialist big fair well is not only a measure to hit at capitalist activities but also a practical step to educate the peasants, transform small production, and restrict bourgeois rights. In the period of socialism, there inevitably exist bourgeois rights such as the trade fair, the exchange of commodities, private plots, family side-occupations, distribution according to work, etc. Their existence is allowed by the Party's policy. But they should not be given oxygen and blood and be allowed to grow unrestrictedly. Instead they should be gradually restricted under the dictatorship of the proletariat. Running the socialist big fair provides fresh experience for blocking the channel which leads small production to capitalism, effectively restricting bourgeois rights in the sphere of exchange of commodities in the countryside and gradually removing the soil and conditions engendering capitalism.

On the basis of heightened awareness, the Party committee of Ha-erh-t'ao Commune has at all times taken guiding the masses along the socialist road as an important task in the process of running the socialist big fair. Through continuously instilling socialist ideas into the peasants, it has enabled them to consciously break with the concept of private ownership and with established traditions. In this commune, the political night schools of various brigades constantly launched such activities as "line education," "discussing everything," etc. Before a big fair was held, they organized the masses to study the Party's basic line and the theory of the dictatorship of the proletariat. At times they also invited the old poor peasants to recount histories of their families, villages and cooperatives, so as to impart education by making comparison between the new and the old societies and between the conditions before and after the Great Cultural Revolution. Through these activities, they praised Chairman Mao's revolutionary line, criticized the revisionist line, and brought political and ideological work to every house and every heart, so as to strengthen continuously the people's consciousness in following the socialist road. Thus, a still broader ideological foundation was provided for the socialist big fair.

## Leaders Stand in the Van of the Movement

"The root lies in the line and leadershp is the key." This equally applies to the struggle of operating a socialist big fair.

The Party committee of Ha-erh-t'ao Commune held that in order to make the masses grasp the theory of the dictatorship of the proletariat and consciously restrict bourgeois rights and follow the socialist road, the Party committee of the commune should first take the lead in breaking with established traditions and waging a resolute struggle against capitalism. Secretary Nashun (a Mongolian) of the commune Party committee is an old comrade. After receiving education in the Great Cultural Revolution, he looked upon the operation of the socialist big fair as a struggle to continue the revolution. He led the way in recalling the painful lessons he learned by carrying out the revisionist line before the Great Cultural Revolution. He took the initiative to criticize the bourgeois influence in himself and took the lead in restricting bourgeois rights. His act of persisting in continuing the revolution inspired the ideological revolutionization of the leading bodies at the commune and brigade levels. Young cadre Shih Ya-wen, vice chairman of the revolutionary committee of the commune, took the initiative to persuade his mother to be the first in selling to the state at the quoted price the tobacco crop from her private plot, thus playing a forward role among the masses. The ideological revolutionization of the leading body also set the pace for the ideological revolutionization of the broad masses of cadres and Party members. In the whole commune, there appeared a revolutionary scene of vigorously criticizing revisionism and capitalism and vigorously building socialism.

## Turn the Supply and Marketing Cooperative into a Tool of the Dictatorship of the Proletariat

In the past, under the influence of the revisionist line, Ha-erh-t'ao supply and marketing cooperative did not put proletarian politics in command but only concerned itself with talking about buying and selling behind the counter and cared nothing about class struggle beyond the counter. In the course of purchasing agricultural produce and by-products, it practiced many restrictive rules. It refused to handle one thing and purchase another, and thus it could not meet the needs of the socialist countryside. When it started to run the big fair, the commune Party committee took the correct orientation of the operational line of the supply and marketing cooperative as an important task. It pointed out that the rural commercial departments should persist in putting politics in command, serve the broad masses of poor and lower-middle peasants, become a special army in hitting at capitalism, use socialism to occupy the commercial position in the countryside, and serve as a tool of the dictatorship of the proletariat.

Under the leadership of the commune Party committee, the working personnel of this supply and marketing cooperative conscientiously studied the theory of the dictatorship of the proletariat and resolutely carried out Chairman Mao's revolutionary line. Their idea of doing business went through a tremendous change. They energetically widened the scope of business and regarded the handling of one more kind of product as the occupation of one more position and the removal of one more plot of soil engendering capitalism. In the past year and more, the commodities handled by this supply and marketing cooperative rose to over 350 varieties. The agricultural produce and by-products purchased were 41 items more than those handled before the socialist big fair. Meanwhile, additional points were set up in the commercial network. This gave the masses every facility and production every support. In addition, they also supplied small earth stoves. This gave the commune members every convenience in retrieving the old and utilizing waste materials. Small carts were sent to the countryside to bring goods to the doorsteps, while purchases were made in the brigade. Various sales departments also offered additional services such as cloth cutting, book lending, free glass-cutting, etc. Thus, even on the days when the fair was not held, the masses could also keep in touch with the state-run commercial network. This left no room for capitalism.

After the establishment of the socialist big fair, in order to insure the steady supply of commodities on the market, Ha-erh-t'ao Commune took market demands into consideration while arranging production in accordance with the guideline of "developing the economy and insuring supplies." While seeing to it that no adverse effect was produced on food crops and not a cut was made in the planted acreages planned by the state plan, when implementing the state cultivation plans, the various production teams made unified arrangements for certain economic crops needed by the market and gradually substituted the products under the collective economy for those formerly obtained from the commune members' private plots. Meanwhile, the production teams not only continuously encouraged individual commune members to raise pigs, but also made energetic efforts to develop collective pig-breeding and collective side-occupations and to combine development of diversified economy with the organization of sources of market supplies. Thus not only in the area of commodity circulation but also in the link of commodity production, the initiative was seized in fighting against capitalist influence, and the steady supply of commodities on the market was effectively guaranteed. This was hailed by the broad masses.

## 33. Representatives of Ten Big Department Stores in Nine Cities Denounce Teng Hsiao-p'ing and Demand "Bourgeois Right" Be Restricted (Source 4, pp. 166-168) July 16, 1976

Representatives from ten big state-owned department stores in nine Chinese cities held a meeting recently in Tientsin to exchange their experiences in criticizing Teng Hsiao-p'ing and repulsing the Right deviationist attempt at reversing correct verdicts. The stores represented were the Peking Department Store, the Tung-feng market of Peking, the First Department Store of Shanghai, the Tientsin Department Store, the State Department Store of the Nan-fang Hotel in Kwangchow, the Chungking Department Store, the Wuhan Market, the First Department Store of Harbin, the Hsin-chieh-kou Department Store of Nanking, and the Min-sheng Department Store of Sian.

At the meeting, the representatives angrily denounced Teng Hsiao-p'ing's crimes of negating the Great Proletarian Cultural Revolution. Through a review of the struggle between the two classes and between the two lines on the commercial front, they came to realize more deeply the correctness of Chairman Mao's instruction, "The current Great Proletarian Cultural Revolution is absolutely necessary and most timely for consolidating the dictatorship of the proletariat, preventing capitalist restoration, and building socialism."

They recalled that in this revolution the commercial workers, together with the people of the whole country, are criticizing the counterrevolutionary revisionist line pushed by capitalist-roaders in the Party and have seized back that portion of power which they had usurped. An excellent situation now prevails on the commercial front throughout the country. Markets are flourishing, prices are stable, and both purchase and supply are on the increase. New socialist things continue to emerge, and a wealth of fresh experience has been created. The "three-in-one" leading bodies combination of the old, middle-aged, and young are full of vigor; the theoretical contingent of commercial workers is growing steadily; "July 21" workers' colleges are mushrooming; and the support of commerce to industry and agriculture is growing. All these things testify to the further and better implementation of Chairman Mao's general principle guiding commercial and financial work: "developing the econom and ensuring supplies." They have also helped to enhance the role of commerce as a bridge and bond linking towns and countryside, industry and agriculture, and production and consumption.

The representatives agreed unanimously that the newly emerging socialist things are fruits of the Great Proletarian Cultural Revolution, which have restricted bourgeois right in the realms of distribution, exchange, and the relations among people. Proceeding from his reactionary bourgeois stand, Teng Hsiao-p'ing, the arch unrepentant capitalist-reader in the Party cherished a bitter hatred toward the Cultural Revolution. He concocted a revisionist program and spread the fallacy that "the present is not as good as the past" in an attempt to destroy the fruits of this revolution and of the entire socialist revolution and to turn history backward. China's commercial workers will never tolerate this but will struggle against him to the very end.

Through their exposure of Teng Hsiao-p'ing as a teacher by negative example, the representatives came to realize that the main danger in the historical period of socialism consists in the capitalist-roaders usurping Party and state power, changing the line of the Party, and pushing revisionism. The bourgeoisie is in truth right inside the Communist Party, they said.

In their speeches at the meeting, the representatives pointed out that bourgeois right provides the vital economic basis for the emergence of capitalist-roaders in the Party. In view of the existence of commodity production and exchange through money in Chinese society, certain people are bound to take advantage of this by using some legal and many illegal means to amass money and become new bourgeois elements. These new and the old bourgeois elements form the social basis for the capitalist-roaders to restore capitalism. They work hand in glove with each other to wage a desperate struggle against the restriction of bourgeois right. Socialist commerce in China is carried on not merely to do business, but to consolidate the position of the dictatorship of the proletariat. Workers on the socialist commercial front are proletarian revolutionary fighters and shoulder the important task of restricting bourgeois right in the sphere of commodity circulation and combating the forces of restoration and retrogression, so as to eradicate the hotbeds that engender new bourgeois elements.

The representatives declared: "We are determined to take class struggle as the key link, firmly keep to the socialist direction in running shops, conscientiously implement the Party's policies, distribute commodities in a reasonable way, resist the unhealthy tendencies, and deal heavy blows at those engaging in embezzlement and theft and speculation, thereby turning the shops into a real bastion for consolidating the dictatorship of the proletariat."

## 34. All-China Supply and Marketing Co-op Mass Criticism Group Exposes Crimes of the "Gang of Four"* in Sabotaging Agricultural and Subsidiary Production and Rural Markets (Source 25, pp. 94-97) November 30, 1976

The great leader and teacher Chairman Mao taught us:

*The "gang of four" was a group of top political leaders purged immediately after the death of Chairman Mao Tse-tung in September 1976. They generally espoused policies on the "left" of the Chinese political spectrum. — G. B.

"Policy and tactics are the life of the Party." Chairman Mao has formulated for our Party the basic line for the historical period of socialism and according to the tasks of the Party in different periods all kinds of proletarian policies. Only by conscientiously carrying out the Party's policies can the basic interests of the broad masses of the people be represented, the socialist enthusiasm of the broad masses of the people be brought into play, and the forward development of the cause of socialist revolution and socialist construction along the correct line be guaranteed. Like the Lin Piao-type of political swindlers, the anti-Party clique of Wang Hung-wen, Chang Ch'un-ch'iao, Chiang Ch'ing, and Yao Wen-yüan donned the Marxist mantle, extensively practiced idealism and metaphysics, wantonly cut up the theory of unity of the theory of uninterrupted revolution and the theory of the development of revolution by stages, upset the boundaries of policies and trampled underfoot the various economic policies of the Party in the countryside, thus resulting in serious harm through sabotaging the movement to learn from Tachai in agriculture, production and the market.

The rural economic policies of the Party clearly stipulate that the production teams of people's communes should actively develop a diversified economy and that under the condition of insuring the absolute predominance of the collective economy, the commune members should be allowed and encouraged to develop proper domestic side-occupations. However, the "gang of four" insidiously made a big negative issue of the question of diversified economy and domestic side-occupations. Whenever you intended to develop a diversified economy according to state plans, they branded you as practicing capitalism; whenever you said that commune members should be allowed to develop proper domestic side-occupations, they slandered you as "supplying oxygen and transfusing blood" to capitalism. They violated the Party's policies and confused people ideologically so that the cadres of all levels were afraid of discussing the Party's current policies, of grasping diverse economic undertakings, and of guiding the commune members to develop proper domestic side-occupations. When production was sabotaged and the procurement of agricultural and subsidiary products was affected, they also made false charges to lay the blame on others — the leading cadres of Party organizations at all levels and those responsible for economic work.

How could the active development of the collective diversified economy and the granting of permission for commune members to practice proper domestic side-occupations by people's communes be confused with the development of capitalism? It is true that a part of the diversified economy and domestic side-occupations still belongs to commodity production and constitutes a condition giving rise to capitalism. However, in order to prevent this from growing into capitalism, we could never adopt the method of giving up eating for fear of choking to stifle it, but must strengthen the Party's leadership, carry out the Party's line and policies, restrict it under the dictatorship of the proletariat, and gradually incorporate it into the orbit of socialist planned economy.

The "gang of four" equated diversified economy and domestic side-occupations with capitalism, and even denounced the Party's relevant policies as "Right-deviation." They pinned the label of "capitalism" on anyone who wanted to grasp this aspect of work according to the Party's policies. Really, metaphysics was rampant! This actually called on us to renounce Party leadership, abolish the Party's policies, and allow diversified economy and domestic side-occupations to spread freely so as to disrupt revolution and production. This was really out-and-out capitalism.

Viewed from the actual situation in our country, the diversified economy is by no means unimportant. At present, 70 percent of the raw materials for light industry come from agricultural and subsidiary, native and special products, waste and obsolete materials. As for the domestic side-occupations of the commune members, they are also by no means nonessential. Among the agricultural and subsidiary products procured by the commercial establishments, one-quarter of them comes from the domestic side-occupations of commune members. Without boosting agricultural and subsidiary production as fast as possible, increase of industrial raw material for enriching market supply, improving the living standards of the people, and supporting export in foreign trade would become empty talk! In fact, it was precisely owing to the interference and disruption of the "gang of four" that some agricultural subsidiary products in our country developed at a slow rate, with some even registering decline in output. This was not in correspondence with the need for the development of the national economy. Is it not very clearly a disastrous result the "gang of four" has brought through confusing the line of demarcation between socialism and capitalism?

The crimes of the "gang of four" in undermining the Party's policy on rural fair trade are also very serious. Since the Great Proletarian Cultural Revolution and especially after the issue of Chairman Mao's important directive on the question of theory, under the leadership of the Party committees at all levels, the rural commercial establishments have strengthened their leadership and control over rural fair trade. In accordance with the policies relating to rural fair trade they have adopted many effective measures according to local conditions to further consolidate and extend the socialist rural market battlefront. However, the "gang of four," singing the high-sounding tune of "revolution" and flaunting the signboard of the "advanced," indiscriminately and frenziedly demanded the immediate lopping off of rural fair trade with no regard for the actual situation. They took one cap after another from the "cap-making factory" and one big stick after another from the "iron and steel factory," and in the name of "upholding the old relations of production," "opposing socialist revolution," etc., they vainly attempted to use the vile means of branding and clubbing to attack the revolutionary leading cadres from the Central to the local organs who correctly carried out the Party's rural fair trade policies.

On the question of rural fair trade, we are advocates of uninterrupted revolution. We know that rural fair trade belongs to the traces left by the old society and is the soil and condition engendering capitalism. It plays a negative role toward the deepening of socialist revolution and the development of the movement to learn from Tachai in agriculture. Therefore, we must persist in taking class struggle as the key link, adhere to the Party's basic line, adopt methods of restriction and transformation under the condition of the dictatorship of the proletariat, and unceasingly attack the capitalist force so as to enable socialism to further occupy the rural battlefront and gradually create conditions under which the bourgeoisie can neither exist nor emerge again.

We are also advocates of development of revolution by stages. Because at the present stage, when the majority of places in the whole country are taken into consideration, the production and livelihood needs of commune members still cannot be entirely underwritten by rural socialist commerce, and some small and piecemeal resources of the third category still have to go through rural fair trade so that the commune members can help supply one another's needs and adjust surplus and deficit. If we turn a blind eye to this point, ignore this objective reality, and do not carry out the current economic policies of the Party, a disastrous result is bound to be brought to the development of rural economy.

The consistent policy adopted by our Party toward rural fair trade is to make use of its positive role to restrict its negative role, strengthen leadership, exercise strict control, deal blows at speculative and profiteering activities, criticize the capitalist tendencies, protect the proper exchange effected among commune members, actively create conditions politically and economically, and gradually replace it with socialist commerce. This policy of permitting and restricting [rural fair trade] fully embodies the theory of unity of the theory of uninterrupted revolution and the theory of development of revolution by stages, and is in correspondence with the present objective conditions of our countryside.

The "gang of four" gave people a false image as if only they were the "most revolutionary" and the "most advanced." As a matter of fact, wherever their gang meddled, revolution and production were in a mess, rural fair trade was left to follow its own course, capitalism ran wild, speculators and profiteers were rampant, state plans were battered, and the unified market was undermined. Particularly in those places where there were still not the conditions for closing rural fair trade at the moment, they arbitrarily insisted on closing it down artificially. As a result, the open ones were closed, but secret ones emerged. This on the one hand opened the door of convenience to the speculators and profiteers and on the other hand affected the development of diverse economic undertakings and proper domestic side-occupations, thus bringing many difficulties to the livelihood of the people. It is all very clear that what the "gang of four" practiced was definitely not "revolution" but disruption and definitely not "progress" but regression.

Lenin pointed out: "The dictatorship of the proletariat is the proletariat's leadership in policies" ("On Food Grain Tax," Collected Works of Lenin, Vol. XXXII, p. 332). The "gang of four" vainly attempted, by way of undermining the leadership of the Party over rural economic policies, to oppose the dictatorship of the proletariat over the bourgeoisie from the sphere of production to the sphere of circulation in the countryside, disintegrate the collective economy of the people's commune, sabotage the worker-peasant alliance, and further realize their criminal aim of usurping leadership in the Party and seizing power, subverting the dictatorship of the proletariat, and restoring capitalism. How venomous the wolfish designs of the "gang of four" were. They were really a gang of pests that brought disaster to the country and the people.

At present, the broad masses of commercial staff members and workers in the countryside are high in spirit and strong in morale. They are resolved to rally most closely round the Party Central Committee headed by Chairman Hua, thoroughly expose and criticize the "gang of four" politically, ideologically and organizationally, consistently carry out the policies of "taking food grains as the key link to insure all-round development" and "developing the economy and insuring supplies," conscientiously carry out to the letter all rural economic policies of the Party, vigorously grasp revolution and actively promote production, recover the losses caused by the "gang of four" through disrupting production and the market, and make new contributions to the development of the national economy.

PART THREE

# Money, Banking, and Investment

China's financial policies aim at three important goals — controlling inflationary pressures, contributing to the mobilization of savings for investment, and enforcing planned allocation among enterprises. Financial policy can be distinguished from fiscal management of government revenues and expenditures, and from economic planning which is mostly physical materials allocation. Monetary policy naturally is inseparable from fiscal management, planning, commerce, enterprise management, and labor policy. Nonetheless, most of the emphasis in this section is given to the financial system itself.

The first goal — controlling inflationary pressures — is a direct responsibility of the financial system. Inflation is of course harmful to consumers whose incomes are relatively fixed. But more than that, inflation can be politically dangerous when it grows severe and long lasting. Though the relationship remains to be established scientifically, casual empiricism suggests that high, uncontrolled inflation is a symptom of political instability, perhaps even a harbinger of revolution. It indicates that sitting authorities have lost their capacity to manage the economy and calls into question their general right to rule. The Chinese inflation after 1935 is legendary by now. Shanghai wholesale prices rose several million percent just between May 1946 and March 1949, a thoroughly unrestrained resort to the printing presses![1] This frightening experience led the Chinese Communist Party to nationalize banking first before setting out to reorganize any other sector of the economy. The new People's Bank was established in 1948, a year before liberation; the new "people's currency" (jen-min pi) replaced all other notes in circulation shortly after 1949, and as early as 1952 complete monetary stability was restored.

This impressive achievement, logged even while the Korean War was in progress, was not equivalent to final victory over inflationary pressures, however. Official prices continued to rise slowly. In the 1950s, retail prices appear to have risen slightly under 2 percent per year, and in the 1960s and 1970s, at an even lesser rate.[2] According to one leading estimate, the index of retail prices in eight large cities (1952=100) rose in 1963 to 118 but declined again by 1971 to 116.[3] But official list price indexes do not tell the whole story. When goods are available in insufficient quantity, black markets appear with prices two or three or more times the state's list prices. And if some goods are not available at all, "repressed inflation" – excess demand and purchasing power with no outlet – occurs.[4] The government's weapons for controlling inflation include discouraging conspicuous consumption through inculcation of egalitarian values, increasing supplies of consumer goods wherever possible (including occasional resort to grain imports), freezing wages, rationing, administering prices, restricting market activity, encouraging voluntary private saving, and inducing involuntary saving (in the form of high profit margins for state enterprises).[5] These various measures reinforce one another. For example, if the real value of the yuan holds steady, then people have an incentive to maintain savings accounts since they need not fear their savings will be inflated away. Conversely, if individuals deposit their savings at modest interest (in 1972 around 2.2 percent on current demand deposits and over 3.2 percent on fixed deposits of one year or more), then fewer yuan of "people's currency" chase available goods.[6]

The new regime after 1949 was committed to the second goal – a high investment rate leading to rapid economic growth – as one of its chief priorities. The aspirations of Chinese Communist leaders were guided by the Soviet precedent of successes with Stalin's "forced draft" industrialization, even though they realized the economic challenges they faced in the 1950s were substantially different from those faced by an earlier generation of Soviet leaders. For one, labor in populous China was much more plentiful than in Russia; hence, forced industrialization would create less competition for labor and be less likely to pressure wages upward. Labor discipline would be easier to achieve.[7] For another, China's revolution had been rural, and the CCP was better prepared to manage the transformation of its rural economy — land reform, collectivization, rise in farm productivity, and mobilization of political support from farmers. Moreover, the Chinese were driven by stronger emotions of nationalism against foreign powers who had dominated their culture and the modern sector of their economy for many decades, emotions that were reinforced by the racial distinction between Chinese and all imperialists except Japanese. Although these differences between Russian and China gradually induced the Chinese to adopt their own unique approaches to development culminating in the so-called "Maoist model," China like the Soviet Union moved rapidly to achieve an impressive rate of investment. The percent of Gross Domestic Expenditure accounted for by Gross Domestic Investment rose from only 6 percent in 1933 (a rate undoubtedly static throughout the Republican period) to 16 percent in 1952, 23 percent in 1957, and an estimated 28 percent by 1970, all calculated with constant 1957 yuan.[8]

This rapid increase suggests to some economists that a significant potential surplus above mass consumption existed in the economy of the Republican period, a surplus probably equal to almost 37 percent of Net Domestic Product. The Nationalist government of the time could not tap it, but the Communist government, with its more effective leadership, later could. To oversimplify two competing interpretations of the "surplus" issue, writers taking the "technological" side question the actual existence of a surplus available for investment. They hypothesize that under the dangling sword of population expansion, traditional agriculture was approaching the limit of land and labor productivity possible under primitive, age-old farming methods. Only "inputs created by a fairly advanced stage of an industrial-scientific revolution" could save China's agriculture from sharply diminishing returns. Only by bridging gaping "discontinuities" in transport and farm technology could agricultural growth even match an annual population increase of 1.5-2 percent. What small and diminishing marketed surplus did occur before 1949 mostly can be traced to the tiny coastal and riparian treaty port sector and to unequal distribution of income, in particular to the estimated 20 percent of grain output controlled by landlords who counted for only 4 percent of the rural population. Writers taking the "distributional" side assert, to the contrary, that a rather large potential surplus existed in Republican China. Only part of it was actually realized, mainly as a result of the exploitative social structure, and even that part was frittered away by the classes who controlled it on luxury consumption, comfortable town living, and wasteful personal services (including private armies). Military spending was also the chief villain in the public sector. The new Nanking government devoured at least 67-85 percent of its revenues with overinflated military expenditures and with repayment of military loans floated between 1928 and 1935. The rapid increase in the investment rate achieved after 1949 lends support to the "distributional" interpretation.[9]

All Chinese investment outside the collective sector comes from the state budget. Of the possible sources of state revenue to finance the budget, China has moved steadily toward principal reliance upon the profits of state enterprises (Table 1).

Table 1

Principal Sources of Budget Revenue
(in percent)

| Revenue source | 1952 | | 1970-72 | |
|---|---|---|---|---|
| Taxes | 56 | | 36 | |
| Industrial and commercial | | 35 | | 30 |
| Agricultural | | 15 | | 6 |
| Other | | 6 | | - |
| State enterprise profits | 27 | | 60 | |
| All others | 18 | | 4 | |
| | 101 | | 100 | |

Source: Figures rounded from Table 5-2 in Alexander Eckstein, China's Economic Revolution (New York: Cambridge University Press, 1977), p. 184. Eckstein's 1970-72 data came from his interview in 1972 with Fu Tse-hao, Director of Budget Administration in the Ministry of Finance.

Other than approximately two billion dollars of Soviet credits accepted for First Five-Year Plan (1953-57) projects, China has eschewed foreign loans and foreign investment. Domestic sales of government securities, which at one point financed about 10 percent of government expenditures, were phased out by the mid-1960s. And even though individual savings deposits have risen dramatically since the regime's early years, their relative proportion of total revenue is still small. These facts, coupled with the absence of a private securities market in China, confirm that the role of financial institutions (primarily the People's Bank) in mobilizing investment capital is minimal, especially when compared with a capitalist economy.

Bank credit is supposed to be available to enterprises mainly for working capital. Most fixed capital investment is financed through interest-free budgetary grants. In reality enterprises like to turn a blind eye to regulations and seek working capital loans to finance new construction illicitly. Even though after 1961 interest rates for working capital loans above the planned quota in China (about 7 percent) were higher than in the Soviet Union (about 2 percent), they were still low relative to the marginal efficiency of capital in China. They were also low relative to the rates that probably would have been offered if China had a free market for credit.[10] As a result of its tight money policies, the Bank often found itself in a position of restraining unauthorized capital investment. This allocation problem is discussed separately below. Since higher interest rates paid by an enterprise must be subtracted from profits, the amount of the interest rate was most important only during periods when profits were most emphasized as an enterprise success indicator. When profits were relatively unimportant, enterprises would be willing to pay any rate of interest to expand their capital.

The third goal — enforcing planned allocation among enterprises — joins the financial system with the planning system. Even if physical planning were to work comprehensively and smoothly in China, which it does not, a positive role for financial institutions would still exist. On the one hand, enterprises with too little credit might not be able to command enough resources to fulfill their output plan; or they would be left with insufficient flexibility to overcome bottlenecks in their planned supply of inputs or to deal with emergency orders. On the other hand, enterprises with too much credit could disrupt the physical plan by commanding more inputs than they were slated to receive, or by diverting credit to unplanned new construction. Actually China does not have the capacity to make physical planning work comprehensively and smoothly. Their general approach has been to decentralize as many planning decisions as possible to provincial or local levels, and then to arrange "balance transfers" of key items (steel, machine tools, foreign exchange, etc.) in demand countrywide. To oversimplify, "balance transfer" works this way. Once Hupei Province, for example, drafts its provincial plan and determines it will produce 20,000 tons of rolled steel more than it will consume in the year to come, central planners allocate surplus Hupei steel to other provinces. In reality, of course, central authorities must consider varieties of rolled steel (by width, thickness, alloy composition, hardness, heat resistivity, etc.). They must negotiate with Hupei authorities if they think the provincial planners claim too much native steel for themselves. And they must consider delivery dates and transportation costs. Audrey Donnithorne argues that conditions for centralized planning were most favorable in China toward the end of the First Five-Year Plan period (1953-57), and that more recently "the inability of the centre to implement an effective national plan is connected with the fall in the proportion of resources available to it and to the fact that a high proportion of the centre's available resources have been pre-empted for military purposes."[11]

Under conditions of limited, decentralized physical planning, financial statistics necessarily take on greater importance for central authorities. The "comprehensive financial plan" is an instrument for checking physical balances, thus allowing officials at the center to keep their finger on the pulse. As outlined by the Chinese in 1960, six components form the comprehensive financial plan: budgets, extrabudgetary receipts and expenditures, granting and repayment of bank loans, cash receipts and payments, receipts and payments of ministries in charge of enterprises, and items concerned with investment and working expenses in the budgets of units of collective agriculture. Certain summary statistics were to be calculated as well, such as rate of profit, rate of reduction of cost, and the expected impact fulfilling plan targets would have upon the circulation of money.[12] Chinese leaders debated in the early 1960s the desirability of using enterprise profit (reckoned on capital) as the chief indicator of enterprise success. Profit rate, ran one side of the argument, could reflect the combined effect of several narrower indicators. Output alone could be raised simply by spending more on labor and material inputs, or by producing great quantities of cheaper varieties regardless of demand. Quality or product variety alone could be raised by reducing overall output and taking more care with each unit of production. Labor and cost plans could be met by ignoring effects on the output and distribution sides. The profit rate supposedly would be greatest when all other specific targets were optimized.

The other side of the argument was that profit targets too are capable of abuse. Enterprises could use bank loans to remit the planned amount of profits, even when they have not fulfilled output and sales plans. And the absence of a free market in China means that sometimes the most profitable items to produce are not the ones in greatest demand. In the wake of the Cultural Revolution profits were still said to be important and enterprises were supposed to make profits. But no longer were they regarded as a comprehensive indicator of everything desirable about enterprise performance.[13]

In sum, since China's planning system is fairly loose to begin with, and since no consensus obtains on which success indicators should be most important, planning authorities themselves are helpless to enforce enterprise discipline. This job falls to the banking system. Large enterprises often have a representative of the local People's Bank actually stationed on the site. This representative is supposed to make sure that bank credit is used for its intended purpose, to insure that accounts are kept properly, and to inspect warehouses and inventories in search of hoarding or improper use of credit for unintended purposes. All enterprises are supposed to keep no more than three day's supply of cash outside their Bank account. And no credit is supposed to be extended by one enterprise directly to another — the Bank should always act as intermediary. Enterprise managers tend to regard such controls as "tight" and

Figure 1

Basic Organization of Financial Institutions, 1970s

| Level | Party (CCP) | Administration | |
|---|---|---|---|
| Center | Central Committee Finance-Trade Work Department (FTWD) | State Council Finance-Trade Office (FTO) | |
| | Bank Party Committee | Ministry of Finance | |
| | | Tax Affairs General Bureau | |
| | | Budget Section | |
| | | People's Bank of China, General Office | |
| | | Bank of China | |
| Province | Provincial Committee FTWD | Revolutionary Committee FTO | |
| | Department and Bank Party Committees | Department of Finance | |
| | | People's Bank, Provincial Office | |
| | | Urban | Rural |
| City or District (<u>ti-ch'ü</u>) | Municipal (or District) Committee FTWD | Municipal Revolutionary Committee FTO | District Administration FTO |
| | Division and Bank Party Committees | Division of Finance | Division of Finance |
| | | People's Bank, City Office | People's Bank, Central Branch |

| | | | |
|---|---|---|---|
| Town or County | Municipal (or County) Committee FTWD<br><br>Bureau and Bank Party Committees | Municipal Revolutionary Committee FTO<br><br>Bureau of Finance<br><br>People's Bank, Branch (chih-hang) | County Revolutionary Committee FTO<br><br>Bureau of Finance<br><br>People's Bank, Branch (chih-hang) |
| Local levels | Party committee members with special responsibility for finance and trade<br><br>Bank Party committees or branches | People's Bank, neighborhood branches (fen-hang) | Commune<br><br>People's Bank, Branch (fen-hang)<br><br>Credit Cooperative<br><br>Agricultural Tax Office<br><br>Brigade<br><br>Credit Cooperative, Branch |

routinely avoid them whenever possible.

Thus a sort of tension system has emerged whereby planning is loose, management and much distribution are decentralized, and a monolithic central banking system tries to exercise tight control. One hypothesis about the creation of a separate Agricultural Bank of China in 1963, for example, sees it as a victory for local forces who wanted to ease agricultural credit by getting it out of the hands of the People's Bank. Two years later, in 1965, a further decentralization of agricultural credit was effected with a new system of "fixed management" whereby fixed allocations of farm loan funds to provinces came under the control of local financial departments for ultimate allocation to borrowers within their province. Significantly, this raid was staged against the more vulnerable Agricultural Bank, not against the People's Bank itself.[14]

Throughout these debates in China, someone on the ideological "left" has always felt compelled to advance the position that money and profit are pure evil, thus necessitating the counter-argument that only over-reliance upon them, or unrelieved pursuit of them, are undesirable: making money and raising profitability in the service of the people are good; individuals simply must be on their guard ideologically. It is only wrong for profits to dominate all other considerations. Looking through Chinese articles on the subject of finance and trade, one sees this concern reflected in career preferences by students. Many wish to avoid commercial careers not only because jobs in finance and trade traditionally have low status, but also because in China contact with money is often regarded as potentially corrupting. As the saying goes, "It is impossible to walk by the riverside without getting one's feet wet."

## Guide to the Documents in Part Three

Selections 35 and 36 provide overviews of China's financial institutions. Selection 35, following two opening sections on the theoretical role of public finance in a socialist state, describes the state budget, state credit facilities, finance departments of state enterprises, tax departments, and other state-administered funds. Selection 36 is an article by a former official of the French National School of Administration who interviewed representatives of the Chinese People's Bank in Peking in 1972.

Selection 37, in the form of praise for a model Service Group of an office of the People's Bank, reveals how Chinese authorities would like their banking personnel to perform. Such articles indicate where present performance is unsatisfactory.

China's approach to fiscal policy — striving for a balanced budget, minimum resort to credit at any level, and a stable currency — is extremely conservative by other countries' standards. One reason for the emphasis upon repressing all visible signs of inflation appears in Selection 40: the years of the previous regime's dramatic political decline were accompanied by a runaway inflation. Selections 38 through 41 give additional perspectives on China's conquest over visible inflation. The term "people's currency" (jen-min pi, or renminbi as it is spelled now in China) is used in phrases like "Renminbi savings accounts have become very popular in Hongkong recently." But the currency is denominated in yuan; one receives a "two-yuan bill," and a bicycle is said to cost "120 yuan."

A separate but related development, elaborated in Selections 42 through 45, that Chinese leaders interpret as a sign of confidence in their economic policies is the steady increase in long-term individual savings accounts. As explained in Selection 45, at least four general benefits flow from the successful mobilization of personal deposits, not the least of which is some contribution to price stability through the evening out of seasonal peaks in farm income.

Selections 46 through 52 give several perspectives on the continual choice that has to be made between reserving more collective income for local investment (accumulation) and distributing more of it directly to workers (consumption). Judging from the variety of arguments presented in these selections that defend a higher accumulation/consumption ratio, as opposed to a stable or smaller ratio, fairly strong pressures must have been generated in production teams and brigades to favor increased consumption.

Selection 53 picks up the theme of thrift introduced first in Selections 8 and 9. Here it is explained how a model sugarcane industrial chemicals plant which used to lie idle after each sugar harvest was processed, and which used to pay to have effluent hauled off for disposal at sea, has found economical "multiple uses" for sugar pulp waste and has begun year-round operation.

Selections 54 and 55, both of which appeared during a time when the gang of four's influence was still strong over official publications, counter what the authors believe to be erroneous arguments about the role of money under a dictatorship of the proletariat. While they find money to be functional for the present period of transition, they conclude with a wistful reference to Lenin's utopia where gold would be used for the construction of public lavatories.

Selection 56 shows how a model bank office actively uses its strategic place in the financial life of the enterprises in its jurisdiction to check deviant management practices that "tend toward capitalism."

Notes

1. Alexander Eckstein, China's Economic Revolution (New York: Cambridge University Press, 1977), p. 163.
2. Ibid.
3. Dwight H. Perkins, "Growth and Changing Structure of China's Twentieth Century Economy," in China's Modern Economy in Historical Perspective, ed. by Dwight H. Perkins (Stanford: Stanford University Press, 1975), p. 153. In constructing this index, Perkins accepts an official report that the Shanghai price level dropped 2.4 percent between 1965 and 1970, a drop he assumes occurred in the other seven large cities.
4. Eckstein, China's Economic Revolution, p. 175.
5. Ibid., p. 172.
6. John G. Gurley, China's Economy and the Maoist Strategy (New York: Monthly Review Press, 1976), p. 276.
7. Eckstein, China's Economic Revolution, pp. 172-76.
8. Ta-Chung Liu and Kung-Chia Yeh, The Economy of the Chinese Mainland: National Income and Economic Development 1933-1959 (Princeton: Princeton University Press, 1965), p. 80. Perkins, "Growth and Changing Structure," p. 165.
9. Carl Riskin, "Surplus and Stagnation in Modern China," in Perkins, China's Modern Economy in Historical Perspective, p. 72.
10. Audrey Donnithorne, China's Economic System (London: George Allen and Unwin, 1967), pp. 424-26.
11. Audrey Donnithorne, "The Budget and the Plan in China," Contemporary China Papers No. 3 (Canberra: Australian National University Press, 1972).
12. Donnithorne, China's Economic System, p. 471.
13. Ibid., p. 162.
14. Ibid., pp. 427-28.

## 35. Economist Gives Comprehensive Overview of Socialist Public Finance (Source 20, pp. 3-27) June 1966

The function and work of socialist public finance are an important and integral part of socialist reconstruction. A clear understanding and appreciation of the nature, system, and characteristics of socialist public finance are a matter of importance in the development of the socialist revolution and socialist reconstruction. In this essay, an attempt is made to investigate, in a preliminary way, the problems arising from these areas. Should there be any incorrectness or shortcomings, criticism and guidance are welcomed.

### 1. The Nature and Substance of Socialist Public Finance

What the true substance and nature of the public finance of a socialist state should be is one of the problems over which there has been much current theoretical discussion, and various opinions have been expressed in our country.

Whether the problem of the socialist state is one of distribution is a problem about which there is as yet no unanimous opinion. Some of our comrades are of the opinion that the problem of socialist public finance is one of distribution. Other comrades are of the opinion that the problem of socialist public finance is not one of distribution.

Which of these opinions is correct?

It is my feeling that the former of the two opinions is correct because it is more in accordance with the objective facts of our socialist financial tasks.

In order to establish and consolidate the dictatorship of the proletariat, our socialist state effectuates the various functions of the state: it organizes the total mobilization of the whole economy; it develops the socialist economic reconstruction and the socialist cultural reconstruction; it consolidates our national defense; it strives to continually raise the living and cultural standards of the working people. To do this it has to centralize the power of the state, using various organized means and bringing together and absorbing a large proportion of the population's income, so that it can be redistributed directly and centrally for the various needs and requirements of our socialist revolution and reconstruction. In this way, the state actually participates, financially and economically speaking, directly in production and in raising people's incomes, thereby effecting distribution and redistribution.

Naturally, when we say that public finance is a matter of distribution, we cannot go into the matter of distribution and study it independently and in isolation.

All matters of distribution have to be established on the foundation of production. Without production there can be no distribution. Naturally, public finance is something that cannot be considered apart from production. It is only in a situation where there is a large volume of production of socially usable goods that the state can step in to appropriate a portion of it for distribution. Hence the proper basis for considering and studying finance is on the plane of production.

We should study not only the part played by public finance in all forms of social savings and accumulation, but also the part played by public finance in the development of production. The relation of production to public finance is really the same thing as the relation of production to distribution. On the one hand, production determines distribution; on the other hand, distribution can have a positive influence on production. The two are related in a dialectical manner. In our study of the nature and substance of public finance, we are on the one hand opposed to the study of distribution in isolation from production; on the other hand, we are opposed to regarding the process of distribution as something secondary, which does not occupy a counterbalancing position to production, and as capable in a socialist society of playing an important and special role in the sphere of production.

To study the nature and substance of finance, it is necessary to raise high the red flag of Mao Tse-tung's thought.

It is necessary to clarify to oneself not only the relations between production and distribution, but, by using class struggle as a basic concept, to advance to an understanding of the relationship between the state and finance; the state is a necessary product of class struggle, and finance can come into being only after the coming into being of the state. History has shown that the state and its finance have always been the instruments of the ruling class, used to uphold its position and for its various other requirements. Thus, public finance and the state are essentially linked; without the state there can be no public finance.

Under the socialist system, the state's finance is used as an instrument by the proletarian government to carry out its socialist revolution and socialist reconstruction.

At the 10th Assembly of the 8th Party Congress it was pointed out in the Public Bulletin: "During the period of the proletarian revolution and proletarian dictatorship — that is, the historical period of transition from capitalism to communism (this period can extend for several decades or even longer) — there is implicit in the society the class struggle between the capitalist class and the proletariat class, between the capitalist road and the socialist road."

This clear and illuminating statement and guidance from the Party Central Committee is of the greatest importance to all those who are involved in the discussion and theorizing about public finance. Because the socialist society is the transitional society in the progress from capitalism to communism, it naturally follows that socialist public finance is the finance of a state of this transitional period.

During the whole extent of the socialist period both classes and class struggle exist; consequently, socialist public finance naturally assumes the role of the instrument of the proletariat in its victorious class struggle against the capitalists. If public finance is treated apart from the position of the state, from the problems of class struggle, from the dictatorship of the proletariat, there is no way of defining the relationship between politics and finance, and in consequence there is no way of resolving the concept of what are the substance and nature of the state's finance.

Since the establishment of our state, from both the actual and practical point of view, the fact that public finance has functioned and been utilized as an instrument of class struggle cannot be clearer.

In 1956, during the high tide of the cooperative movement in agriculture and the absorption of capitalist commerce and industry into joint ventures of state and private enterprises, the government promulgated a number of financial measures to facilitate the socialization of agriculture and handicraft enterprises, as well as the socialization of capitalist commerce and industries. After having achieved these processes of socialization, in order to guard against the restoration of capitalism, further measures were adopted to consolidate the position of socialism.

From all this it can be seen that the financial work of a socialist state has not only an economic function but also a political one.

For the purpose of consolidating the dictatorship of the proletariat, the state undertakes the basic work of laying the foundation of the socialist revolution and the development of socialist reconstruction in a planned manner; it raises the living and cultural standards of all the working people by degrees. To do this, it absorbs and concentrates a portion of total national income, which is in turn centrally redistributed to fulfill the needs in the various sectors of the economy. The achievement and formulation of its role in distribution constitute the substance and function of the state's finance during this transitional period.

## 2. The Peculiarities of Socialist Finance

Socialist public finance is a part of the function and machinery of socialist distribution. Financial distribution of this kind has its own peculiarities. The experience of our socialist finance in practice shows that it includes the following major points:

### a. National Finance Is the State's Direct Effectuation of Distribution

In all societies, the state's financial activities constitute an expression of the state's function — to use the state power to absorb and distribute a portion of the society's income, thus performing an economic function.

A socialist economy is a planned economy; a socialist state has an economic function and capability. In a socialist economy it is necessary to absorb a portion of the social production and people's income into the hands of the state, so that the state may effect a distribution. This is so not only because it is necessary to maintain the machinery of a proletarian state, but also because it is the objective demand of the planned development of the socialist economy. On the basis of the planned development of the society's various economic and cultural projects and enterprises, which are in turn planned in accordance with the needs of the various phases and stages of development, the state formulates its various guidelines, directives, and policies. Thus the state, basing its finance on these guidelines, directives, and policies, absorbs or collects a portion of the national income and distributes it in a planned manner to fulfill the requirements of the planned development of the national economy.

All that the state can use in distribution is only a part or portion of the national income, and not the whole of the national income. Through the institution and application of measures in the form of taxes, the state collects and absorbs a part or portion of the output or revenue of the agricultural communes or urban industries or handicraft cooperatives into the hands of the state. The bulk of the production of organized bodies and units cannot be distributed by the state; it can only be left to be distributed by the organizations themselves, although under state guidance and direction.

In this case then, in the instance of an enterprise wholly owned by the people, is it possible for the state to undertake to effect distribution directly? To this we answer: no. Although the state-owned enterprises are in fact state enterprises, where all the properties — whether they be fixed assets or current funds — are supplied by the state and are, therefore, owned by the state, and although the sales and distribution of such enterprises are carried out according to the direction and resolution of the state, such enterprises are nonetheless independent operational units under the national accounting structure; on the basis of the principle of the dissemination and ramification of responsibility, under the guidance of the state they can independently organize their productive activities as well as their sales and distribution activities. With the revenues derived from the sales of goods they defray the various outlays and expenses, such as the cost of labor and depreciation; finally, they turn over the bulk of the accrued income in the form of taxation or profit.

Thus, what the state can use for distribution consists primarily of the taxation or income turned over by the state enterprises — in other words, the bulk of their net profit, in the form of taxation or revenue. Then what the state can use for direct distribution, as it were, is made up of what has been turned over as taxation or profit from the state enterprises that are wholly owned by the people — i. e., the net income of such enterprises and not the whole output of such enterprises.

### b. Value Expressed in Cash, or Monetary Value, Is the Usual Method of State Distribution

Before the time of the capitalist system, much of the state's finance was based on goods or expressed in kind. After the development of commodity and currency, the nation's finance and distribution gradually came to be based on monetary value. The capitalist system of finance is based on monetary value or currency.

Under the socialist system, owing to the retention of commodity and currency, distribution is also largely carried out on the basis of monetary value. The use of monetary value as a means of distribution is more flexible and mobile than the utilization of actual goods for this purpose. Under certain circumstances, however, it is sometimes necessary for a socialist state to use actual goods in distribution; such a step can only be regarded as a special measure of the government.

Whether the state uses monetary value or actual goods for the purpose of effecting distribution, we are only dealing with distribution; we are not examining or dealing with the nature and substance of distribution. In any case, in the end, the adoption of monetary value for the purpose of effecting distribution must ultimately result in a distribution of actual goods. Thus, distribution by monetary value is only a step and not the purpose of distribution. In point of fact, the purpose of distribution by monetary value through the use of the state's finance, by varying the values appropriated for various objectives, is to enable the state enterprises and the various units of enterprises, both organized bodies and individuals, to receive their various appropriate allocations so that they can make their contributions to the socialist revolution and reconstruction.

Consequently, in our financial task we should give our attention not only to the allocation of capital funds, or to such matters as pricing and the control of market conditions, but we should also always consider the effect of such an allocation of resources on the eventual distribution of actual goods. For instance, in the course of the centralization of financial capital and eventual allocation and distribution, we must study the effect of such a distribution on the whole nation's resources for production and consumption and on total accumulation and consumption, as well as the problem of the balance or equilibrium between the volume of the currency and the volume of the actual goods in circulation. In the matter of the allocation of capital, thought and attention must be given to the effect of such an allocation: whether such an allocation is counterbalanced by the availability of actual goods, thus achieving a state of equilibrium; how such an allocation might affect the capital and current resources of all the bodies and organizations concerned, their reserve deposits and administrative problems, etc. In our study and consideration of financial problems, we must therefore not confine ourselves to the sector of the distribution of monetary value; we must go further and examine the problems of the whole balance and equilibrium of our national economy.

### c. The Allocation of Our National Resources Through Public Finance Is Fundamentally Carried Out on the Basis of "Nonrepayable Distribution"

Our financial distribution of a portion of our national income and resources is fundamentally based on the principle of "nonrepayment." That is to say, the capital resources accumulated and centralized through revenue and taxation — whether received from national enterprises owned by the whole people, from collective enterprises, or from the people and workers at large — are as a rule "nonrepayable." At the same time the funds and capital payments allotted by the state — whether as capital funds invested in state enterprises, or for the purpose of establishing welfare or educational institutions, or for paying salaries and wages — are also made on the basis of a "nonrepayment."

We have pointed out this basis and principle of nonrepayment because it is not necessarily a part of the nature or substance of socialist public finance. In our system of finance, we not only adopt the "nonrepayment" system but we sometimes also adopt, in certain sectors of our economy, the system of repayment with interest, as in the case of certain long-term loans, etc.

### d. Public Finance Is Principally Concerned with the Distribution of the "Net Income" of the Society

As we have noted, the public finance comprises principally the distribution of a portion of social production and national income. But what part or portion of the national income and social production does the socialist state distribute?

My feeling is that the portion of the national income and social production that the state distributes should be the "net income" of the society.

The first phase of the distribution of the national income of a socialist society takes place in the bodies and organizations where physical production is carried out. With the income of the national enterprises, which are owned by the people, the first distribution takes place in the form of wages paid to workers. What remains from the revenue is considered the "net income." The bulk of this "net income" is turned over to the state; only a small portion is retained by the enterprises for various fixed uses, according to the decisions of the government. In the case of agricultural communes, production units, or handicraft cooperatives, the revenues produced and accrued after the deduction of the payments needed for wages or any rewards made for work are considered their net income. In such organizations, a smaller portion of the "net income" is turned over to the state, and a large portion of it is retained by the respective bodies and organizations to defray their various expenses or to apply to various other uses. Thus, in the distribution effected by the state under the socialist system, the earliest stage of the distribution is effected by the productive organizations in the distribution of the net income of the society.

Clearly, public finance consists principally of the distribution of the society's "net income." Then why do we say that public finance is the distribution of a part or portion of the national social output and the national income? This is because only the principal income of the state is derived from the "net income" of productive enterprises; there is still a small portion of the state income that is derived not from the productive units and organizations and enterprises, but from the redistribution of the distributed income — namely, the taxes and duties collected from individual persons and the incomes derived from the various state service organizations, which are spread over a wide mass of people. Thus, we often say that the state revenue is derived from the distribution of a part of the national income and from its redistribution. The portion of the state's income derived from the direct taxation of individuals becomes comparatively and progressively reduced in relation to the revenues derived from the net income of the productive enterprises, as the socialist economy develops and the state's capital and scale of accumulation continuously expand.

## 3. The State's Financial System and Organizations

After the foregoing analysis of the nature and substance of the socialist state's public finance, I believe that the finance of a socialist state should consist of the following: the state budget, the state credit facilities, the financial departments of the state enterprises, the taxation departments, and the other various state-administered funds — a total of five sections. Among the five sections an intimate interrelationship exists simultaneously with a clear demarcation of activities. All in all, they make up a complete system of socialist state finance.

### a. The State Budget

The state budget is an important and integral part of the state's financial system.

The state's finance and the state's budget are intimately related. The state's budget reflects and involves the distribution of the bulk of the social production and national income. Speaking generally, all the finance and resources that can be distributed and appropriated by the state should come within the scope of the state budget.

In certain circumstances, however, for the sake of more efficient centralized control, and in adherence to the principle of the division of managerial responsibility into administrative levels, certain financial activities and funds are not included within the budget. It is felt that in this way the efficiency of the financial system and administration will improve through the greater awareness at all levels of management of their individual responsibilities and, in consequence, their increased desire to contribute positively to the greater efficiency in the employment of capital resources. Because of this arrangement and system the scope of the state's financial activities is very much greater than that covered by the budget.

There is a basic difference between the budget and the state's finance. The difference exists not only quantitatively but also, and more importantly, in the matters with which they deal. The state's finance concerns distribution; the budget deals with planning.

The state's finance concerns itself not only with the state's financial distribution but with the distribution of the whole society. It has to manage and deal with the relationships between the state and state enterprises, the state and the collective enterprises, the state and the broad masses of individuals, the state and various bodies and departments, the state and the various areas and regions, including the relationship between the areas and regions themselves. Whether the management of these relationships is efficient or not has an important bearing on the rate of development of the progress of the whole program of socialist reconstruction. At the same time, because the state's financial distribution does not exist in isolation — indeed, it exists as an organic part of the whole process of social distribution — the correct and efficient management of the state's financial distribution has an immensely important bearing on the whole of social distribution. Thus, in the work and management of the state's financial activities, although every effort should be made to achieve correct and efficient financial distribution on the part of the state, every effort should also be made to see that correct and efficient financial distribution is achieved in all levels and related sectors of the whole socialist economy. For instance, the state's financial activity should concern itself with the distribution and payment of wages and salaries not only to the state's own employees, but also to the employees of all the state-owned enterprises.

Because of the need for the correct handling and management of finance and distribution, the state participates in the handling and management of the whole socialist distribution. To do this it has to evolve and formulate an organized financial direction and policy. The financial direction and policy are what the party and the state have determined to be the main road of socialist reconstruction — that is, the financial formulation of this main road and direction, which act as the guideline and orientation for all financial distribution and activities. As such it is a matter of extreme importance in the whole financial context.

In the practical application of this financial policy and direction, a whole system of financial control and management has to be evolved, together with all the attendant measures and regulations, which all operate to serve and facilitate the whole financial task of the national and social distribution.

The budget is the basic financial plan of the state. It embraces the basic aspects of the state's financial distribution. It reflects the state's policy and the extent and direction of the government's activities. Under the direction and provision of the budget and financial policy, the state appropriates and mobilizes the basic capital funds and provides detailed plans for their distribution and utilization. According to the provisions of our constitution, each year both the budget and the final state balance sheet have to be submitted to the People's National Assembly for review, auditing, and acceptance. After the budget has been passed and accepted by the Assembly, it is then ready for the executive branch of the government to carry out its provisions. Consequently the budget must be considered a state instrument and a document of the greatest importance. The correct planning and formulation of the budget, and the efficiency with which its provisions are carried out, ensure that the state's basic distribution is being smoothly and efficiently realized and substantiated.

Some comrades have expressed the view that, although on the one side the state's finance is concerned with distribution, on the other side the state budget is a basic item of financial planning and forms a part of the state's financial organization. Such a view is neither coherent nor logical. My own view is that there is no contradiction between the two sides. Because the state's finance is a part of the organized economic activity of the socialist state, and because its purpose is to carry out the distribution of a portion of the social product and the national income, it needs various ramifications of organization to achieve this purpose. In this context the budget acts as the basic plan. It serves in the state's basic activity of distribution.

Although the budget is an organized product of the state's finance, it also exists as an independent function of the state's activity. At the same time — through the activities evolved and formulated by the budget, which forms the most basic formulation of the state's distribution and from which all other distributive activities stem — it acts as a brake and a regulator and finally as a controller of all the interweaving threads and factors of financial activities.

In spite of the extreme importance of the budget, however, it must not be confused with the whole or with other parts of the state's finance itself, nor must it be regarded as standing on the same basis.

### b. The State's System of Credits

In our country, a part of our state financial distribution is based on interest-bearing, repayable credits — for example, the funds that have been transmitted by the state to the banks for the latter to use or lend as long-term credits. These long-term loans, where the period of loan exceeds a year, or loans provided for the provision of goods, etc., all belong to this category. This type of financial distribution, which takes the form of loans and credits, can be termed government or state credits. They are different from bank credits.

There are some comrades who feel that because this type of distribution is returnable and bears interest, it should not belong to the sphere of the state. My feeling is that such an interpretation cannot be sensible. As we have mentioned, the substance of the state's finance consists primarily of the distribution of a part or portion of the social product and the national income, with the state acting as the principal. The form this distribution takes — whether interest-bearing, repayable loans or noninterest-bearing, nonrepayable loans — is only a matter of operational method; it does not affect or concern any demarcation in the sphere of activity; it is only a matter of different measures adopted. Because interest-bearing, repayable loans constitute the form adopted for the granting of state credit as a form of distribution, the state still acts as the principal in effecting the distribution. Thus, this activity is still very much within the sphere of the state's financial activities.

There are other comrades who feel that because the granting of state credit is only a part of the state's budget, there is no need to regard it as an independent facet of financial activity. In my opinion, such a viewpoint is also erroneous. The whole financial system of the state is divided into a number of sectors and facets. The sector or facet in which a particular financial activity is placed is not determined by whether or not the activity is an integral part of the state's basic planning; it is determined by whether, in the whole financial system, that particular sector or facet of activity is, indeed, an independent one. The granting of state credit in the form of interest-bearing, repayable loans has an independent function in the whole financial system of our state. Its principal manifestations are as follows:

1. It possesses a highly flexible form, capable of mobilizing various dormant and scattered resources that are normally beyond the ability of ordinary financial means to mobilize. It also enables the state to meet different requirements at different times, adapting as it goes along.

2. By using the state credit system, it is possible to meet some of the special demands for capital investments in special circumstances: for instance, for advancing the policy of the development of agriculture as the foundation, and of industry as the main road; to assist agricultural development, the state's finance uses the banks to grant credit in the form of long-term agricultural loans, so as to assist the consolidation and development of agricultural production.

3. The state credit system can be used to provide capital for current funds and for the provision of commercial stock, which helps to facilitate financial control and accounting.

From these various angles it can be seen there is a difference in nature and character between the application of state credit and other forms of financial distribution; it is a form of distribution, which is a facet of its own.

What we need to study here is whether the short-term loans and credit facilities provided by the banks can come under the state's financial activity. There are at the moment various views on this matter.

In my opinion the loans and credit facilities granted by the banks (usually for terms of under one year) should belong to the sphere of the banks, and therefore they should not be listed directly under the financial activities of the state.

For this reason, such short-term credit facilities have the purpose, in part, of mopping up the scattered fragments of capital that might be afloat in the society — for example, the deposits of state enterprises, ordinary enterprises, government and institutional offices, agencies, and collective organizations. There is a continual interflow of deposits and withdrawals under these credit-facility accounts within any given period of time; they should probably belong to the sphere, and under the provisions, of currency and capital adjusters and regulators. If we were to classify these items under state finance, such funds could easily be utilized by the state for one purpose or another, resulting in their being unavailable to the banks for meeting withdrawals when required.

As the economy develops, however, and the standard of living of the people rises, the banks will always maintain a minimum level of deposits, and these deposits should increase in volume with the passage of time. In other words, few accounts will withdraw all the funds and deposits during the course of the year; further, the actual volume of deposits should increase with the advance of each year. In this way the state should be able in the long run to make use of this increase in deposits for the purpose of lubricating the general flow of currency; thus, this portion of funds should be considered as belonging to the sphere of state finance.

Some comrades are of the opinion that the division of credits into state-grant credits and bank-grant credit is quite unnecessary; it might be detrimental to the unity and centralized control of the country's finance. My opinion is that such confusion is unnecessary. This division of credits into state and bank credits is an objective fact of the society; it does not stem from the subjective wish of any individuals or groups of people.

There is a difference in nature and substance between state credit and bank credit. State credit consists of the distribution of the whole national income; bank credit consists of the regulation in the utilization of available capital resources. Otherwise there is, of course, a very intimate relationship between the two types of credits.

Both forms of financial activity, however, take the form of credits, where there are both deposits and withdrawals; on the other hand, both forms of credits are capable of changing from one into the other — from state credit into bank credit, or vice versa.

Furthermore, in a socialist country the activity of the bank is nationwide; it is the center of all cash and currency transactions as well as of their accounting. All the state expenditures and revenues are in fact handled by the banks. Thus, both state credit and bank credit are in point of fact handled and managed by the state banks.

### c. The Finances of the State Enterprises

The state enterprises are the foundation of the state's finance. The main source of the state's revenue consists of the state enterprises (this occupies over 90% of the state income). At the same time, in the distribution of capital resources a very large portion is allotted to investment in capital construction on the part of the major industries or to various current funds they require. Thus, the status and management of these enterprises have a great bearing on the whole revenue of the state.

The finance of the state enterprises differs from that of other forms of state finance in that it is concerned directly with physical production. The economic account adopted by the state enterprises determines that there are two sides to their character. On one side, these state enterprises derive capital and funds directly from the state to carry out productive or commercial activities, and hand back the main bulk of their net income to the state. From this point of view, the financing of these enterprises is directly related to and forms the very foundation of the state's finance and financial income; it is, therefore, an integral part of the state's financial organization. On the other hand, the state enterprises also exist as independent bodies or units, which operate according to the plans laid down by the state; so long as the capital invested in any enterprise is secured, it is in a position to operate independently in the use of the fixed capital and in the purchase of raw materials, and to organize the employment of mass labor to carry out its productive activities. From this point of view, the finance of the state enterprises should belong to comparatively independent spheres of the finance of physical production and should not be incorporated directly into the sphere of the state's finance.

Because of this — that is, because the finance of the state enterprises belongs to the comparatively independent sphere of independent enterprises — their finances cannot and are not incorporated directly as items under the state finance. But because the finances of the enterprises form the foundation of the state's finance, it is necessary for the state to strengthen its control over the management of these enterprises. In actual practice the state does not merely limit its concern to the points of contact between the enterprises and the state in the deposit and withdrawal of bank funds; it also concerns itself with the financial and organizational work and management within the enterprises themselves; for it is only by acting in this manner that the state is able to give better direction and guidance to the various sectors and facets of public finance under its control.

Some comrades fail to recognize this dual character of the state enterprises. They are of the opinion that because the state enterprises are a part of the state, all their revenues and expenditures should come under the state's revenues and expenditures, and all their organizations should be a part of the state organizations, and therefore all the capital invested should be regarded as part of the state funds – that is, all the revenues derived from the sale of goods produced by the enterprises should be regarded and classified directly as revenues of the state. It follows that all the expenditures incurred by the enterprises in all the phases and facets of their production should be classified as direct expenditures of the state. If this were to be the concept and classification, the sphere of the state's activities would have to be greatly enlarged, which would not only be difficult to accept theoretically, from the practical point of view, but would also lead to many new problems.

First, such a concept would reduce the clarity of socialist finance, which is based on centralized leadership and the dissemination of responsibility through the various levels of management and organization. The socialist economy is a centralized one, but in a country as vast as ours, where reconstruction is carried out on the largest scale, if all matters large and small were attended to directly by the state, an impossible situation would soon arise. Thus, under centralized leadership, we must practice division of labor as well as of responsibility, and the dissemination of management through the various levels of organization.

Centralized leadership and the dissemination of responsibility and management are not only the concern and problem of the state enterprise; they are also the concern and problem of the party and the policy of the mass line. If the revenues and expenditures of the state enterprises are all regarded and classified as the direct revenues and expenditures of the state, it would be difficult to assume centralized leadership or to practice the principle of the dissemination of responsibility and management to the various sectors and levels of organizations.

Second, such a concept would be detrimental to the present accounting and auditing system and policy. If all the revenues and expenditures of the state enterprises were to be taken as state revenues and enterprises, there would be no way of ensuring the financial independence of the enterprises, of being certain that its revenues would meet their expenditures, or of determining what portion of their net income should be remitted to the state; a contradictory situation of concept and demand would then be created in practice. Such a situation would reflect to the disadvantage of the concept of independent responsibility in management and of the consolidation of the present accounting and auditing system.

Finally, to allow the revenue and expenditure of the enterprises to be classified as state revenue and expenditure is to increase the enterprises' psychology of dependence on the state. All this will also be a detrimental influence on our concept and policy of "resurgence through self-endeavor" and "success in enterprise through industry and thrift."

Further, although some comrades do not believe that the revenues and expenditures of state enterprises should be classified and regarded as the direct revenues and expenditures of the state, they feel that the wages of the workers of the state enterprises should belong to the sphere of state expenditures. Their reasons are as follows: the rate of pay — that is, the wages and salaries of the workers in the enterprises — are fixed and determined by the state in the same centralized manner as the rate of pay of the members and employees of the government offices and other bodies and units of state employment; therefore, no distinction should be made. It is my feeling that such a conception is neither sensible nor correct. The classification of payments should not be made in accordance with the rate of payment or with the persons who determine the rate. The classification should be made according to the economic activities involved. The wages of the workers in state enterprises arise from activities of physical production; they are expenditures of physical production. It is only after the deduction of expenditures on raw materials and wages that the state enterprises arrive at their net income, which is turned over to the state. The wages paid by the enterprises to the workers cannot, therefore, be regarded at this stage as a direct part of the state expenditure. As for the wages and salaries of the administrative officials of the state and the payments made to the employees of other units and offices, where no physical production is involved, these are expenditures paid by the state from the net income previously turned over by the various units of production and state enterprises; they therefore consist of the distribution of net income, and thus they should fall within the sphere of state finance.

## d. State Taxation

The state's levies and taxations occupy a special position in the state's finance, constituting a very important instrument of state revenue and income. In capitalist countries, the capitalist and propertied classes impose duties and taxation that constitute a very severe aspect of their exploitation of the working classes. In socialist societies, the state-applied taxation absorbs a nonrepayable revenue, which is a portion of the people's national income, to meet the expenses and costs of the development of socialist revolution and socialist reconstruction. In substance, therefore, by imposing taxation the state is actually effecting a distribution and redistribution of a portion of the people's national income.

Taxation, however, is something quite different from any other form of distribution. It is applied through the use of political power — by formulating the rules, means, and measures by which all persons concerned must pay what is due to the state under these rules and measures. Because of this, there is a certain amount of coercion behind taxation, which makes it very different from any other form of revenue.

Some comrades believe that taxation cannot form a separate and distinct sector of the state's finance. Their reason is that, organizationally speaking, taxation is simply an integral part of the state's activity and is already included directly under the state's budget. The budget, therefore, has already provided for all the details of taxation.

My contention is that such a conception would greatly lower and reduce the position and function of taxation. As previously mentioned, the various sectors of the state's finance should not be divided and determined by whether or not it occurs within or outside of the budget; because if it were so divided and determined, the state's finance could only be divided into two sectors — those that occur within the budget and those that occur outside it. In our study of the range of the state's finance we should give our attention to the study and examination of the special position and the special function of all the various sectors of the state's finance. The fact that taxation has a vast contribution to make to the socialist revolution and reconstruction has long been proved by the facts. Any denial of this, or any playing down of the function of taxation in a socialist society, is bound to have an unfavorable influence on the development and initiative of the socialist revolution and reconstruction.

### e. Various Other Funds and Capital Resources

By other funds and capital resources we mean those not included in the aforesaid four categories: that is, those that have been left to the various levels and organizations of government to organize and administer. Such funds and capital have the distinction of being directly administered by the state, yet at the same time they differ from similar types of capital funds, being organized and administered in a more dispersed and fragmented form owing to their having to meet the demands and requirements of varying conditions. Capital funds of these types that are current in our country today fall largely into the following categories:

1. The various surcharges and subsidies administered by the various local and municipal governments (such as the surcharge and subsidies for industrial and commercial, agricultural, and municipal and public enterprises) and their relevant expenditures.

Funds of this type are administered by the local authorities under the appropriate direction of the party and government, and are administered and distributed in a unified manner; they cannot be touched or utilized by any other unit or body. Because of their fixed nature, they can be incorporated into the state's basic financial planning. It was decided, for example, that this should be done, from 1963, under the finance administrative regulations. They do not constitute, however, the most important part of the national budget and planning;

they are only the local mechanism, which exists to help in furthering the unity and balancing of national finance.

2. The management of funds applicable to cultural groups, student bodies, and forestry and water conservation enterprises (or for such fees as hospital charges, admission fees for theatrical performances, etc.), to subsidize a part or the whole of their expenditures. The activities of such bodies and enterprises are by nature different from those of productive units. They are services to production and to people's ways of living, and they do not come under normal accounting and auditing. As a rule these bodies and enterprises use their income or revenue to defray as much of their own overhead as possible; where their income falls short of their overhead, the state provides a subsidy. Because the circumstances of each type of body or enterprise is different, however, the methods adopted for the administration also vary according to circumstances. The income and expenditures of all such bodies are included under the state's finance.

3. The miscellaneous revenues of all the different units and levels of administration. Because such categories of funds and finances are comparatively small, it is left to each body or unit to handle both its revenue and its expenditures. These are also considered a part of the state's finance, however, although they are not listed among the major items of the state's financial planning. They are administered under the category and regulations of special funds.

As for other types of funds, from the point of view of the major items of state finance, they are only small and fragmentary items, which can have little bearing on the main body of national finance as a whole. All the same, they do occupy a definite place and function in the whole system of public finance; the administration of these funds has a bearing on the development of the positive factors in the management of local finance, as well as on the development of local economy, and especially on local welfare and public works.

At the same time, although these funds and finances which are included in and are related to national finance constitute only a small proportion of the local or unit finance, they can have an important and positive influence on the more efficient management and financing of these units and localities as a whole, spurring them to greater care in the sectionalizing of financial items and to a greater return and productivity in regard to the funds deployed. Taken together, therefore, they have a significant meaning in the whole process and development of socialist reconstruction.

On the whole, the nation's budget, the various state loans and credits, the state enterprises, the state's duties and taxations, and the various administered special funds possess their special positions and functions, although they are all embraced and covered by the umbrella of the state's finance. They all make their own contribution and have their own meaning in speeding up the planned development of our national economy.

## 36. Pierre-Henri Cassou, "The Chinese Monetary System" (Source 3, pp. 82-97) 1973

For approximately the last five years, that is, since the end of the Cultural Revolution, the People's Republic of China has slowly been opening up. The number of visitors coming from Europe has steadily increased, and the nature of their visits has diversified. The diplomatic, parliamentary, and commercial missions have been succeeded by scientific and medical delegations and political, economic, or administrative study groups. The Chinese tourist agency is trying to vary the types of meetings it organizes for all these visitors. The travelers are no longer only received in factories, secondary schools, universities or communes, but also in schools for executives, local administrative offices, and economic organizations.

During a trip to the People's Republic of China last June, a group of young officials from the National School of Administration was able to have several extremely interesting meetings, especially in Peking, with two experts from the People's Bank.

It is, to our knowledge, the first time since the Cultural Revolution, and perhaps even long before, that visitors have been able to gather some information about the current monetary affairs of the People's Republic of China and about the role of the People's Bank in the economic life of the country.

Very little information has been published on the subject. The studies published in 1966 in Japan by Tadao Miyashita (1) and in 1971 in the United States by Katharine Huang Hsiao (2) only cover the period from 1949 to 1961. The articles which appeared in 1971 and 1972 in Italian and English journals (3) are in fact translations of interviews which appeared in Chinese newspapers describing the credits that the People's Bank should grant to firms. And it appears that the last article which appeared in French is dated 1967. (4)

The experts really only described the internal aspects of the Chinese monetary system. In fact, exterior financial relations are not directly dependent on the People's Bank but instead on the Bank of China. This bank is already well known by exporters, importers, and Western bankers, and several articles (5) which have appeared recently in Great Britain and in Switzerland have described its role and methods.

## 1. The Foundations of the Chinese Monetary and Financial System

In 1949 when the Communist Party came to power, it had to face a catastrophic economic and financial situation: reduced industrial production due to conflict with Japan and civil war, a large deficit in foreign trade, an unbalanced budget, and large debts.

Galloping inflation prevailed everywhere. Some notes issued by the Kuomintang government were in 1948 drawn up in billions of yuan. The inflation was naturally accompanied by a considerable rise in prices. According to M. J. Stoffels: "From September 1945 to August 1948, the gross price index in Shanghai went from 100 to 1,368,049. After a currency reform in August 1948, the same index rose from 157 in August 1948 to 95,552 in the third week of February 1949 and to 5,057,889 two months later."

### Control of Liquidities and Credit Control (1949-1951)

The first task of the new government in monetary policy was

to stablilize the value of the yuan.

The Communist Party already had a certain amount of experience in this field. In the provinces which it controlled, it had already created its own banks, each issuing its own currency and rigorously controlled. (6) As of 1945, the value of the revolutionary currency was superior to that of the Kuomintang regime. Depending on the area, the exchange rate was from 1 to 2 or from 1 to 3. This advantage developed further in subsequent years, because by 1948 it was approximately 1 to 1,000.

To create a healthier monetary situation, the Communist government had to have its own apparatus. To this end, it created the People's Bank by merging three banks controlled by the Party: the Bank of Northern China, the Bank of the North Sea, and the Bank of the Peasants of the Northwest. This was accomplished in 1948, even before the assumption of power in Peking. Subsequently, in 1949 and 1950, as the influence of the new regime grew, the People's Bank absorbed the banks of the nationalist government, in particular the Central Bank of China and several local Communist banks. The exchange of notes was achieved at the same time throughout China.

In 1949, the new People's Bank took several steps to control the existing private banks. Among these were measures taken to freeze 20 percent of the deposits at the People's Bank, to limit the approved credits to 50 percent of the deposits, to forbid withholding of participation in commercial or industrial societies, to establish a minimum capital, and to fix the rates of interest on deposits as well as on loans. Furthermore, in 1950, the Bank of China was placed under the direction of the People's Bank in order to undertake overseas financial transactions.

Having thus submitted the credit organizations to a strict set of rules, the new government also sought to control the circulation of currency. A bill dated March 3, 1950, fixed the maximum cash amount that the nationalized industries and their public establishments could withhold and ordered these organizations to deposit their surplus funds with the People's Bank. As a general rule, the amounts so deposited were equivalent in value to three days of current expenses.

On November 25, 1951, a new bill was published setting forth financial rules for the state enterprises; the enterprises were supposed to establish treasury plans consisting of forecasts of receipts and expenses and mentioning the methods of payment. This text established the conditions of payment for the purchases and expenses of these organizations. They were specifically forbidden to accumulate delays in payment and, of course, credits of any kind.

## The Nationalization of Credit and the Stabilization of the Currency (1951-1960)

These measures of control allowed certain forms of private financial activity to remain: nonnationalized banks and the circulation of titles and bills. These disappeared progressively between 1951 and 1955 in order to make way for a unified financial system entirely in the hands of the state.

First, the necessity to work with the minimum of capital, the limitation on interest rates and on the volume of transactions, and the administration by the People's Bank of all of the funds of the nationalized sector obliged the private banks to cease their activities or to merge. Those which were still in existence in 1952 regrouped around a new organization, the "joint publicly-privately operated bank." The role of this bank progressively diminished, and in February 1955, the People's Bank took over the headquarters and the agencies of what remained of the private sector.

Furthermore, transferable shares were entirely eliminated. The deeds issued by the state after the liberation were reimbursed between 1958 and 1968. Since this date, there have been no more public debts, either internal or external.

The steps taken in 1949 and 1950 were not adequate to maintain the value of money. The rise in prices continued rapidly until 1951 and more moderately from 1952 to 1955. At Shanghai, the net retail index went from 100 in July 1949 to 1,100 in July 1950 and to 1,400 in July 1951. It subsequently rose by approximately 25 percent in three years.

In 1955, the Chinese government found it necessary to undertake a new monetary conversion to complete the task of stabilization initiated six years earlier. The new unit, the "Renminbi" (people's money), usually called the yuan, equaled 10,000 old yuan. Unlike previous reforms, the exchange of notes was rapidly completed. According to official declarations, only two months were necessary for the transaction.

Since then, all observers agree that prices have not varied to any great extent, and the buying power of the yuan has been maintained. Several articles which have recently appeared in the Chinese press have asserted that the "Renminbi" is the most stable currency in the world.

## 2. Savings and Credit in the Present-Day People's Republic of China

Chinese financial structures were thus defined in the period between 1948 and 1955. Since then, monetary policy has only been translated into practical terms by variations in rates of interest and modifications of grant conditions for credit. We have no precise information on the exact content of these steps, nor on the motives which inspired them.

In particular, we have very little information available on the monetary events which took place between 1961 and 1972, that is to say, in the period which followed the Great Leap Forward, during the Cultural Revolution, and in the stabilizing period which followed it.

Current financial life is extremely simple, probably totally adapted to the current level of economic development. There are no checks, no stock exchange, and no banking network. One can define the monetary and financial system by the following formula: The People's Bank, the only autonomous financial institution, receives individual deposits and deposits from firms, communes, and state organizations and lends to firms.

### Deposits

There are two types of deposits in the People's Republic of China: those of collectives and firms and those of individuals.

The administrative services of the state, public establishments, and firms under public control, since 1950, have been obliged to deposit their funds in the People's Bank, any sum above a certain level to be held as cash. On the other hand, the autonomous rural collectives, the production brigades and people's communes are not subject to this rule and have access to the sum total of their cash balance.

All commercial dealings between firms, the payment of taxes, and the profits of the state take the form of bookkeeping transactions, whereas salaries and pensions, as well as certain agricultural dues, are cash outlays.

The credit accounts of the state services and public establishments are not remunerated. On the other hand, those of the firms are, at the rate of 0.15 percent per month, or 1.8 percent per year. This last rate has been in force since 1972. Previously, since 1955, it appears to have been at 0.18 percent per month, or 2.16 percent per year.

Private persons are not allowed to have checking accounts. The only type of investment possible is a deposit at the People's Bank. The characteristics of the accounts are comparable to our savings accounts. The deposits are completely free as far as the total is concerned as well as the frequency. In effect, contrary to what has happened at certain periods in other countries run by Communist parties, the Chinese receive their total salaries, pensions, or agricultural revenue in cash and are not immediately obliged to deposit part of it in a savings account. Similarly, withdrawals are completely free, and our informants assured us that the savings had never been frozen against the will of the depositors.

These accounts give rise to the deposit of interest. This amounts to 0.27 percent per month, or 3.24 percent per year, for time deposits, that is to say, for a duration longer than one year, and 0.18 percent, or 2.16 percent per year, for open accounts. This last rate appears to have been in force since 1959, whereas the first has been notably reduced; it reached 7.92 percent per year in 1955 and was 4.8 percent in 1959. The deposited interests are tax-exempt, like all personal income.

Confidentiality is guaranteed for all accounts. The sums deposited are thus unknown either to the administrative authorities or to the employers. The savings are furthermore transmittable to legatees.

It has not been possible for us to find out the average deposit of individuals because statistical secrecy was decreed in 1961, and since then, no data have been published. We have only been told that in the twenty years from 1951 to 1971, the number of depositors multiplied 100 times, whereas the total savings increased tenfold. If this last indication is true, it would imply that the level of savings has hardly increased since 1957, because, according to Mrs. K. Huang Hsiao, individual deposits in that year were nine times higher than in 1951.

It would, in fact, not be impossible that the level of savings in 1973 would overtake that of 1957. Between these dates, the Great Leap Forward, the ensuing economic difficulties, and the Cultural Revolution probably brought a drop in individual savings, which could only resume in 1968.

This hypothesis was confirmed in a bulletin published in 1965, according to which, the value of savings increased fivefold from 1952 to 1964. According to figures published up to 1961, individual deposits had already quintupled between 1952 and 1957. Thus, the deposits in 1964 were of the same order of magnitude as those of 1957, which would confirm the extent of economic difficulties encountered from 1958 to 1961, that is to say, after this phase.

The last indication we have about savings concerns the partitioning between time deposits and open accounts. In 1973, 80 percent of individual savings were time deposits, that is to say, for terms of more than one year. This proportion is identical to the one indicated for the year 1964 in an article published in 1965. There had thus been no notable evolution in the structure of savings during the previous ten years, whereas the same article indicated that between 1952 and 1964 a modification of approach had been observed: the proportion of open accounts went from 60 percent to 20 percent.

## Credits

In spite of the fact that the methods of investment have been reduced to only a few types, the credits accorded by the People's Bank conform to very simple characteristics. The rulings concerning the financial structure of state enterprises, adopted in 1950 and 1951, still remain unchanged and apply to the totality of industrial and commercial sectors because the entire means of production is actually in the hands of the state, except for agriculture which is managed collectively but decentralized by the communes and the production brigades.

There are no more shares, bonds, or loans directly accorded by the enterprises to other production units. Furthermore, when taking into account the options adopted with regard to economic organization, the totality of financial needs linked to productive investments is directly taken care of by the budget, which assures the distribution of available resources according to criteria defined in the plan. The industrial and commercial enterprises receive endowments in capital for investment projects which need external resources: the acquisition of machines and the purchase of construction materials.

The intervention of the People's Bank is limited to the granting of short-term credits which are intended to cover current treasury needs linked to the procurement of stocks of raw materials or to the establishment of stocks of manufactured goods. Bank loans thus play the role of supplying credit and the discounting of bills of exchange.

Only the enterprises which depend on the state or on public collectives can obtain such credits. On the other hand, the public service administrations, enterprises, and private persons cannot benefit from them. The rules for distribution of credit thus contribute to limiting the importance of the private sector (small businessmen and artisans) whose capacity for self-financing is further curtailed by the fixed prices of the administration.

To obtain credit, an enterprise has to fulfill two conditions. First of all, its budget plan has to be approved by the bank. The financial needs then have to be seen to correspond to certain types of transactions. In industry, credits are intended to finance production (the acquisition of raw materials and intermediary goods) or the marketing of the finished product. Commercial enterprises can borrow internally or externally for their sales. A special category of loans is consented to for enterprises for the marketing of cereals. Credits for industry and commerce are accorded for up to twelve months and are taxed at a rate of interest of 0.42 percent per month, or 5.04 percent per year.

Loans to the agricultural sector, which according to our informants only represent a limited part of the credit of the bank, are subject to somewhat different regulations. First of all, short-term credits exist at a rate of 0.36 percent per month, or 4.32 percent per year, with the aim of encouraging production (the purchase of seed, fertilizer, insecticides, and so forth) or representing advances on the sale of agricultural products. Furthermore, the People's Bank grants loans for agricultural equipment from state funds for terms of one to five years and taxed at an interest of 0.18 percent per month or 2.16 percent per year. Thus, one observes an important difference between agricultural investments and industrial or commercial investments. The external resources necessary to the communes must be repaid within a maximum of five years, whereas the capital grants established by the state budget for the firms are definitely acquired by them. In fact, this formal difference in treatment has no economic consequence because it appears that the state exacts a very large interest on invested capital and thus obtains a rapid return on investments.

The rates indicated previously have been in force since September 1972. They were previously 0.48 percent per month for industry, 0.60 percent for commerce, and 0.48 percent for short-term agricultural credits. Generally, all rates have fallen considerably since the Communist Party assumed power, as is shown in the table below (showing monthly rates) (7):

| | 1953 | 1955 | 1958 | 1959 | 1961 | Before September 1972 | After September 1972 |
|---|---|---|---|---|---|---|---|
| State industrial firms | 0.45 to 0.48 | 0.48 | 0.60 | 0.60 | 0.60 | 0.48 | 0.42 |
| State commercial firms | 0.69 | 0.60 | 0.60 | 0.60 | 0.60 | 0.60 | 0.42 |
| Agricultural collectives | 0.75 | 0.60 | 0.48 | 0.60 | 0.48 | 0.48 | 0.36 |

It is difficult to give an exact interpretation of this progressive reduction in interest rates. It is possible that the leaders of the People's Republic of China want to avoid representing financial costs as too heavy a load for industry and commerce. If this hypothesis is true, it would mean that these last resort to credit even more as their production grows, and in consequence, the stocks of raw materials and semifinished and finished goods increase.

This probable development of credit in present-day China could be further confirmed by another indication brought to our attention by the experts. In 1973, a firm could obtain loans for up to 70 percent of the necessary resources, the balance having to be financed out of its own funds, that is to say, by the state budget. According to Mrs. K. Huang Hsiao, from 1952 to 1962, the quota of financial needs with recourse to credit has always been less than 30 percent, except during the period of the Great Leap Forward, that is, from 1959 to July 1961, during which time the People's Bank could provide 100 percent of the necessary resources.

This increased lending capacity certainly allows the People's Bank to play a more active role to encourage economic growth. However, the official doctrine refuses to present the increase of distributed credits as a means for motivating an increase in production. The granting of loans to firms is only considered as a possibility to facilitate productive activity and the circulation of goods; economic decisions concerning the volume of production and investments having already been taken by the authorities in charge of planning.

## 3. The People's Bank and the Conduct of Monetary Policy

As the only autonomous financial institution, the People's Bank carries out multiple functions. It is concurrently the issuing body, the state bank, a credit establishment for industry and agriculture, an organization for financial compensation, and an agency for financial and economic control.

### The Internal Functioning of the People's Bank

Organized in a uniform fashion throughout the country, the

People's Bank owns more than 10,000 subsidiaries, excluding local agencies and the temporary offices accountable to the subsidiaries. Its internal organization is based on that of the public administration: At the headquarters of each constituency (province, region, district, municipality) is an agency of the bank which is its direct liaison with the local economic accountables.

These agencies seem to have a fair amount of autonomy at their disposal. They render an account of their activities every ten days. This decentralization of power is justified both by the difficulties of communication still existing in China and by the wishes of the managers to avoid such strict control that it would impair production.

The accounts of the People's Bank are not published. According to our informants, it would appear that two types of situation are recorded: on the one hand, an account of financial functions and resources and on the other hand, an account of work.

The functions of the bank essentially take the form of previously mentioned credits and eventually of loans to the "Bank of China." On the other hand, its resources are more diverse. These consist first of all of the portion of profits which are not transferred to the state (in practice this means of the amortization accounts and of the reserves). Subsequently, the People's Bank profits from capital investments as well as budgetary subventions intended to finance loans for agricultural equipment. A third category of resources consists of cash issues. Finally, the most important funds come from deposits from the state, public services, firms, and individuals.

The only revenue from the active accounts is the interest paid in by the firms, always higher than the interest paid in by the bank on the deposits of individuals or firms, the main entry of expenses. These further comprise the costs of operation. The surpluses are in part reverted to the state in the form of taxes, and the balance is set aside or established for reserves.

## The Public Service Missions

Among the functions carried out by the People's Bank, some involve works of general interest which are assumed everywhere by public organizations.

The bank is first of all a loaning institution, and under this title, it assures the issuing of notes and the placing of methods of payment throughout the country. It controls the circulation of money and attempts, by its policy of savings credit, to stabilize currency. On the other hand, it is not directly responsible for exchange transactions. This function is entrusted to the Bank of China, an institution founded in 1908 and under the control of the People's Bank since 1950. The Bank of China is notably in charge of administering the assets of China in foreign currency and the accounts of deposits of Overseas Chinese. It also distributes credit for export.

In its capacity as the state bank, the People's Bank keeps the accounts of the public administrations. It centralizes tax resources and deposits of the nationalized organizations. However, the bank is not in charge of debt recovery, which is the responsibility of the specialized administrative services.

One of the important tasks of the bank is also to ensure correct commercial practices. In this respect, it plays the role of our clearing houses and our centers for postal checks. As indicated above, all sales by the nationalized industries have to be paid by transfer, and only salaries and certain purchases by commercial firms of agricultural goods for communes are settled in cash. Thus 85 percent of bank transactions take the form of transfers from account to account, the remainder being made up of withdrawals or deposits of notes.

## The Economic Functions Exercised by the People's Bank

One of the goals pursued consistently by Chinese monetary policy seems to be a search for adapting solvency to the quantity of available goods. The adjustment of the offer of cash is accomplished, on the one hand, by a detailed examination of demands for business credit and, on the other hand, by systematic encouragement of individual savings.

When studying a credit, the People's Bank rigorously controls the financial situation of the industry and the profitability of expected expenses. It sees to it that all sales have been settled, that the withheld liquidities do not exceed the budget, and that previously accorded credits have been used effectively. Expenses which produce treasury needs are subsequently carefully examined, with the bank advising the industry on the profitability of the planned transactions and the technical and financial means of achieving the most economical solutions. When the expenditures do not correspond to forecasts, the bank can demand immediate reimbursement of the agreed credits.

Thus, the process of control of the bank can lead it to the exercise of too strong a control over the operations of industry. Since the Cultural Revolution, and particularly since 1970, the emphasis in articles published in the Chinese press has largely been on the role of administrative advisers that bank employees should assume. (8) Applying Mao Tse-tung's directive "Develop the economy and assure provisions," procedures have been simplified and excessively restrictive financial criteria for the granting of loans have been abandoned in favor of a more economic evaluation of expenditure programs of enterprises.

The bank is currently conducting an active policy encouraging savings, probably in order to limit the growth in demand resulting from salary increments granted since 1968. One of the incentives is the deposit of interest. Despite their relatively low level in comparison to Western or other rates, they remain attractive since such income is free from tax and the stability of buying power has been assured since 1955.

It is largely by propaganda and persuasion that the monetary authorities act to develop savings. An article in Red Flag [Hung-ch'i] (which appeared in 1972) relates a significant anecdote (9): "One day, an old woman appeared at the agency to withdraw some money. On receiving her money, she murmured: 'My son is getting married. The wedding must be nicely prepared.' The comrades at the agency demonstrated to her that such expenses reflected a bourgeois outlook and spoke of the importance of the economy and of industry. Three days later, the same old lady brought back half of the money saying, 'My neighbors, my son, and my daughter-in-law all hold the same opinion as you do.'" Further on, the same article indicates that savings deposits rose in this agency to 50 percent in two years.

A third way of encouraging savings is by the growth in the

number of bank branches. Each urban or rural subsidiary assures the functioning of several offices, permanent or temporary, in the neighborhoods, firms, or villages. In particular, headquarters are found in large production units so that employees, who are paid in cash monthly, can conveniently withdraw or deposit.

Finally, it should be noted that the impossibility of recourse to credit forces individuals to save before buying durable consumer goods. The purchase of a bicycle, a watch, furniture, a camera, or a sewing machine, the prices of which represent two to five months of the average salary, forces households to save for several years. According to indications by our informants, an employee saves approximately 4 to 5 percent of his income each year. This percentage is notably lower than that of Western countries. But one must remember that in China a large saving is redeemed by state firms, which assure the financing of all productive investments of industry and commerce.

## The Originality and Adaptation of the Chinese Monetary System

In terms of this description of the monetary system, two features seem to characterize it: its originality and its adaptation to the current economic situation of China.

The originality of the Chinese system is twofold. [It is not simply an extension, after nationalization, of systems prior to 1949, which had proven incapable of maintaining a stable currency, saving 4 to 5 percent of its income each year, and which had a larger diversity of institutions and procedures for saving and credit.]

It is largely due to its simplicity that the Chinese system is well adapted to the current economic situation. In a country where industry and services consist only of a limited part of the gross national product, the existence of numerous financial institutions or of fairly elaborate systems like the check or bills of exchange would probably be unnecessary. A multiplicity of agencies or procedures would even be contrary to the will of the Chinese directors to carry out a dynamic economic policy over a wide territory and without external assistance insofar as industries and households would then have a freedom of choice which could run counter to the options of the plan.

Finally, it appears that the Chinese monetary system has proven its efficiency since 1949. The controls exercised at the level of enterprise liquidity and on the distribution of credit has, it appears, contributed to the total elimination of speculation on commodities, especially foodstuffs, which characterized economic life before the Communist Party came to power. Furthermore, the maintenance of the yuan's buying power, which all observers recognize and which the Chinese press boasts of at every international monetary crisis, shows that the policy of credit and savings has been conducted in a manner totally in accordance with the policy of production and distribution of goods and with a policy of price control.

## Notes

1) Tadao Miyashita, The Currency and Financial System of Mainland China, Tokyo, 1966.

2) K. Huang Hsiao, Money and Monetary Policy in Communist China, New York, Columbia University Press, 1971.

3) Chinese Economic Studies, Winter 1972-1973; Documentazione sui Paesl dell'.Est, December 15, 1971.

4) "Monnaie et financement en Chine," M. J. Stoffels, Bulletin du Centre d'études des Pays de l'Est (1967). (N.D.L.R. de P.E. — Cf. Problèmes économiques, no. 1.038, November 23, 1967).

5) The Banker, February 1972; Neue Zürcher Zeitung, September 24, 1971. (N.D.L.R. de P.E. — Cf. Problèmes économiques, no. 1.273, May 24, 1972).

6) See Tadao Miyashita, op. cit.

7) Sources: K. Huang Hsiao, op. cit.; Tadao Miyashita, op. cit.; information gathered by the author.

8) K. Huang Hsiao, Money and Monetary Policy in Communist China, New York, Columbia University Press, 1971.

9) See Chinese Economic Studies, Winter 1972-1973.

## 37. Red Flag Correspondent Reports the Advanced Experience of a Model Banking Office (Source 2, pp. 26-39) February 1971

During the new upsurge of industrial and agricultural production, what should a bank do? The broad revolutionary masses of the People's Bank in Fushun Municipality, keeping abreast of the new circumstances of revolution, have joined the workers, peasants, and soldiers in holding high the banner of revolutionary mass criticism. They have thoroughly criticized the counterrevolutionary revisionist line implemented by the renegade, hidden traitor, and scab Liu Shao-ch'i and his agents in banking circles. They have simplified their administrative structure. Being at the front line of the Three Great Revolutionary Movements, they have set up 35 comprehensive service groups oriented to production, to the basic level, and to the workers, peasants, and soldiers. These groups are striving to serve the workers, peasants, and soldiers and the development of socialist production.

The Chien-hsin Service Group of the Chungho Road Bank Office is one of them.

Our great leader Chairman Mao points out: "Developing the economy and ensuring supplies — this is our general principle governing economic and financial work" ("Economic and Financial Questions During the Period of the War of Resistance Against Japan"). The Chien-hsin Service Group, as soon as it was established in December 1968, regarded the above teaching of Chairman Mao as a direction in which to advance, as the criterion for its work, and as a guide to its action, and started a revolution in banking operations. Members of the group criticized the purely financial viewpoint and such black goods as "regulations in command" and "financial management by experts," instituted the idea of developing the economy in a fundamental way, relied upon the broad masses in managing finance, and exercised financial power properly in the interest of the consolidation of the proletarian dictatorship. Everyone in the service group has striven to be a propagandist for Mao Tse-tung thought, a combatant for class struggle, and a servant of the people, thereby turning the group into a center for propagandizing of Mao Tse-tung thought. Praising the bank, the masses said: "The People's Bank has come to the people and is doing what we want."

## Serving the Workers, Peasants, and Soldiers at the Front Line of the Three Great Revolutionary Movements

Workers, peasants, and soldiers are the main force of the Three Great Revolutionary Movements. Establishing the concept of serving the workers, peasants, and soldiers is an important prerequisite for carrying out the general principle of "developing the economy and ensuring supplies."

In the past, Liu Shao-ch'i and his agents, pursuing "bigness and modernity," advocated a privileged and mystified position for the bank, promoting a kind of scholasticism. The masses angrily recalled, "What Liu Shao-ch'i had done was to put up the socialist signboard but actually to follow the capitalist road." The service group revolutionized such practice by moving from the bustling city into the factories and mines and into the midst of the masses. Instead of waiting for customers in the office, members of the service group have gone out to serve the masses. Their hearts turned toward the workers, peasants, and soldiers; they are serving the people heart and soul.

The Chien-hsien Service Group was located in what was formerly a "small man's bookstore," surrounded by 36 enterprises and business units and more than 9,000 households consisting of more than 50,000 residents. It has undertaken a creative study and application of the "three constantly read articles" and brought proletarian politics to the fore. The group's comrades said: "Small as the office is, we must still contribute to revolution. The ceiling of the office may be low, but we must scale the peak in serving the people." They regard performing every business transaction successfully as adding bricks to the edifice of revolution. They would go through all kinds of trouble if, in doing so, they could better satisfy the needs of the masses. They operate 365 days a year, handling every request made by the masses to their satisfaction. One morning, before the office was opened for business, some poor and lower-middle peasants who had come from Kai hsien to Fushun to mine shale for fertilizer rushed to the service group to settle their accounts, because they wanted to return home by the eight o'clock train. At that time, the shale fertilizer had just been loaded onto the train, the consignment papers had not yet been delivered to the office, and the cash of the bank had not been taken out of the vault. But the train would start in less than an hour. What could the comrades of the service group do? They thought: "The difficulties of the masses are our difficulties, and to serve the workers, peasants, and soldiers is our responsibility." So the whole group went into action. Some went to the office to get the cash, and some went to the railway station to help the poor and lower-middle peasants complete the consignment procedure. Within an hour, everything required was done properly, and the more than 70 poor and lower-middle peasants returned to their work in time.

Standing behind their counter, the comrades of this service group think of their work far beyond their counter. When they work away from their counter, they think of their work behind the counter. They continue to improve their work in the light of the needs of the workers, peasants, and soldiers. When the group was established initially, two queues used to appear in front of the office of the service group on the day wages were paid by the enterprises. In the morning, the financial personnel of the enterprises queued up to get their cash; in the afternoon, the workers queued up to deposit their savings. The group members thought: "The masses work busily day and night; if we delay them by one more minute, that would mean their having one less ounce of energy to work for revolution. We therefore should think more of the masses." Subsequently, on the day when wages were paid out, they would go to the office earlier so they could deliver the cash to the factories. Having done this, they would then handle the savings deposits on the spot. In addition, the comrades of the service group would frequently go to the homes where both husband and wife work, to handle deposits and withdrawals. They are deeply convinced that only by going frequently to the grass roots among the workers, peasants, and soldiers can they better serve them.

The comrades of the group are never satisfied with the service they render to the workers, peasants, and soldiers. They always regard the concern of the masses as their own concern. There is a shale hill some seven or eight li from the Chien-hsin Service Group. Nearly a thousand poor and lower-middle peasants in the province used to go there all year round to mine shale for fertilizer. It is inconvenient for them to make deposits or withdrawals. So the comrades of the service group, carrying their packs, go there by turns to take part in labor, to accept reeducation from the poor and lower-middle peasants, complete the procedures for the consignment of shale fertilizer, unsew their quilts, wash their clothes, and do any work required. Once, the axle of a big cart belonging to a production team was damaged. For two days and nights the repair could not be done and the fertilizer could not be removed. The commune members were worried. A woman comrade of the service group, acting on Chairman Mao's great teaching of "serving the people heart and soul," climbed over the shale hill and went to several units before she finally found a new axle and brought it back quickly to have the cart repaired. On another occasion, a production team brought some food grain with it, but did not know where it should be processed. The commune members, who often mined fertilizer there, said: "Go to the comrades of the Chien-hsin group. They serve the masses. They'll do anything for you." Indeed, the comrades of the service group helped the team to get its food grain processed properly and in good time.

During the past two years, 100 groups of commune members, involving no less than 10,000 persons, have gone to the shale hill one after another. Every one of them praised the Chien-hsin group for its good service. Some commune members who come to Fushun from the rural areas always insist on visiting the service group to say hello to the comrades. In August of last year, representatives of the 23 fertilizer mining teams of poor lower-middle peasants from hsien and districts in Liaoning, beating drums and gongs, came to the office of the service group, where they hung up a red tablet on which was inscribed: "The People's Bank is for the people."

## Going All Out to Help Enterprises Develop Production

Chairman Mao teaches us: "On financial and economic questions, we should use 90 percent of our energy to help the peasants increase their production and the remaining 10 percent to collect tax revenues from them. If we do a good job of the first, it will be easy to do a good job of the second" ("Launch the Movement for Rent Reduction, Production, Supporting the Government, and Cherishing the People in the Base Area"). A socialist bank must act in accordance with this great teaching of Chairman Mao and make great efforts to help the enterprises develop production in the light of the requirements of state plans and policies.

Before the Great Proletarian Cultural Revolution, Liu Shao-ch'i and his agents advocated views such as that the bank "must hold the fate of the enterprise" and the bank "must be the locomotive of the national economy." Influenced by the revisionist line of Liu Shao-ch'i, a bank used to center on itself; the practice was, "when you visit a factory, see the manager, look at charts, pick faults, and come back to write a report." Money was used to restrain production. The Chien-hsin Service Group thoroughly criticized this fallacy of Liu Shao-ch'i. Said the comrades of the group: "What Liu Shao-ch'i peddled was capitalist monopoly of finances! The People's Bank is a logistics department for industrial and agricultural production, and everything it does is for the front line." The comrades regard as their political task the fulfillment of Chairman Mao's great policy of "independence, seizing the initiative in our hands, relying on our own efforts, hard work, and plain living, and building the nation with industry and frugality." They go deep into reality to carry out investigations and studies, rely on the masses, practice "five-togetherness" with the workers, and serve industrial and farm production heart and soul.

The following are the main methods they have used in helping enterprises develop production:

1. With an eye to promoting the development of production, they take the initiative in helping the enterprises to tap their internal potentials, practice austerity severely, and solve the

problem of funds actively. In March of last year, Fushun Cement Plant, aiming at comprehensive utilization, was determined to build a power generating station which would utilize the residual heat from cement production. Due to lack of sufficient depreciation funds, it asked for a short-term loan of one million yuan. The comrades of Chien-hsin Service Group made an analysis of the problem. Some said that comprehensive utilization would turn a factory into several plants and thus would be an effective measure for building socialism with greater, faster, and better results at lower costs. Therefore, they said that they should grant the loan, whatever the amount. However, the majority of the comrades took the view that while active support should be given, this did not mean that all support should be in the form of money, for the first need was to help the enterprise tap its own internal potentials. So they went to the plant the same night to hold talks with the leading comrades. They went deep into the workshops and assisted the plant in drawing up an inventory and tapping potentials, thereby reducing the need for external funds by 300,000 yuan. They also checked the cash standing of the plant and discovered that credits amounting to more than 1,000,000 yuan had not been collected. So, on their own initiative, they helped the comrades of the plant collect 400,000 yuan of credit. But despite repeated efforts, a portion of the required capital was still lacking, whereupon the comrades of the service group warmly made out a loan to the plant, thus meeting its urgent need. As a result, a thermal generating station was built in only 128 days, and it has enabled the plant not only to achieve self-sufficiency in power but also to recover the whole investment made in the power station within half a year. The workers of the cement plant told the comrades of the service group: "You have really tried one thousand and one means to support production. That is the way a bank should be run."

2. Rely on the worker masses in managing finances and making a success of financial management in enterprises. The comrades of the Chien-hsien Service Group, acting on Chairman Mao's instruction that "it is necessary to rely on the working class wholeheartedly," have gone deep into various enterprises. In these units, with the support of the leadership

and the masses, they help in setting up organizations for workers to participate in management. They rely on the workers in controlling credit plans and the use of funds and making a success of socialist economic accounting. They have deeply realized that if a few specialized personnel are relied on for fund control, then "while one item is controlled, a hundred items would be missed" and nothing would be done properly. They know that only by depending on the worker masses, who have the greatest understanding of production and the richest practical experience, can the funds be properly controlled and used and Chairman Mao's principle of building the nation on the basis of industry and economy be implemented. There was a small plant that produced vacuum pumps in Fushun. When mapping out its 1970 production plan, it intended to increase personnel, equipment, and funds to boost the production of vacuum pumps from 46 to 100 units. Later, the plant's revolutionary committee, with the help of the Chien-hsin Service Group, organized and strengthened the organ for workers to participate in management and mobilized all the workers in the plant to discuss the production plan, tap its internal potentials, and launch technical innovations. Surplus material valued at 110,000 yuan was handled, more than 20 items of technical equipment were improved, and 3 indigenous machines were produced, thus meeting the urgent needs for funds and equipment. As a result, while no personnel, no equipment, and no funds were increased, 120 vacuum pumps were produced and the production task for 1970 was fulfilled in its entirety 50 days ahead of schedule.

3. Help the various factories better develop socialist large-scale cooperation, so that the experience of one plant can be turned into the wealth of all and the difficulties of one plant can be tackled by all. Because the vacuum equipment manufacturing plant was very successful in its socialist economic accounting, the Chien-hsin Service Group quickly made the experience of this plant available to all plants. The big chimneys of Chemical Industrial Works No. 2 emitted heavy smoke all year round, and the comrades of the service group encouraged all the plants to participate in solving this prob-

lem. Those comrades who took part in this project said: "If a single plant is red, that means that only one spot is red, but if every plant is red, the whole area is red. Socialist co-operation is wonderful. The Chien-hsin group has done everything conceivable."

## Firmly Grasp Class Struggle in Making "Collections and Payments"

"Socialist society covers a fairly long historical period. In this historical period of socialism, there still exist classes, class contradictions and class struggle, the struggle between the road of socialism and the road of capitalism, and the danger of capitalist restoration." The comrades of the Chien-hsin Service Group, bearing in mind this great teaching of Chairman Mao and extending the revolutionary traditions of revolutionary banks of workers and peasants in Chingkangshan, conduct financial work on the principles of classes and revolution. They use the viewpoint of classes and class struggle to criticize the counterrevolutionary revisionist line of "putting business in command," controlling money but not ideology, controlling money without distinction of lines, and controlling money without distinction of classes. They take the bank as the battleground for class struggle and stand guard for the consolidation of the proletarian dictatorship.

The comrades of this service group pay constant attention to developing struggle between the two kinds of ideology in the course of "payment and receipt," seeing that to control money, it is first of all necessary to control ideology, namely, to use proletarian ideology to triumph over bourgeois ideology.

One day, an old woman happily came to the service group to make a withdrawal. While collecting her money, she murmured: "My son is taking a wife. The wedding must be well prepared." The comrades of the service group took the view that extravagance was a way of bourgeois thinking, so they warmly told her about the great significance of industry and frugality. Three days later, this old woman happily redeposited over half of the money she had withdrawn, saying: "My neighbors, my son, and my daughter-in-law — all of them like your idea." In order that the proletarian ideological style of hard work and plain living take root among the masses of the people, the comrades of the Chien-hsin Service Group view the savings work from the standpoint of "preparing against war, preparing against natural disasters, and doing everything for the people." They have overcome the idea that nothing can be usefully done; they take the whole situation into consideration and together with the neighborhood revolutionary committee, they have launched among the vast masses of residents "five-economizing and one-saving" activities – economizing on grain, economizing on coal, economizing on water, economizing on electricity, controlling childbirth, and saving money for revolution. These activities are very popular among the broad revolutionary masses. The outlook of the neighborhood has been brightened, and savings deposits alone increased by 50 percent within two years. The masses remarked: "The service group has brought home Chairman Mao's principle to thousands of households!"

The comrades of this service group also view fund allocation from the viewpoint of the struggle between the two lines, controlling not only money but also the line and firmly and unswervingly working in accordance with Chairman Mao's proletarian revolutionary line. One enterprise was extravagant in its practices. It already had a small sedan, but it wanted to purchase parts to assemble another small car itself. The service group discovered this problem while making the payment, and held that the struggle between extravagance and frugality was a struggle between the two lines. Comrades of the service group went deep among the masses and enthusiastically propagated Chairman Mao's great teaching about "running factories with industry and frugality." They helped the enterprise concerned to return the auto parts it had bought and use the funds instead for the urgent needs of revolution and production. Once, a production team of Hsinglungtien Commune of a certain hsien, which was mining shale on the hill, received a remittance. The comrades of the service group suspected that this remittance came from a questionable source and sought information from the poor and lower-middle peasants. The poor and lower-middle peasants pointed out straightforwardly that some people were secretly selling shale fertilizer through illegal channels. Acting on the suggestion of the poor and lower-middle peasants, they set up a Mao Tse-tung thought study class with the comrades of this production team on the shale hill. With the help of others in this production team, the personnel concerned recognized their mistake of not following the road indicated by Chairman Mao and promptly returned the money.

The comrades of the Chien-hsin Service Group also often examine the essence of a matter through its outward manifestations. While taking charge of money, they have not forgotten class struggle, and dealt firm blows to the small handful of class enemies who vainly attempted to undermine the proletarian dictatorship in the economic realm. In May of last year, the chemical fertilizer plant of Fushun hsien allocated to a neighborhood multipurpose plant a sum of 700 yuan for sinking wells. The comrades of the service group asked: "How could wells be sunk in the streets? Could it be that some bad people were behind this?" After an investigation, they discovered that there was indeed a "well-sinking team," and that it really had sunk wells for the chemical fertilizer plant. The problem seemed to have been settled. However, the comrades of the service group analyzed this matter from the viewpoint of class struggle and carried out further investigations of the multipurpose plant. They discovered that originally the plant did not have this project on its list, but since a bad person had entered the plant, its direction of service was changed. In the name of sinking wells, it aimed at reaping fabulous profits, corrupting the cadres, and undermining the collective economy. They promptly reported their findings to the neighborhood revolutionary committee, quickly exposed this bad person, and helped the neighborhood in managing its finances in a more proper way.

The comrades of the Chien-hsin Service Group never forget class struggle, viewing "payment and receipt" from the standpoint of the struggle between the two classes, two roads, and two lines, thereby safeguarding the financial power of the proletariat and the socialist economy. The broad revolutionary masses praise them as the "red sentinels" on the socialist financial front.

## Revolution in Banking Depends on Revolutionized People

A revolutionary small bank symbolizes a big revolution in banks. The most basic reason why the Chien-hsin Service Group has been able to advance further on the road of continuing revolution and has constantly made new contributions to struggle-criticism-transformation in banking work is that it has firmly grasped the ideological revolutionization of men and used Mao Tse-tung thought to continuously transform people's world outlook.

In a bank, the educated predominate in number, there is a lot of work to be done in the office, and the work is highly specialized. In the past, poisoned by the revisionist line, the bank was divorced from politics, the masses, and reality. It followed regulations and ignored politics. The Chien-hsin Service Group, taking the People's Liberation Army as its model, brings proletarian politics to the fore, insists on the "four firsts," and places creative study and application of Mao Tse-tung thought above other spheres of work, thereby achieving the "three supports."

First, support the creative study and application of Mao Tse-tung thought to transform world outlook. They read every day and discuss the results of their application every day; nothing could force them to desist from doing so. Before work, they arm themselves with Mao Tse-tung thought, during work they use Mao Tse-tung thought to command battle, and after work they use Mao Tse-tung thought to sum up results. After the Chien-hsin Service Group made some achievements, it was commended by the higher level and praised by the masses. Its deeds were given press publicity. However, some failed for a time to learn from the advanced experience, could not work in depth, and could not march in strides along the revolutionary road. Grasping this problem, the leader of the group organized every member of the group to study Chairman Mao's teaching "modesty makes one progress, conceit makes one lag behind" so as to fight against conceit and prevent complacency and remove the inadequacies. As a result, everyone realized that work could never be perfected and revolution never completed, and consequently raised his consciousness of continuing revolution and continued to revolutionize himself in the revolution of banks.

Second, support depending on the workers, peasants, and soldiers in the control of the service group and in stepping up political and ideological work. Members of the service group voluntarily invite representatives of workers, peasants, and soldiers to supervise their work. They frequently invite the workers, peasants, and soldiers to hold ideological commentary meetings, and to hold classes on class education recalling the past hardship and reflecting on the present happiness so as to help the comrades of the service group raise their consciousness and transform their world outlook. A woman comrade had been working in the bank for 20 years. In the past, she put heavy emphasis on business activities and ignored politics. With the help of the worker representatives, she studied and applied the "three constantly read articles," criticized the purely business viewpoint, and persisted in taking the road of identifying herself with the workers, peasants, and soldiers. She performed outstanding deeds in her work and gloriously joined the Chinese Communist Party.

Third, support taking part in collective productive labor by rotation. The comrades of the Chien-hsin Service Group have in the course of labor tempered their red hearts loyal to our great leader Chairman Mao and strengthened their proletarian sentiments. A university student professed to be "sound both in mind and body," and he often complained that the organization made little use of him. After nearly two years of training in labor, his thoughts and feelings changed markedly. While working in a plant, he also insists on helping the workshop in cleaning the floor every day and delivering water and hot meals to the workers. Once, when a lathe was being installed, a "three-step tower" threatened to fall. Some workers were in danger of being hurt and the lathe of being damaged. While chanting Chairman Mao's great teaching of "fearing neither hardship nor death," he charged forward at the risk of his life and used his body to hold an iron stand weighing a hundred catties. Although his shoulders and hands were injured, he protected the lathe and ensured the safety of the workers.

For the past two years, out of the 14 comrades of the Chien-hsin Service Group, 7 have been assessed to be "five-good" workers and 4 attended the municipal meeting on creative study and application of Mao Tse-tung thought. The whole group has become an advanced collective in the creative study and application of Mao Tse-tung thought in the city, and has been named "Red Flag Service Group on Fiscal and Financial Front in Fushun Municipality." In November of last year, the Fushun Municipal Revolutionary Committee made the decision to learn from the Chien-hsin Service Group. The comrades of the Chien-hsin Service Group treat themselves correctly with Chairman Mao's brilliant philosophic thinking of "dividing one into two." They do not become complacent in the face of their glory. They search for inadequacies amidst achievements, and find their weak points from their strong points. They are determined to continue to forge ahead on the broad avenue of building socialist banks!

## 38. "Red Bank" [Homonym] Lauds the Long-term Stability of the Jen-min pi (Source 8, pp. 180-182) July 6, 1969

The long-term stability of China's People's Currency has been demonstrated by the long-term stability of commodity prices. Since the establishment of our regime, the retail prices of our commodities have remained stable in the face of the rapid growth of industrial and agricultural production. The prices of food grains, cloth, coal, and salt have been stable. Many daily commodities and other goods also enjoyed basically stable prices. Charges for living quarters, utilities, postal services, and transportation, which affect the people's livelihood directly, have been low and stable. In order to adjust the inequitable relative prices of industrial and farm products left behind by the old China, to further consolidate the worker-peasant alliance, and to promote industrial and farm production, the government has systematically raised the procurement prices for food crops, cotton fibers, oil seeds, hemp, cocoons, tea leaves, sugar cane, hogs, and other farm and subsidiary products. The selling prices, however, have not been raised. With the development of industrial production, the government has also lowered the prices of many industrial products, especially farm inputs and many daily industrial commodities, such as chemical fertilizers, farm machines and tools, pesticides, diesel fuel, kerosene, medicines, and medical equipment. In this way, the peasants can get more industrial products in exchange for the same amount of farm products. During the Great Proletarian Cultural Revolution, the government has drastically reduced the prices of books, newspapers, magazines, radios, and other cultural and educational supplies in response to the enthusiasm of the broad worker, peasant, soldier masses in learning Mao Tse-tung thought.

China's People's Currency is at the service of the broad working people, our socialist revolution, and socialist construction. It has the full confidence of the broad masses. Since the establishment of the People's Republic of China, the government has reduced the interest rate on savings deposits several times. But savings deposits have grown steadily. Compared with figures in 1952, the amount of deposits in urban areas has increased seven times, and deposits in rural areas one hundred times. Holders of these savings accounts are largely working people of the urban and rural areas. During the Great Proletarian Cultural Revolution, savings deposits in the urban and rural areas increased even faster. One-third of the amount of savings deposits were made within the last three years. The present total urban and rural deposits exceed the amount of currency in circulation. Many patriotic Overseas Chinese in Hong Kong and Macao have also requested the local Chinese banks to institute deposits in People's Currency. This attests to their affection for the great socialist fatherland and their confidence in the People's Currency.

China's People's Currency has also won very high international prestige. Lately, amidst the daily worsening monetary crisis of the capitalist world, our foreign trade, foreign aid, and other economic transactions formerly conducted in other currencies, have been conducted in the People's Currency with many countries. The number of countries and regions using the People's Currency is increasing.

## 39. "Red Bank" Draws Contrasts between the Currencies of China and the Soviet Union's Ruble (Source 8, pp. 184-185) July 6, 1969

The Soviet revisionist clique turned the clock back by resorting to the wholesale restoration of capitalism, bogging the economy down in difficulties. They squandered away the socialist accomplishments that the Russian people had struggled to achieve under the leadership of Lenin and Stalin. In the ten years between 1956 and 1965, they sold gold totaling U.S. $3 billion. They even auctioned off their natural resources in exchange for handouts from the monopolistic international finance groups. In 1961, the replacement of the old ruble by the new ruble was actually a substantial devaluation of its foreign exchange value. The bourgeois privileged class repeatedly raised prices to plunder and squeeze the working people. Since 1966, the Soviet National Prices Commission has stipulated the successive implementation of new prices in the textiles, knitting, leather shoes, and food industries, and in heavy industries and other industries, thus substantially raising the wholesale prices of many industrial products. On July 1, 1967, the prices of many types of industrial products were raised. Among them, the price of coal was increased by 78%, and the price of electricity for industrial use by 20% to 22%. At present, food, clothing, and daily necessities are in short supply in the Russian market. The black market is rampant. Even the price of bread has sharply increased in some regions. As prices shoot up, the purchasing power of the currency keeps going down. This arouses all the more the violent discontent and resistance of the Russian people.

Two currency systems, two kinds of fate: a sharp contrast exists between the currency of socialist China and the currency of the capitalist world. The former has, like the rising sun, a bright future; the latter has, like the setting sun, faded glory. "Watching the world across the ocean," "the scenery is far superior over here." The long-term stability of the People's Currency indicates the vitality of our socialist enterprise, the unsurpassed superiority of the socialist system.

## 40. "Red Bank" Draws Further Contrasts between the Jen-min pi and Currency under the KMT and under the Line of Liu Shao-ch'i (Source 8, pp. 186-190) July 6, 1969

As soon as the country was liberated, we abolished the financial privileges that the imperialists had previously enjoyed in our country; we confiscated the financial institutions of bureaucratic capitalism, established our banking system, reformed private banks and money exchanges with speed and deliberation, and instituted a unified, nationwide socialist financial system with the help of the invincible thought of Mao Tse-tung, the strength of the proletarian government, and the support of the broad masses. We thoroughly wiped out all the currencies issued by the reactionary KMT [Nationalist] government; we drove capitalist currencies out of circulation so that the People's Currency could rapidly circulate in the city and the countryside. An independent, unified, and stable socialist currency was born. Thus, all possible effects that the monetary crises of the capitalist world might have on our monetary system were completely eliminated.

As early as the Second Plenary Session of the Seventh Central Committee of the Party, Chairman Mao earnestly taught us: "We must master the art of political, economic, and cultural struggle against the imperialists, the KMT, and the bourgeoisie." Otherwise, "we will not be able to maintain our political power, we will not be able to hold our ground, and we will fail."

On the eve of liberation, the reactionary KMT left us with a devastated economy. In the twelve years from the start of the Sino-Japanese War to May 1949, the reactionary KMT government increased the currency issue by more than 140 million times. Prices soared. What formerly cost one KMT yuan ended up costing more than 8,500 million yuan. The broad working masses were miserable. In the early period of the People's Republic, the remnant KMT elements and bourgeoisie again engaged in massive speculation, price manipulation, and sabotage. At the same time that the U.S. imperialists were waging the war of aggression against Korea, they imposed an economic blockade and trade embargo on China. They also froze our foreign assets without justification; and they acted in collusion with the Chiang [Kai-shek] gang to forge large amounts of banknotes to create confusion in our monetary system in an attempt to strangle new China economically. Liu Shao-ch'i, the capitalist agent and the backstage boss of the bourgeoisie, actively responded by peddling the reactionary proposals of "red compradors" and "exploitation has its contribution." He wanted the bank to fix the foreign exchange rate according to the wishes of the capitalists, to open a stock exchange, and to extend credit to the capitalists for speculation and manipulation so as to upset the market.

But, under the leadership of the great leader Chairman Mao, we have relied on the massive strength of the proletarian government and the socialistic state economy to deal a severe blow to the speculative activities of the bourgeoisie. As early as March 1950, prices had been stabilized all over the country and the inflationary spiral lasting for more than ten years under the reactionary rule of the KMT was arrested. During and immediately following the Korean War, we persistently and simultaneously prosecuted the just war, advanced socialist construction, and stabilized the price level and the currency. In response to the banditry of the unreasonable freezing of our foreign assets by the U.S. imperialists, we froze the U.S. assets in our country. In 1952, we beat back the frantic attack of the bourgeoisie by launching the seething "Three-Anti" and "Five-Anti" campaigns. Beginning in 1953, the unified procurement and marketing scheme for major farm products was implemented to sever the links between rural and urban capitalism and to promote the development of the socialist economy. In 1956, the socialist reform of agriculture, handicraft industries, and capitalist industry and commerce was completed. The thorough implementation of a series of guidelines and policies of the great leader, Chairman Mao, contributed to the significant development of the socialist economy, the consolidation of the proletarian dictatorship, and the creation of favorable conditions for the long-term stability of the People's Currency.

The great leader Chairman Mao teaches us: "The general guideline of our economic and financial work is to develop the economy and to ensure supply." Our people have put his teaching into practice by making revolution command production, stimulating production, and forging ahead along the general line of "going all out, aiming high, and achieving greater, faster, and better results with lower cost in building socialism."

Liu Shao-ch'i, the renegade, traitor, and scab, was disheartened by the swift progress of socialist revolution and construction. He strongly advocated the "theory of extinction of class struggle" and opposed continual revolution, on the one hand, and resisted the general line of socialist revolution of the Party as "reckless adventure," on the other. If the counterrevolutionary conspiracy of Liu Shao-ch'i had succeeded, the foundation of the socialist economy would have been destroyed and capitalism restored. On the financial and monetary side, resources would have dried up, supplies dwindled, and currency devalued. But the wheel of history cannot be reversed. All domestic and foreign obstruction and sabotage are futile.

A sound, stable, and balanced national budget is an important condition for the safeguarding of currency stability. The great leader Chairman Mao teaches us "to consolidate and unify the management and leadership of financial and economic work, to balance revenue with expenditure, and to stabilize prices." The major source of China's revenue is the domestic accumulation of state enterprises. The main expenditure goes to the development of the socialist economy. If revenue and balance do not balance, we should make necessary adjustments in economic plans, increase production, and wage austerity campaigns. We will not rely on domestic or foreign debts, or the issue of banknotes. The issue of banknotes in our country is based on the needs of economic development, and on the need to expand production and circulation. As a result of the thorough implementation of Chairman Mao's guidelines, China has achieved a balance between state revenue and expenditure, while running a surplus in its balance of payments. Not only has the problem of tapping resources for building socialism and strengthening defense been solved, China has also become a socialist country with neither domestic nor foreign debts.

Liu Shao-ch'i, the renegade, traitor, and scab, has long advocated the reactionary nonsense of "deficit spending and inflation." He said, "It is all right to have budget deficits"; "We can increase revenue by issuing more banknotes"; and, "Inflation is all for the good"; "The more inflation there is, the richer the people." Especially during the three years when China's economy suffered temporary setbacks due to natural calamities and the sabotage of the Soviet revisionist clique, Liu Shao-ch'i once again acted in collusion with the domestic and foreign class enemies to stir up trouble. In 1962, he called for a 50% increase in commodity prices. In December 1963, when the economy was fully recovered, he repeatedly raised the reactionary demand for a general increase in prices and a decrease in currency value. The Chinese people have had enough of inflation and soaring prices to realize that the implementation of Liu Shao-ch'i's proposals would only subject the broad working people to repeated hardship. Faced with the frantic attacks from the domestic and foreign reactionary forces, the whole people responded to the call of the great leader Chairman Mao: "Never forget class struggle." With the spirit of arduous struggle, self-reliance, and building the country with diligence, frugality, and determination, they carried out the policy of adjusting, consolidating, strengthening, and improving the economy; and they worked hard to raise production and income and to cut down expenditure to ensure the balance between revenue and expenditure. Meanwhile, market management was strengthened, and prices and currency value stabilized. Once again, the scheme of Liu Shao-ch'i and his followers to restore capitalism was thwarted.

Now, the Great Proletarian Cultural Revolution launched and led by the great Chairman Mao has won a smashing victory.

This great revolutionary storm has destroyed the command headquarters of the bourgeoisie led by Liu Shao-ch'i, the renegade, traitor, and scab, and shattered their plots to restore capitalism. This has made China's proletarian dictatorship more solid, the socialist economy more flourishing, and the financial foundation sounder than ever before. During the Great Proletarian Cultural Revolution, the whole people, armed with Mao Tse-tung's thought, has waged a great revolutionary criticism against Liu Shao-ch'i and a handful of other Party persons taking the capitalist road and swept the reactionary nonsense of "deficit spending and inflation" and their black proponent, Liu Shao-ch'i, into the garbage dump of history.

For the last 19 years [of the People's Republic], there has been a fierce struggle between the two classes, the two roads, and the two lines on our financial and monetary front. China's People's Currency has withstood every severe test. Its continual stability testifies to the unparalleled superiority of the socialist monetary system under the guidance of Mao Tse-tung's thought. Today, when financial and monetary crises are sweeping the capitalist world and countries under modern revisionist rule are suffering from serious difficulties, China's People's Currency stands rock steady in the world as an independent, unified, and stable socialist currency.

## 41. *Red Flag* Author Explains Why the *Jen-min pi* Has Remained Stable (Source 7, pp. 75-78) November 1974

The Renminbi's long-term stability derives mainly from the fact that the state possesses a large stock of commodities which is put on the market at stabilized prices. This is a peculiar feature distinguishing the socialist from the capitalist economic system. Money serves as a universal equivalent of commodities; "The circulation of money is merely a manifestation of the metamorphosis of commodities" (Karl Marx, *A Critique of* the Political Economy). The value of the currency can be kept stable when the socialist economy develops, with goods in ample supply and the state possessing a large stock of commodities and always putting them on the market at stabilized prices. Since the founding of New China, the Chinese people, guided by Chairman Mao's revolutionary line, have held fast to the principle of "developing the economy and ensuring supplies." This leads to steady development in agricultural production, a substantial growth of both light and heavy industrial production, and a large increase of consumer goods on sale in the market. State purchase of commodities and total retail sales in 1973 increased more than sevenfold compared with the early years of liberation. The state is keeping a growing stock of commodities. The commercial departments at the end of last June had in stock nearly twice as many goods as in June 1965. To date, every single yuan in circulation in our country is backed by commodities worth several yuan. This enables the currency in circulation to be commensurate with the supply of commodities, thus ensuring a long-standing stability of the value of the Renminbi.

Another important condition for the Renminbi maintaining long-term stability is to work out a state budget under the socialist system, a budget which is steady and sound and in which revenue and expenditure are balanced. In the early days of the People's Republic, Chairman Mao already had pointed out that "the balance of revenue and expenditure and the stabilization of prices should also be consolidated" ("Fight for a Fundamental Turn for the Better in the Financial and Economic Situation," China Wins Economic Battles, Foreign Languages Press, Peking, 1950, p. 7). Whether a balance between revenue and expenditure can be brought about or not has a direct bearing on the issuance of the currency and the stability of its value. "The issuing of notes by the state bank is based primarily on the needs of economic development" ("Our Economic Policy," Selected Works of Mao Tse-tung, Vol. 1, Foreign Languages Press, Peking, 1967, pp. 144-45).

In the course of socialist construction in China, the principle of balancing revenue and expenditure has all along been adhered to, and it is impermissible to increase the fiscal outlay by issuing more notes. The implementation of the state budget generally results in a favorable balance with a slight surplus so that the state's reserve is continually reinforced. In special circumstances, like natural calamities, the revenue and expenditure balance is ensured by increasing production and practicing economy, tapping the state's reserves, making adjustments in a planned way, and using what has been set aside in the bumper years for the lean years. Our country never relies on getting loans to solve the problem, still less on the issuing of more bank notes. Today, China is one of the few countries with neither internal nor external debts. Thanks to the consolidated and balanced fiscal position, currency in circulation is limited to a scale just enough to meet the development of production and the enlarged circulation of commodities. The kind of monetary inflation that occurs in capitalist society as a result of issuing notes indiscriminately can never happen in our country.

The long-term stability of the Renminbi is also due to the state's centralized and unified control of the issuing of notes through adjusting, in a planned way, the amounts of money put into circulation and to be called in. Issued by the state bank in a unified way and subject to its centralized control, the Renminbi is the only currency in circulation in China. Money put into circulation by the bank flows back mainly through supplying commodities in a planned way. The amount of wages paid by the state, the quantity of farm and sideline produce purchased by the state, the amount of money to be put into circulation, and the corresponding quantity of merchandise to be supplied — all these are arranged annually by the state according to plan. This makes it possible for the currency to be released and called back through planned channels and so ensures the normal circulation of the currency. When a temporary, partial imbalance takes place in an unexpected situation in the course of implementing the plan, the state is free to make adjustments through planning in order to reach a new balance. This is the superiority of the socialist planned economy.

## The Line Decides Everything

"The correctness or incorrectness of the ideological and political line decides everything." The long-term stability of the Renminbi is, in the last analysis, a fruit of Chairman Mao's proletarian revolutionary line triumphing over the revisionist line of Liu Shao-ch'i and Lin Piao. Babbling that "it is all right to have budgetary deficits" and "to issue more bank notes," Liu Shao-ch'i and Lin Piao and their gang tried to justify their reactionary stand for currency depreciation and monetary inflation. Their vain attempt was to open up a breach on the financial and monetary front — the chief link in the entire national economy — to undermine the socialist economy, subvert the proletarian dictatorship, and restore capitalism. With Chairman Mao's revolutionary line pointing out the way, these sabotaging activities were rebuffed in time and failed to succeed. The two bourgeois headquarters of Liu Shao-ch'i and Lin Piao have been demolished by the Great Proletarian Cultural Revolution, and their criminal schemes for capitalist restoration smashed. The present Campaign to Criticize Lin Piao and Confucius is being broadened and deepened in a sustained way Socialist construction in China is about to enter a new phase of development. The socialist economic system in China, the financial and monetary system included, is becoming daily more consolidated in the struggle between the two lines. Prospects are infinitely bright.

## 42. Economist Observes a Shift since 1949 in the Profile of People Making Personal Savings Deposits (Source 10, p. 64) June 1964

In New China there is a radical change in the proportion and percentages of savings depositors; the principal depositors today are peasants, workers, and elements of the intelligentsia.

Although the depositors include a number of capitalists, drawing a fixed interest, they do not form an important section of the people's savings; nor are the savings activities focused on them. The people's savings of New China are principally the savings of the working proletariat. All this deeply reflects the profound social changes that have taken place as a result of the socialist revolution, the fact that the people at large have become the owners of the country.

## 43. Economist Reports Increase in Proportion of Fixed Savings Deposits to Total Deposits, 1952-1963 (Source 10, pp. 74-75) June 1964

In recent years, not only has the volume of savings in the People's Bank rapidly risen, but the composition of savings deposits has also undergone marked changes. It is of interest to note, for instance, that fixed savings deposits have increased as a ratio to total deposits. In 1952 the proportion of fixed savings deposits amounted to 46.6%; at the end of 1957 it rose to 70.3%, and by 1963 it climbed to 82.5%. These changes reflect the profound economic and social changes that had taken place during this period. This is a healthy sign of the continuous economic development and expansion of the national economy and of the rapid improvement of the people's standard of living.

## 44. People's Daily Correspondent Explains Continued Increase in Savings Deposits through 1973 (Source 17, pp. 90-92) January 23, 1974

(NCNA, January 22, 1974) With the incessant penetration of education with respect to ideology and political lines and the sustained growth of agricultural production, the livelihood of the broad masses has gradually improved. Once again in 1973 the rural and urban savings deposits in our country have expanded by big margins: urban savings deposits increased 10.5 percent compared with the end of 1972; rural savings deposits, 32 percent. Nearly half of the existing bank deposits in the urban and rural areas have been saved in the seven years since the Great Proletarian Cultural Revolution.

On one street of a new housing estate for workers of K'ai-luan Coal Mine, all of the 267 households had bank savings. Among them, they had 400-odd bicycles, 200-odd radios, 110 sewing machines, and 200-odd watches. But before liberation, the miners here lived in a run-down temple and slept on worn mats. More than 10 people were packed together on a heated earth bed, subsisting on salted vegetables and moldy kao-liang. Earnings from a whole year's labor were insufficient to support a family, and their dependents had to beg for extra food.

In Lin hsien, Honan Province, the Red Flag Canal, built on the precipices of the Tai-hang Mountains, has brought water to irrigate 600,000 mou of farmland. The total value of agricultural production has increased 1.3 times since the Great Proletarian Cultural Revolution. The per mou grain yield increased by 74 percent and the savings of the members of the commune credit co-op doubled. This very fact of an increase in urban and rural savings deposits reflects the incomparable superiority of our socialist system and forcefully rebuts Lin Piao and his anti-Party clique's shameless lies that "the national economy is stationary"; it "enriches the state and impoverishes the people."

The fundamental reasons for the expansion of the people's savings in 1973 were the strengthening of education regarding the Party's basic line, the criticism of Lin Piao's revisionist line, the alerting of the people to resist the corrosion of bourgeois ideology, and the fostering of the superb Party tradition of plain living and hard work.

The Party committee of the Peking Wool Blanket Works regularly educated the staff and workers about the fine revolutionary tradition of plain living and hard work, using the Party's basic line as the key link. They held discussions, organized the staff and workers to visit exhibitions on class education, and invited old workers to compare the new and old societies in order to make the staff and workers realize that only by fostering the revolutionary tradition of plain living and hard work can Chairman Mao's revolutionary line be correctly implemented, corrosion by the bourgeoisie be resisted, and socialist revolution be carried to the end. They actively increased savings to support socialist construction. More than 90 percent of the staff and workers in this factory now save, and the amount of deposits has increased yearly.

With the education about the Party's basic line, the residents of the Yang-p'u area of Shanghai voluntarily saved grain, water, electricity, and coal; they practiced family planning and joined bank savings programs. K'ung-chiang Street residents formed a mutual aid fund whose deposits had increased twenty times at the end of last year compared with the beginning of the year.

With the Party's basic line as the key link and under the leadership of the Party committee of the commune, the Ying-lan Credit Co-op of Jung-ch'eng hsien, Shantung Province, helped the poor and lower-middle peasants to save grains, hay, and money and practice family planning. They criticized bourgeois ideology and fostered the new trend of industry and thrift. The deposits of members at the end of 1973 reached 110,000-odd yuan, averaging 172 yuan per household. The number of households in the credit co-op represented 85 percent of the total agricultural households.

The bank deposits of China's urban and rural population have become an important source of finance in supporting socialist construction. New deposits alone in rural credit co-ops in 1973 represented 25 percent of the extended agricultural loans.

## 45. Economist Explains the Importance of People's Savings to Economic Construction (Source 10, pp. 66-73) June 1964

### Economic Prerequisites for the Existence of People's Savings Under Socialism

Under our socialist system, people's savings are based on

the objective fact that there is still an intimate relationship between money and commodities. Where a commodity-money relationship still exists, in order to accumulate and build up capital for reconstruction, it is necessary to mobilize all means and resources to gather all the untapped and scattered fragments of capital in order to assure the rapid development and realization of socialist reconstruction. People's savings are a form of this mobilization. They are a suitable method and measure to be adopted for this purpose. At the same time, the individual should also save what he has earned in anticipation of future need; therefore, personal saving is necessary.

Under socialism the presence of an idle cash balance in the people's hands can be explained by the present distribution system, which is based on: from each according to his ability and to each according to his work. Since there are differences in work and, therefore, in incomes, some will receive more and others less. Even if the people receive the same pay, those who have a large family and a heavy burden will save little, while those who have no family burden will have some surplus.

The crucial question is: what are the people going to do with their spare money? Because they are patriotic and class-conscious, they will either turn it over to the state through savings in the banks, so as to speed up socialist reconstruction, or they will use it as a sort of revolving mutual fund to help their fellow-workers for welfare purposes.

Second, a good proportion of savings has arisen from the people's desire to improve their own living conditions, their material and cultural livelihood. Although what they have left over is not much, still savings will have to be made from their daily and weekly expenditures and be put aside as savings to purchase some expensive consumer goods, or for other purposes.

Furthermore, there are seasonal fluctuations in the income and expenditures of some groups of the people, and it is necessary to put aside and save that income which is accumulated but is not immediately needed. An example is the peasant's supplementary production (such as handicrafts), which may yield one lump-sum income in a year but the expenditure may have to be drawn out, spread, in the course of the whole year. All seasonal workers have to calculate and anticipate those expenditures which occur in low-work and low-income seasons.

Finally, in the urban areas the monthly payments of wages and salaries, which are required for expenditures during the course of the entire month, will also accrue some money for which there is no immediate use.

Since there are always some idle cash balances in the people's hands, there must be a place where they can be safely stored and secured. This situation gives rise to the demand that the state and the collective organizations provide the people with savings facilities. Meanwhile, on the other hand, when the state is engaging in large-scale socialist reconstruction, it requires an immense amount of capital and working funds. To meet this demand the state should mobilize and tap all means and sources of savings so that production can be expanded, construction accelerated, and the people's standard of living raised.

Under these circumstances, it is obvious that to tap the people's savings is one of the vital functions of the state banks and of the credit cooperatives and agencies. It is a measure and activity instituted to meet the demands and needs of the people at large and the requirement of socialist reconstruction. It is a useful and beneficial measure, both from the public and the private point of view.

Because of the differences between the forms of people's incomes, the national banks, the cooperatives, and the savings societies provide, in the main, three different types of savings accounts for the convenience and facility of depositors.

The first type is the long-term, fixed period deposits. These are provided mainly for those whose incomes exceed their expenditures and who are therefore likely to have savings to accumulate. As regards those national capitalists who are drawing interest on their former investments, their interest is based on the same mode of calculation. Under this category, funds are generally deposited for more than one year. Originally the maximum period for interest-bearing deposits was one year. However, on expiration dates, there were a great number of depositors who wished to extend the period of their deposit; some even had their deposits extended or renewed several times. It became obvious that the need for long-term savings required extension. The People's Bank, in order to meet these actual demands, extended the maximum period of fixed deposits to three years.

The second type is the seasonal fixed deposit account. In general the maximum period of deposit under this category is one year. This type of deposit is most common in the rural areas.

The third type is the current savings account, where funds can be deposited or withdrawn at any time. These are suitable for urban requirements and are particularly convenient for workers and peasants who may need cash for daily transactions. For instance, a worker may receive his monthly wage; he deposits it with a savings account, and later on he can make withdrawals as he needs funds. In this way such a savings account becomes a workingman's treasury. Whether in the form of fixed deposit accounts or of current savings accounts, all this increases the bank's services, such as paying interest to the accounts and seeing to it that all the details concerning deposits and withdrawals are attended to. Hence the People's Bank is primarily concerned with the convenience of the depositors and the security of the deposit.

## The Function and Use of People's Savings

Because of the total difference in the nature of savings under socialism and under capitalism in Old China, there is also a sharp difference in the effects on the economy. The effect and influence of savings on our national reconstruction and on the people's livelihood are expressed in the following principal forms:

First, one of the most important functions of savings is to concentrate the capital required for our reconstruction. Savings also form a reliable source of the funds and cash required by banks and cooperatives. In a country such as ours, with our enormous, checkered population, savings take on a special meaning.

Chairman Mao stated: "For the development of the nationalized economy, for assisting the economy of the cooperatives . . . to rely on the strength and ability of the masses for raising the capital for reconstruction is at the moment the only way to do it, and a very likely way of doing it. . . ."

He also pointed out: "In raising and amassing capital for rural reconstruction, there is in fact a considerable amount of capital that can come from the peasants themselves . . . the peasants themselves possess an innate strength in the storing of capital. In the collectivization of agricultural enterprises, the state should give the peasants every assistance, but in the formation of capital the peasants should primarily rely on themselves to raise most of the funds needed for capital formation. It would indeed be a tragedy to underestimate the peasants' potential to accumulate capital."

As Chairman Mao pointed out, the people's savings both in the rural and urban areas are one of the main sources of funds which can be tapped for our economic reconstruction. Capital can be accumulated by the efforts of the masses themselves. Confidence in the people and in their rejuvenation is one of the principles in our socialist reconstruction — a principle to which we always adhere, a principle which forms one of the major components of our revolutionary tenets.

Second, people's savings tend to stabilize the market. It is an instrument that can be employed to regulate the supply and demand for money and, thereby, for products. One of the means to channel surplus and idle funds into the various economic projects is to encourage people to practice economy and industry and to deposit their savings with the national banks. This principle should not only be practiced in state agencies, but also be carried into every household. Meanwhile, savings enterprises should expand and streamline their organization and extend their facilities. In this way, through the channels of these savings organizations, the bulk of the idle and scattered funds which are afloat in the community will flow back again into the national banks. Such a flow of cash will help to stabilize the market and is beneficial to our economic reconstruction, enabling it to advance along planned lines.

A process of reinvestment and reallocation of resources

starts when savings funds begin to accumulate; what originally existed for consumers' purposes is transformed into investment and capital formation. All this adds to the large-scale scope of our reconstruction and, in due course, to the expansion of our total productive power and supply.

People's savings, and especially peasants' savings in rural areas, are a great regulator in the flow and control of currency. This has a profound bearing on the various aspects of our economic life. Because rural savings are largely seasonal, the savings device and facilities play an important part in regulating the flow of cash, and hence serve as stabilizers.

We all know that in a country as vast as ours, whenever there is a fluctuation in our agricultural production — a bumper harvest or a failure — it has a tremendous bearing on our whole financial budget and planning, as well as on the volume of cash turnover, which in turn has a direct influence on the market. This is especially the case when seasonal variations accentuate the fluctuations. During the harvesting season in the autumn (that is, in the fourth season and the last quarter of the year), the state makes large-scale purchases in rural areas; as a result, a great deal of cash is released into the countryside, resulting in a sharp rise in the demand for consumer goods. By the second and third seasons (second and third quarters), most of the cash released will have returned again into the banks; this often results in a shortage of cash or a tight-money situation in the rural areas. Such a money flow situation is not ideal. This is where the savings movement comes in: to break this contradiction. At the height of the season, when the state releases the maximum amount of cash to make its large-scale purchases from the land, the savings organizations should mobilize all their manpower to encourage their members to deposit in banks of the credit cooperatives, all their spare cash or any funds for which the peasants have no use in immediate transactions (these are, in turn, passed on to the national banks).

In this way the surplus money on the market will be somewhat reduced. During the lean season, when cash becomes tight on the market, the peasants will start to withdraw the savings which they deposited in the banks. In this way, regulation of the supply of money will prevent market fluctuation. At the same time the savings accumulated after the autumn harvest could also be used by them to purchase those supplies and equipment necessary for supplementary rural production (handicrafts, etc.). In this way the state will be able to reduce the total volume of cash that would have to be issued, as well as prevent the overconcentration of cash during the "high" seasons.

Third, within the savings activities, there also exists scope for mutual help and mutual assistance among the workers. In our present stage of development, the rewards and wages in the communes, which are still organized on a socialist collective principle, are still largely based on work or exchange, and, in consequence, there can be a considerable difference in the cash available to commune members, and this difference is likely to exist for a long time to come. Under these circumstances, one of the basic functions of the various savings cooperatives is to draw in the excess cash balance in the hands of some rich members and to use it to relieve the shortage of cash among the poor members. In this way, by balancing the surplus with the deficit, it will be able to help in maintaining a smooth flow of funds and production.

Parallel with this is the situation in the urban areas. Although the workers will use their increased pay to improve their standard of living, the majority of them still have spare money to save. Conversely, there are always some workers who, for a variety of reasons, find themselves short of money. In order to regulate the flow of money, there should be a savings bank or mutual fund, or a savings cooperative, in every factory, school, organization, and on every street. People should be encouraged to join the cooperatives and to pool their resources so that they can help each other. This is another form of people's saving.

Fourth, saving will influence people to live in an orderly fashion; it will encourage them to see the advantages and benefits of industry and economy in their domestic life. Under our socialist system, people enjoy the security of jobs, and because of this their livelihood is secured; there is no need for them to save in order to secure themselves against unemployment.

An expansion of the national product would tend to raise the average income of the people; in consequence, their standard of living will rise. It is true that the people's standard of living is much higher today than what it was in the days of Old China. But the fact remains that there is a big gap between the present standard of living and what we would like it to be.

Chairman Mao said: "It is necessary for our youth to know that our country is still very poor, and that this state of affairs cannot be changed overnight.

"It will take the youth of this country several decades of unremitting labor and struggle before they can turn China into a wealthy and powerful country. The socialist system has given us a chance to traverse a road that will in due course lead us to an ideal society, but the building of such a society will depend entirely upon our own efforts, determination, and continued hard work."

All of us must therefore learn from Chairman Mao's teaching; we must unceasingly extol the virtue of "practicing economy and industry as the basic principles of building our country," of "being inspired and zealous in our effort to become powerful," of "practicing economy and industry in our domestic life." Only in this way will we be able to improve our livelihood. To positively practice saving is one of the ways of bringing about the realization of this goal.

## 46. Economist Raises the Problem of the Ratio of Accumulation to Consumption in Rural Communes (Source 23, p. 32) March 1965

The ratio between accumulation and consumption in rural people's communes reflects the relationship among the state, the collective, and individuals. It also reflects the relationship between the rate of enlarged agricultural reproduction and the rate of enhancement of the peasants' standards of living. It further reflects the relationship between the peasants' present interests and their long-range interests. Correct handling of the ratio between accumulation and consumption in rural communes is an important factor in correctly handling the contradictions among the people, and in mobilizing the positiveness of the broad mass of peasants, and in further developing agriculture as the basis upon which the new leap forward of the entire national economy can be launched and accelerated.

## 47. Economist Details Three Attributes of the Accumulation/Consumption Ratio (Source 23, pp. 33-36) March 1965

Because the important characteristic of agricultural reproduction is the close link between the economic reproduction process and the natural reproduction process, and because at the present time the rural communes in China are still using the collective ownership system, accumulation and consumption in rural communes have the following attributes:

First, in rural communes, the accumulation fund and the consumption fund are not stipulated centrally by the state. The level of accumulation and the level of consumption are determined generally and directly by the production levels of the various collective units, a greater portion of the gross income being generally retained in the respective units, and the proportion between accumulation and consumption being determined by the members' representatives meeting on the basis of the specific conditions of the production team. Among different communes and production teams, there are certain differences in the levels of accumulation and consumption, and some of the differences are rather large. Of course, the economic support of the state and the all-people's ownership system have direct effects on the accumulation and consumption of rural communes. For instance, through such patterns as farm loans, the supply of means of production for agriculture at low prices, and the undertaking of larger capital constructions on the part of the state, massive support has been given to rural communes. This has had important repercussions on developing agricultural production, on increasing state and collective accumulations, and on raising the peasants' consumption level.

Moreover, in the present stage of the development of rural communes in China, there are still the remnants of such privately owned economies as the members' private plot and home subsidiary industries, etc., which also have certain effects on the consumption of peasants. We all know that "where the collective ownership system has not yet been elevated to all-people's ownership, and where the remnants of private economy have not yet been completely eliminated, the peasants will inevitably retain some of the inherent characteristics of the original small producers. In this circumstance, there arises unavoidably the spontaneous tendency oward capitalism. . . ." Thus, the relationship between accumulation and consumption in the rural communes is bound to reflect directly the two-way struggle between socialism and capitalism, as well as the relationship between the socialist all-people's ownership system and the socialist collective ownership system, on the one hand, and the remnants of private economies, on the other. Consequently, in handling the relationship between accumulation and consumption in rural communes, it is necessary to pay attention to strengthening socialist education among the peasants, continuously solidifying and developing the collective economy, and striking at and preventing the spontaneous tendency toward capitalism. On this basis, the relationship among the state, the collectives, and the individuals, as well as the relationship between accumulation and consumption, can be handled correctly.

Second, in the accumulation and consumption of rural communes, whether in regard to the means of production or the means of consumption, there is a portion consisting of products for self-sufficiency. Marx said: "What distinguishes agriculture and animal husbandry from the other industries is that . . .the former can be used as their own productive tactics and add them to the process of production from which products are derived." In the meantime, among the means of consumption in agricultural production, a considerable portion is used directly for the personal consumption of the peasants. In the income of peasants from the collective economy, a portion consists of income in kind. Where the peasants' level of consumption is rather low, and where the commodity portion of agricultural products is rather small, the portion of income in kind still forms a considerable ratio to total income. This illustrates the fact that in rural communes, in order to handle correctly the relationship between accumulation and consumption, it is necessary to handle correctly the relationship between the production of a commodity for marketing and production for self-sufficiency, as well as the relationship between procurement and retention. One should not stress one aspect only, to the detriment of the other aspect.

Moreover, the ratio in value terms between accumulation and consumption must be proportional to that in physical terms, so that the accumulation and consumption funds retained in the commune will be in proportion in physical terms to the intra-unit allotment of products for accumulation and consumption purposes; the ratio in value terms between accumulation and consumption for commercial agricultural products must be in proportion in physical terms to the means of production and consumption that can be supplied by various industries.

The trend of development — i.e., the continuous rise in agricultural labor productivity — suggests that the ratio of input of agricultural product to total input will decline relatively, while the ratio of the agricultural products for marketing in total agricultural output will increase relatively. This trend will help promote accumulation. It will gradually increase the portion of agricultural products for marketing (i.e., raise in physical terms the ratio of industrial means of production in agricultural accumulation), and it will accelerate the process of agricultural technological innovation and change the ratio of agriculture in total consumption (by raising the share of industrial products in total consumption), thus raising the peasants' standards of living.

Third, because China's agricultural production still depends largely on natural conditions in different areas and for different communes and brigades, even if the same amount of labor is invested, the level of income may vary. Sometimes the gap is rather large. Of course, with the development of agricultural technology and with the strengthening of the ability of people to change themselves and adapt to nature, the effect of natural conditions on the level of agricultural production and income will gradually diminish. Nonetheless, for a long time to come, natural conditions will have appreciable repercussions in restricting agricultural production and the level of income. Further, differences in the components of crops planted by different communes and brigades in different areas will also cause differences in the level of income. This in turn will lead to differences in accumulation and consumption levels. Thus, in fixing the relationship between the accumulation level and the consumption level, as well as between accumulation and consumption in rural communes, it is necessary to give differential treatment in keeping with the local conditions and to make specific decisions on the basis of such specific conditions as the income levels of the communes and brigades in different areas and their original consumption levels. These levels should not be set uniformly at a fixed ratio.

## 48. Economist Notes Relationship between Consumption and Labor Productivity (Source 21, pp. 41-42) March 1965

In handling correctly the relative rates of growth between agricultural labor productivity and the average consumption level of agricultural laborers, the essential task must be to raise agricultural labor productivity. However, when the rate of the rise of agricultural labor productivity has already been ascertained, the relative rates of growth would then depend upon the rate of the rise in the average consumption level of agricultural laborers. In studying the rate of the rise in the average consumption level of agricultural laborers, it is necessary to consider not only the enhancement of agricultural labor productivity, but also the relative levels of consumption between workers and peasants, so that the rate of the rise in the average consumption level of peasants and the rate of the rise in the consumption level of staff and workers would maintain an adequate proportion, thus becoming conducive to solidifying the worker-peasant alliance and to developing industrial and agricultural production.

In short, in fixing the rate of the rise of the average consumption level of peasants, this rate must be lower than the rate of the rise of agricultural labor productivity, and the enhancement of the consumption level of peasants should be commensurate with the rate of the rise of the consumption level of staff and workers.

## 49. Economist Identifies Views of the Accumulation/Consumption Ratio Held by Different Rural Classes (Source 21, pp. 42-43) March 1965

However, in handling the relationship between accumulation and consumption in rural communes, one must not unilaterally stress consumption and neglect the growth of accumulation. Some would say: "A bumper harvest rarely happens; thus the portion of increased production should be distributed completely." Others remark: "Because the conservation problem has basically been resolved and because there is no lack of means of production, it is not necessary to accumulate further." Still others would say: "It is all right to distribute the products completely among the members because, when there is no production fund, the state will give support anyway." All of these views seem to take account only of temporary and individual interests, and fail to cover long-range and collective interests. Thus, they all reflect the struggle between two opposite views on the problem of distribution. It is mostly the affluent middle peasants who hold this view, while most of the poor and lower-middle peasants advocate a suitable increment of accumulation. This is because the development of the collective economy and their own intimate interests are identical. Under the guidance of the party, they have come to understand the relationship between temporary interests and long-range interests. Only when the collective economy becomes more developed will there be a dependable basis for the enhancement of individual livelihood. Consequently, it is necessary to rely firmly on the poor and lower-middle peasants, to enact a rational distribution program, and constantly to teach the masses to look backward and forward in order to use the bumper harvest to compensate for lean harvests as well as to leave a surplus.

## 50. Economist Refutes View That Accumulation/Consumption Ratio Should Remain Stable (Source 21, pp. 44-45) March 1965

Some people maintain that the ratio of collective accumulation in the distributable income of agriculture should be relatively stable. Where agricultural mechanization has not yet been basically realized and where agricultural labor productivity is still not too high, it would be impossible to raise the rate of accumulation. Such a view cannot be considered correct. First, on the premise of the growth in production and the enhancement in the level of income, unless the rate of accumulation is raised, it would not be possible to enhance the level of agricultural technology and equipment quickly. As we all know, if we should wait until agricultural technological renovations have been completed before the ratio of accumulation is raised, such renovations would inevitably be deferred to the remote future. The people we mentioned have failed to see that on the premise of the rapid growth of agricultural production, a timely and suitable increase in the rate of accumulation in agriculture is one of the prerequisites to accelerating agricultural technological renovation. Second, in recent years, the conditions of China's agricultural production have been improved continuously; the level of agricultural productive forces is being enhanced quickly; the consumption level of peasants has also been raised gradually. Thus, to raise the accumulation rate of agriculture gradually and properly is not only possible but also necessary.

## 51. Mao Tse-tung Legitimizes Interests of State, Collective, and Individual (from "On the Problem of Correctly Handling Contradictions among the People," Peking: Foreign Languages Press, 1957) (Source 21, p. 47) March 1965

When Comrade Mao Tse-tung was speaking about the problem of distribution, he pointed out specifically: "On the question of distribution, it behooves us to pay regard to state interests, collective interests, and individual interests. In regard to the relationship among the tax revenue of the state, the accumulation of cooperatives, and the individual income of peasants, they must be handled properly by paying constant attention to ironing out their contradictions. The state must accumulate, and the cooperative must also accumulate, although the rate of accumulation must not be excessive. We should enable the peasants to increase their individual income from the rise in production year after year when conditions are normal." This guiding principle must be observed in correctly handling the relationship between accumulation and consumption in rural communes. In our practical work, it is necessary to pay equal attention to accumulation and consumption. Where production is developed, we must ensure the steady growth of accumulation and also the suitable enhancement of the consumption level of the commune members, so that accumulation and consumption will be coordinated adequately to accelerate the growth of production.

# 52. Economist Notes How Bumper Harvest Years and Lean Years Should Affect the Accumulation/Consumption Ratio (Source 21, pp. 49-50) March 1965

In bumper harvest years, then, more of the increased gross income from agriculture should be spent for increasing accumulation and less for increasing consumption; in a lean harvest year, everything should be done to ensure the consumption of the members, and accumulation should be reduced suitably. In short, on the basis of specific conditions at different periods of time and for different communes and brigades, specific analyses should be made of the various factors that affect accumulation and consumption and of the methods for properly distributing the increased gross income between accumulation and consumption.

In practice, in order to handle correctly the relationship between accumulation and consumption, attention must be paid to the following problems:

(1) In a preliminary distribution, not much of the increased gross income should be given to the members, so that proper accumulation can be retained. Should an excessive amount be distributed to some members, others may be tempted to overdraw from the commune, thereby affecting the accumulation of the collective economy. When some members overdraw and cannot repay immediately, the nominal surplus in the accounts can neither be converted into the accumulation of the collective economy nor be used to raise the members' level of consumption or to enlarge reproduction. This is true particularly when the distribution is made in kind. If the distribution is excessive and in commodities that are not daily necessities, or even if they are daily necessities, an excess in the amount of the distribution over the livelihood needs of individual members and their families would not only affect accumulation, but would also inhibit the delivery of more agricultural and subsidiary industrial products to the state. It may even, under certain circumstances, entice some peasants toward capitalism.

(2) Wherever possible, some reserve grain should be re-

tained. Reserve grain belongs generally to the accumulation of means of consumption, and it has important functions in coping with serious natural calamities, in ensuring the consumption of the members, and in ensuring the smooth functioning of enlarged agricultural reproduction. Naturally, the amount of reserve grain must not be excessive; more should be retained in a bumper year, while less or even no reserve may be retained in a lean year.

(3) At present, no depreciation fund for fixed assets has been established in the rural communes. This will not only give rise to confusion in inventory, but will also increase auditing costs or reduce labor productivity. Moreover, it would be hard to determine gross income and to handle the relationship between accumulation and consumption, as well as the relationship between simple reproduction and enlarged reproduction. Because of the lack of a depreciation fund, it would be difficult to replenish livestock and farm implements, especially when large farm implements are urgently needed. Thus, on the basis of enhancing the level of operation and management, the depreciation fund should be created gradually, and measures for deducting depreciation on plowing animals, farm implements, and other fixed assets should be adopted. The specific method may be geared to the annual distribution; depreciation may be included in the production cost and may be covered in production costs. With the depreciation fund, it will be possible to ensure the timely replacement of fixed assets. This will be conducive to undertaking enlarged agricultural reproduction on the basis of ensuring simple reproduction.

## 53. Province and Ministry of Light Industry Joint Investigation Group Argues for "Multiple Utilization" to Reduce Waste (Source 9, pp. 151-161) December 1970

Thanks to multiple utilization, the "waste materials" of

the past have now become a treasure. Formerly, the plant spent hundreds of thousands of yuan every year to carry the cinders, silt, and iron pyrite slag out of the plant and to dump them into the sea. Now they are the raw materials for making cinder bricks, cement, carbon steel, and cast iron. Since last year, utilization of these cinders, silt, and slag has created a wealth of several hundred thousand yuan for the state.

As a result of multiple utilization, the potential of material resources has been fully tapped, and one thing can be used for many purposes. Sugarcane, the principal raw material of this plant, is used in making sugar, and its "bagasse" and "waste solution" can be used to make more than 10 kinds of light industrial and chemical products. For instance, bagasse can be used to make paper pulp boards, glossy paper, packing paper, and furfural. The "waste solution" left from the pulp can be used to produce mucilage. The "waste syrup" can be used to make alcohol, yeast, "702" insecticide, etc.

As a result of large-scale multiple utilization, the potential of the equipment has been fully tapped, and one machine can be used to do many jobs, instead of being used for one particular purpose as in the past. For example, the pulp-making equipment can be used in making paper pulp and making artificial fiber pulp; the sugar-making equipment is used to press sugarcane during the sugar production season, the limekiln and the settling equipment are used to produce mild calcium carbonate, the boiling and refining equipment is used to produce microcrystalline fiberin and "702" insecticide when the sugar-production season has passed. In this way, the sugar-making plant operates throughout the year; its production is not suspended even though sugarcane pressing may temporarily stop.

Large-scale multiple utilization brings the subjective initiative of man into full play. Thus workers with specialized skills can do other jobs as well. For example, in the sugarcane-pressing season, the workers engage themselves in making sugar; at other times, they are engaged in the production of mild calcium carbonate, lime, and charcoal. The brewers make alcohol and yeast; but they also know how to make dry ice and "702" insecticide. The mechanics not only make and repair equipment but also are capable of making coke and refining steel and iron. This makes it possible not only to solve the problem of the multiple utilization of most of the manpower but also to substantially raise the productivity of labor. In 1969, the productivity of full-time labor doubled over the early period after the establishment of this plant. What is more important, large-scale multiple utilization helps raise, with greater, faster, and better results at lower costs, a group of "versatile workers" who have the revolutionary spirit of self-reliance and hard struggle.

Now the whole plant not only has completely changed the former practice of letting the sugar refinery carry out production for half of a year, while it lies idle for the other half, but also has broken the barrier between trades. It has turned into a comprehensive factory that is capable of turning out such light industrial products as sugar, paper, and artificial fiber pulp, together with steel, iron, industrial chemicals, medicines, building materials, and polycrystalline silicon.

Practice shows that large-scale multiple utilization is a solid means to carry out Chairman Mao's great strategic directive "Be prepared for war, be prepared for natural disasters, and do everything for the people"; an effective measure for achieving greater, faster, and better results at lower costs in building socialism; an important way of developing new raw material resources and carrying out the policy of increasing production and practicing economy.

## Smash the Argument Against "Departing from One's Own Line" and Conduct Multiple Utilization for the Revolutionary Cause

Chiang-men Sugarcane Industrial Chemicals Plant is a modernized factory completed and put into operation in early 1959. In the past decade or so, it has gone through a violent struggle between the two ideologies and the two lines over the problem of whether efforts should be made to produce by-products and how to produce by-products.

When the plant was established, the broad masses of workers and cadres of this plant, under the guidance of the general line of "going all out, aiming high, and achieving greater, faster, and better results at lower costs in building socialism" charted by Chairman Mao, unfolded scientific experiments in multiple utilization and used the cinders, silt, and slag to make a number of products. However, poisoned by renegade, hidden traitor, and scab Liu Shao-ch'i's counterrevolutionary revisionist line, some people held that "conducting multiple utilization meant departing from one's own line." Others even regarded cinders, slag, and silt as a "burden" and asked for 700,000 yuan and several hundred thousand tons of rolled steel from the state to make three freighters and two tugboats for dumping these cinders, silt, and slag into the sea. Influenced by the erroneous idea of "departing from one's own line," cement production was conducted by fits and starts; the cement workshop went into operation when cement was needed, otherwise it lay idle. With regard to other items of production, some were neglected, and others were directed in a wrong way and suspended soon afterwards.

After its establishment in autumn 1968, the revolutionary committee of this plant led the workers and cadres of the whole plant to study once again Chairman Mao's relevant teachings. They realized that active development of multiple utilization is geared to realizing combat preparedness and to the policy of increasing production and strictly practicing economy; is required for achieving greater, faster, and better results at lower costs in building socialism; is aimed at striking down imperialism, revisionism, and reaction and at aiding the world revolution. They took multiple utilization as their "own line" in revolution. The workers said: "Multiple utilization is by no means an optional 'sideline' but is a revolutionary 'regular line' that must be followed without fail." They were of this opinion: "Whether we fully utilize the material resources and equipment of our plant to create greater wealth for our state, or continue our one-sided emphasis on immediate conveniences at the expense of long-range results so that various 'waste materials' are regarded as a 'burden' and thrown away once and for all — this is in essence a major problem concerning what banner we hoist, what road we follow, and what line we carry out." After leading the masses to sharply criticize Liu Shao-ch'i's counterrevolutionary revisionist line and such trash as "putting profits in command," the plant revolutionary committee made them reckon the political accounts and economic accounts of large-scale multiple utilization. For example, if this plant's slag were to be used totally to refine steel and iron, this would mean an increase of several thousand tons of steel and iron for the state. This would meet the plant's needs for servicing the equipment and further developing production. This also could be an aid to fraternal factories. On the other hand, if the slag were to be dumped as refuse, tens of thousands of yuan would be needed each year to transport it. After reckoning this account, the broad masses understood that, judging from the overall view of revolution, large-scale multiple utilization was of vital importance politically and economically.

After study and reckoning, the workers and cadres of the whole plant destroyed the argument against "departing from one's own line" and greatly raised their consciousness of conducting multiple utilization. They put forward the slogan "Extract precious things from 'waste materials' and make use of cinders, silt, and slag" and quickly stepped up an earth-shaking multiple-utilization mass movement. Various workshops put forward new multiple-utilization targets based on the actual conditions in their units. After extensive mobilization of the masses and on the basis of democratic discussion, they practiced unified planning and management by levels; critical matters are handled by the whole plant, which concentrates forces to fight a battle of annihilation; day-to-day matters are handled individually by the workshops. Thereby prompt action on such important matters as iron and steel, furfural, and artificial fiber is guaranteed. Workers of the sugar-refining workshop learned that the mild calcium carbonate was used in making paper for printing Chairman Mao's works and that thus the making of this substance was important to the publicizing of Mao Tse-tung Thought. In the spirit of revolution, in addition to an all-out effort to work arduously and ingeniously, they fought night and day to adjust and rebuild the equipment. In only 20 days they succeeded in making this product. This fully demonstrates that the workers have infinite creative powers when they are armed with Mao Tse-tung Thought.

## Crush the Idea of "Seeking Things Ostentatious and Modern," Insist on the Policy of Combining Indigenous and Foreign Methods

Should we seek things ostentatious and modern, or adopt indigenous methods and combine the indigenous with the foreign? This is another outstanding problem in the struggle between the two ideologies and between the two lines in the course of multiple utilization.

Before the Great Proletarian Cultural Revolution, some people sought things ostentatious and modern, and they stressed that multiple utilization must be conducted in a "presentable way." They held that "an indigenous enterprise formed by grouping different things together" was incompatible with the appearance of a large modern factory. At that time, the workers demanded an expansion of cement production. They sent to the headquarters of the plant a plan, which combined indigenous and foreign methods. The person in charge of the plant not only did not support them but, on the contrary, he organized others to draw up another plan for a big and modern project, which required a large investment and a great deal of equipment. It was difficult to meet this requirement so that this project long remained only a plan on paper. The workers criticized this erroneous idea of seeking things ostentatious and modern and attaching greater importance to foreign things than to indigenous things, and they criticized the bourgeois style of waste and extravagance. Proceeding firmly from reality, they implemented the policy of adopting indigenous methods and combining indigenous and foreign methods. Working with their own hands and bringing with them iron spades and picks and carts, they went everywhere to look for fire-resistant bricks and earthen bricks, cast-off and used steel and iron wares and tubes. The revolutionary committee of the plant vigorously supported this revolutionary action of the workers. After almost 100 days of arduous fighting, the workers expanded the cement workshop by indigenous and foreign methods. This incident vividly demonstrates that the style of seeking things ostentatious and modern invariably brings about poor results and that the combination of indigenous and foreign methods brings about greater, faster, and better results at lower costs.

Chairman Mao pointed out: "Historical experience merits attention. A line and a viewpoint must be discussed constantly and repeatedly. It won't do to discuss them over with a few people; they must be made known to the broad revolutionary mass." Some time ago, when an experiment was conducted to use reeds in making artificial fiber pulp, some people showed a tendency to seek things ostentatious and modern. They suggested building a new 5-story building, making a 10-ch'ih-deep pool by digging 5 ch'ih below ground for storing the pulp, and installing another 14 units of mechanical equipment. According to this plan, an investment of 700,000 yuan and 70 tons of rolled steel would be needed, and it would take half a year to complete the project. When this plan was assigned to the masses for discussion, the workers sharply criticized it as "putting on new shoes to walk the old road." They put forward another plan in light of their practical experience: no factory building and pulp-storing pool were to be built; the potential of the equipment in use was to be tapped; not one unit of new equipment was to be bought. This plan brought the potential of the existing factory building and equipment into full play, cutting investment by 50 percent and materials by 40 percent. Moreover, production started one month ahead of schedule. Practice shows that there is no construction without destruction. Only by giving the masses free rein and criticizing the erroneous ideas of seeking things ostentatious and modern will it be possible to make the correct policy of adopting indigenous methods and combining indigenous methods with foreign methods materialize and will it be possible for multiple utilization to advance triumphantly in the direction pointed out by Chairman Mao.

## Working with Our Own Hands, Not Stretching Out Our Hands for Aid

In conducting multiple utilization, should we work with our own hands or stretch out our hands for aid? This question reflects the struggle between the two ideologies and between the two lines.

In the past, when multiple utilization was suggested, people hurriedly made reports, asking for investment and materials and equipment from the higher level. They sent in applications, waited, and their applications were turned down. After its establishment, the revolutionary committee of this plant organized the workers to carry out revolutionary mass criticism in light of this plant's failure to conduct multiple utilization. It linked this criticism with the higher level and the grassroots level, eliminated "Liu's poison," overcame the lazy man's idea of asking for aid in everything, and established the noble ambition of striving for prosperity through self-reliance.

Upon deciding to turn out an important new product, some said: "One locality needed an investment of several million yuan and took two to three years to turn out this new product." Others said: "To do the same thing, we need at least several hundred thousand yuan, if not several millions. It won't do if we don't have a few dozen tons of rolled steel!" But the workers, armed with Mao Tse-tung Thought, said unanimously: "We shall go forward if conditions permit. If conditions are lacking, we shall create them!" They worked in a united effort and fought arduously. Eventually, this new product was produced successfully after an expenditure of less than 20,000 yuan and in only 70 days. The workers learned an unforgettable lesson, saying, "We succeed if we work with our own hands. We fail if we stretch out our hands for aid. This is an infallible truth."

In order to put the policy of "self-reliance" and "hard struggle" into effect in every concrete situation, this plant suggested three points in conducting multiple utilization:

1. Raw materials should come from the resources of the plant, chiefly by making use of cinders, silt, and slag and other waste materials of the plant.

2. Factory space, equipment, and materials needed in conducting multiple utilization should come from existing facilities of the plant. For example, the workshop for producing polycrystalline silicon was a renovation of the toilet room and lounge in the sugar-making workshop.

3. Construction of goods for multiple utilization and processing of parts for the equipment should be done through

our own efforts. For example, the 3-cubic-meter blast furnace, the half-ton electric furnace for refining steel, and the steel mill were built through our own efforts. Construction for artificial fiber pulp and starch alcohol was done and the necessary equipment installed by several workshops in a joint effort.

If we adhere to these points, we can do more work with less money at a higher speed and with greater results. For example, in making the "702" insecticide, because the brewing and sugar-making equipment was fully utilized, only four days were needed to build up the workshop and to start production of this insecticide. The insecticide produced was sufficient for use in more than 25 million mou of farmland, giving impetus to the increased production of farm crops. It was warmly commended by the departments concerned and by the broad masses of poor and lower-middle peasants.

## Emphasize Practical Results, Avoid the "Touch and Go" Style

Should we seek vain glory or should we work for practical results? Should we attempt a thing superficially and give up, or hold on to it to the end? This is another manifestation of the struggle between the two ideologies and between the two lines in the course of multiple utilization.

In the past, under the pernicious influence of Liu Shao-ch'i's counterrevolutionary revisionist line of "factories run by experts," the technical know-how of this plant was in the hands of a few technicians. They made experiments behind closed doors and ignored the broad masses of workers, so that theory was alienated from practice and experiment from production. Some technicians had not been remolded ideologically; nor had they adopted the attitude of wholeheartedly serving the people. When their experiment succeeded, they put it aside and no longer paid attention to it.

Now the workers have taken hold of the technical know-how, and three-in-one groups with old workers as the mainstay and with revolutionary cadres and revolutionary technicians taking part have been set up at various levels from the headquarters of the plant to the workshop. They join together to suggest items for multiple utilization, blazing the trail and creating experience. Scientific experiment is closely integrated with production. This makes it possible to put into operation each item of multiple utilization that has been proved successful, and possible to consolidate and develop each item that has been put into operation.

To get a solid grip on multiple utilization, this plant also pays attention to strengthening its leadership, draws up an over-all plan according to the principle of multiple undertakings with emphasis on one line of trade, and arranges and develops multiple utilization on the basis of fulfillment of the state's production plans, so that the principal line of trade and the various sidelines may promote each other. While the material resources of this plant are being used, attention is paid to the needs of other units so as to provide mass coordination and to ensure the fraternal units of a supply of raw materials.

While conducting multiple utilization, the plant pays attention to bringing the workers' spirit as master of the house into full play and earnestly strengthens economic accounting of the products for multiple utilization. From the headquarters to the workshops of the plant, three-in-one groups with workers as the mainstay and with revolutionary cadres and business and technical management personnel taking part are set up throughout to supervise business. Under the leadership of the plant's revolutionary committee, these groups take charge of strengthening business management of by-products. As a result, various kinds of multiple utilization products improve continually in quantity and in quality, and the consumption of raw materials and production costs drop continually. Attention is paid to safety in production and prevention of accidents. In this way, multiple utilization is conducted in an earth-shaking manner and in a down-to-earth manner.

Practice of large-scale multiple utilization by Chiang-men Sugarcane Industrial Chemicals Plant amply testifies to the fact that only socialist revolution, particularly the Great Proletarian Cultural Revolution, can break through the obstacles that fetter the enthusiasm of the masses, can push the broad masses into the vast fields of struggle against Nature and make them masters of multiple utilization and great Nature.

## 54. Group of Theorists at a Branch of the People's Bank Discusses the Importance of Money in a Socialist Economy (Source 6, p. 85) August 18, 1975

Under socialist conditions, as money is still the general representation of wealth, there will be the idea of going after money. Thus, money will stimulate the desire of the new and old bourgeoisie and people more seriously affected by capitalist ideas for the accumulation of wealth through stealing or illegally taking possession of more money, and turn them into the termites of the socialist system of public ownership.

Owing to the existence of money, certain leading cadres of enterprises and units who have not correctly oriented the ideological line will promote "material incentives" and "put profits in command." If allowed to develop, enterprises based on the socialist system of public ownership will actually be turned into enterprises based on the capitalist system of private ownership.

Owing to the existence of money, the new and old bourgeois elements could once again turn money into capital, operate underground factories, lend money at usury rates, and practice manipulation and speculation. They usually adopt the method of "dragging out and storming in" to grasp the leadership in certain units, steal and sell the material resources of the state or the collective, seek profits by unethical means, and swallow up the fruits of labor of the masses of the people.

It can be seen from the several aspects described above that it is still possible for money to disintegrate the socialist system of public ownership. To be sure, whether or not this possibility will be translated into reality has to depend on other conditions. The decisive key lies in whether or not there is a Marxist line and whether or not the leadership is in the hands of genuine Marxists. As long as we resolutely implement Chairman Mao's revolutionary line and restrict bourgeois rights in the aspect of exchange by means of money under the dictatorship of the proletariat we can bring into better play the historical role played by money at the present stage, turn money into a tool of socialist revolution and construction, and constantly consolidate and develop the socialist system of public ownership.

Since the founding of the People's Republic, we have adopted a series of restrictive measures toward bourgeois rights in the aspect of exchange by means of money, for example, the building of a unified monetary system, the exercise of centralized control over issue of money, credit and loans, settlement of accounts and cash by state banks, the dealing of blows at manipulation and speculation, and the prohibition by law of the conversion of money into capital. Meanwhile, we energetically propagate communist ideas, criticize revisionism, capitalist tendencies, and the idea of bourgeois rights. From now on, we must study even more diligently Marxism on the theory of the dictatorship of the proletariat, more thoroughly understand the question of exercising dictatorship over the bourgeoisie on the basis of combining theory with practice, more consciously restrict the bourgeois rights existing in the aspect of exchange by means of money in the practice of work in the future, criticize the idea of bourgeois rights, and consolidate and develop the socialist system of public ownership so that the tasks of the dictatorship of the proletariat can be further implemented.

## 55. Theory Group at a District Office of the People's Bank Discusses Money and Exchange in a Socialist Economy (Source 26, pp. 63-64) October 22, 1975

The line is fundamental in restricting bourgeois rights. We must conscientiously study the theory of the dictatorship of the proletariat in close relation to reality, intensify investigation and study, make a concrete analysis of bourgeois rights in the aspect of exchange by means of money, "study accurately the scope of this kind of phenomenon and find out a suitable method (not repression, or to be more explicit, not prohibition) for the state to exercise supervision and control" (Collected Works of Lenin, Vol. XXXII, p. 375). Only thus can we better adhere to the basic line and various policies of the Party, including all economic policies, restrict bourgeois rights, weaken step by step and even sweep away the soil engendering capitalism and the bourgeoisie, and carry out to the letter the task of consolidating the dictatorship of the proletariat down to the grass roots.

Some people say, "To restrict bourgeois rights in the aspect of exchange by means of money, it is necessary to issue fewer currency notes and cut down the volume of money in circulation." This is a muddled concept. Restriction is preconditioned by recognition of its existence. In actual fact, within a given period of time, owing to the constant development of socialist production, the constant expansion of commodity circulation, the gradual improvement of people's living standards, and the constant increase of actual income, the absolute volume of money in circulation should increase correspondingly rather than diminish. Marx's formula on determining the volume of money in circulation according to the sum total of the price of commodities waiting to be put into circulation and the rate of money circulation is still applicable today. Simply cutting down the volume of money in circulation will not enable us to attain the goal of restricting bourgeois rights in the aspect of exchange by means of money, but will on the contrary restrict the role of exchange by means of money in serving socialist construction and serving the people. Therefore, the need of funds to help socialist construction in conformity with the Party's policies, and with state planning, should be resolutely made available. At the same time, it is necessary to restrict rigidly the investment of money at variance with the policies and not provided in plans, to criticize and repudiate incessantly the idea of bourgeois rights, to broaden the propaganda of communist ideas, and to wage resolute struggle against the spontaneous tendency toward capitalism.

Some people say, "The restriction of bourgeois rights in the aspect of exchange by means of money is economic work and the business of banks." This "theory of having nothing to do with oneself" is actually harmful. The restriction of bourgeois rights bears on combating and guarding against revisionism and preventing capitalist restoration, and is also an important question that must be made known to the whole Party and the people of the whole country. To be sure, exchange by means of money is an economic activity, and the bank is the organ responsible for the issue and control of money. However, we all use money and deal with money every day. Hence, how we treat and use money and how we treat the principle of commodity exchange reflect the struggle between the two kinds of ideology and world outlook. The dictatorship of the proletariat is the dictatorship of the masses. It will not do just to rely on a few people and a few departments. Only when the broad masses have mastered the theory of the dictatorship of the proletariat and consciously restrict bourgeois rights can they deal a more effective blow to the sabotage activities of the bourgeoisie and daily consolidate the dictatorship of the proletariat.

Exchange by means of money is a historical category that will be sent to the museum of history in the future. Lenin once solemnly pointed out with the sense of pride of a Communist that after the victory of the revolutionary cause of the proletariat throughout the world, "gold will be used to build some public lavatories in the streets of a few of the largest cities in the world" (Selected Works of V. I. Lenin, Vol. IV, p. 578). He has thus announced that money is doomed to perish in the end and pointed out that communism is bound to triumph throughout the world in the brilliant future. With unbounded confidence, let us advance triumphantly toward the magnificent prospects pointed out by Marxism-Leninism-Mao Tsetung Thought!

## 56. People's Daily Correspondent Reports on the Supervisory Function of a People's Bank Office (Source 5, pp. 132-135) November 9, 1975

The Ta-ma Road Office of the Changchun Municipal Bank in Kirin Province situated on a busy main street has a total of 131 workers. In the business district covered by this office, there are 364 industrial and commercial enterprises and over 35,000 workers households. For many years, the office workers adhered to the orientation of running socialist enterprises, firmly resisted capitalism, and criticized the tendencies toward capitalism. This won the universal praise of everyone. Through the supervisory function of the bank, they linked concrete business work with the goal of consolidating the dictatorship of the proletariat and strictly carried out the Party's policy and the state's financial and economic systems, thus making a contribution to the further consolidation of the dictatorship of the proletariat.

To meet the needs of the business district with its great majority of industrial and commercial enterprises opening as usual on Sundays, this office, beginning in the second half of 1970, persisted in operating as usual on Sundays. For the 250 or more Sundays in five years, an average daily cash receipt of over ¥ 180,000 was registered, which helped accelerate the balancing of accounts to the amount of ¥ 1,500,000. Because of the continuously strengthened revolutionary sense of responsibility on the part of the workers and their serious sense of responsibility in work performance, the errors made by accountants and cashiers were respectively 76 and 95 percent lower than the permissible percentage stipulated by the higher-level bank. However, they did not rest content with their considerate services, balancing of accounts, and correct statements of accounts.

In the criticism of Lin Piao and the rectification of the style of work in 1972, the Party branch of the office guided everyone to discuss this incident: A lawless element had availed himself of the unsettled accounts of an abolished unit to carry out speculation and profiteering, and this was not discovered for two years by the personnel of the office. Around this question, everyone studied in depth the Party's basic line and, from the plane of the line, tried to recognize the great significance of banking. They realized that a bank was not just an economic organization but a "bookkeeping organ" taking care of the economy of the state, and a tool of the proletariat for exercising dictatorship over the bourgeoisie on the financial front. If attention was paid only to receipts and payments, deposits, money counting and bookkeeping, and no attention was paid to class struggle in the economic sphere, the profiteers would have loopholes to exploit.

Thereafter, they doggedly put proletarian politics in command, combined political work with economic work, and made a political analysis of economic phenomena. In work practice, they gradually summed up the experience in taking the three steps of study, memorizing, and analysis: (1) Study — to study the theory of the dictatorship of the proletariat; (2) Memorizing — to bear firmly in mind the Party's policy and financial and economic systems; (3) Analysis — to analyze the sources of money deposited by enterprises, the purposes for which the amounts withdrawn are intended, and the relations between accounts involved in a transfer.

In the course of conducting business activities, this office resolutely hits out at those acts of making use of money for speculative purposes. It adheres to principle and keeps a close watch for the state over those erroneous practices among the people that run counter to financial and economic rules of discipline. Last year, for the sake of carrying out capital construction not provided in its plan, an enterprise sold a part of supplies allocated by the state under the unified program. Instead of depositing the proceeds realized therefrom in the bank, it even withdrew cash from the bank. In an analysis of the lowest cash deposit this enterprise was allowed to maintain, the office discovered the problem and made an investigation. With the approval of the bank at a higher level and in accordance with the provisions of the state, it sternly dealt with this enterprise which violated the rules of financial and economic discipline. At the same time, the office took the initiative to join this enterprise in calling a general meeting to criticize Lin Piao and Confucius, thus raising the awareness of the masses, further improving the relations between the bank and the enterprise, and strengthening the revolutionary unity between the two units.

Through such daily routine work as accepting money for deposit, granting loans and balancing accounts, this office in the past few years blocked in all 964 irrational payments, resolutely hit out at profiteering activities, and upheld the financial and economic systems of the state. A person in control of money said with deep feeling, "I have been handling money for over twenty years in the bank. Only through study do I understand that without grasping class struggle and the two-line struggle in exchange by means of money, we cannot handle money properly."

Chairman Mao said, "To develop the economy and insure supplies is a general guideline for our economic and financial work." For several years, the Ta-ma Road Office oriented itself toward production to serve and support production, and persisted in staying at selected spots to help factories and shops. It helped enterprises in taking stock and tapping the potentialities of material resources and funds, and carried out work in the units served with very good results.

To help the Changchun Municipal Bicycle Tire Factory lay in urgently needed small-sized equipment, this branch on its own initiative offered it a loan of ¥95,000. This enabled this factory to double its output, and provided the market with increased supply. Based on the actual needs of the Changchun Municipal Nonmetallic Material Experimental Machine Plant, the office loaned it ¥16,000, and helped it buy spare parts and vacuum pumps. This enabled the factory to assemble and supply 16 units of paper-sheet molding machines and to activate funds in the amount of 160,000 yuan. Through banking business, the branch acted as an intermediate for promoting industrial and commercial relations and helped the Hsin-sheng Rubber Plant of Changchun market its accumulated stock of 500,000 pairs of rubber shoes. This enabled the plant to solve the problem of urgently needed funds to meet production expenses, pay taxes and surrender profits to the higher levels, and repay its loan.

Through studying Chairman Mao's important instruction on the question of theory in association with summing up work, this office further understands that in order to support and develop the socialist economy, it is necessary to fight the tendencies toward capitalism and constantly criticize the revisionist enterprise-building line. Over a period of time there appeared in the banking system the tendency toward "abolishing supervision" and "keeping one's hands off." Some people even said that since those industrial and commercial enterprises dealing with the bank were either state-run or collective-run undertakings of the economy based on socialist system of ownership, no matter how much money was allocated them, such money was spent within the framework of socialism. But the majority of comrades did not see things this way, and they said, "Accounts must be kept with an eye on the line, and money must be managed with the key link grasped. In the matter of receipts and payments, there is the two-line struggle!" Through discussion, they distinguished between the right and the wrong line and rectified the tendency toward "keeping one's hands off." They were unanimously of the view that it was necessary to adhere to principle in work and boldly wage an untiring struggle against acts running counter to the state's policies and financial and economic systems.

The emulsified oil produced by a community-operated collective-owned factory was of inferior quality but it was sold at a high price to an enterprise owned by the whole people. At the time of checking the use of enterprise funds, the office discovered this problem, and opportunely reported the finding to a higher level. The relevant departments took steps to check the capitalist tendency adopted by this factory to go after profits by blindly producing emulsified oil. Meanwhile, this factory was helped to switch over to the manufacture of lead powder, a new product urgently needed in the province. The office also took the initiative in inviting technicians to give this factory technical guidance, and helped it establish production, supply, and marketing links. Owing to the energetic efforts of the workers of this factory, the new product of lead powder was very soon successfully trial-manufactured and put on-stream. The working masses praised this way of doing things by the bank as "cutting down the capitalist 'money tree' and planting a socialist 'evergreen pine!'"

In its business activities, this office had a relatively clear idea about what to support and what to restrict. This was inseparable from its paying attention to investigation and study. Young antlers are a famous and valuable medicine of Kirin Province. In the second half of 1973, the office found that in the last ten days of September, the Changchun Medicine Purchase and Supply Station in this business district had only fulfilled 33 percent of the purchase plan for young antlers. This affected the realization of its credit plan. In recent years, since deer-raising made rapid progress in Kirin Province, why was it that young antlers could not be bought? They therefore went deep into the place of origin and among the consumers to make careful investigations and studies. It turned out that certain pharmaceutical laboratories adopted the method of raising the grades and prices to make direct purchases from the antler-producing areas. The comrades of this office waged a resolute struggle against this act that violated the state's financial and economic policies. They also took the initiative to repeatedly publicize the Party's policies among those units that violated the financial and economic systems. Meanwhile, they put forward to the relevant departments concrete suggestions for strengthening of the unified purchase and marketing of young antlers. Later, relevant departments at the higher level strengthened control over young antlers and restored the regular channel for the circulation of antler products. In 1974, this medicine purchase and supply station overfulfilled its young antler purchase plan by 7 percent.

# Sources

1. Anhwei Provincial Revolutionary Committee Writing Team, "Taking Food Grains as the Key Link, Vigorously Develop Economic Crops." People's Daily (Jen-min jih-pao), April 7, 1971. Translated in Chinese Economic Studies (hereafter CES), VI:3 (Spring 1973).

2. "Carry Out the Great Principle of 'Developing the Economy and Ensuring Supplies' — Investigation Report on the Chien-hsin Service Group of the Fushun Municipal Branch of the People's Bank of China, Liaoning." Red Flag (Hung-ch'i), 1971, No. 2. CES, VI:2 (Winter 1972-73).

3. Cassou, Pierre-Henri, "Le Systeme Monétaire Chinois," Le Bulletin de l'Economie et des Finances, October-December 1973. CES, IX:4 (Summer 1976). Published by permission of the author and publisher.

4. "China's State Department Stores Hold Meeting to Criticize Teng Hsiao-p'ing." New China News Agency — English, July 16, 1976. Survey of People's Republic of China Press, No. 6145 (July 28, 1976).

5. "Fight for the Strict Enforcement of the State's Financial and Economic Systems — An Investigation on the Strengthening of the Supervisory Function of the Ta-ma Road Office of the Changchun Municipal Bank." People's Daily, November 9, 1975. Survey of People's Republic of China Press, No. 6009 (January 7, 1976).

6. Group of Theorists of the Industrial Credit Department in the Peking Branch of the People's Bank of China, "Correctly Recognize the Essence of Money and Its Historical Role — Insights Obtained from the Study of the Section 'Distribution' in Anti-Dühring, Part III." Kuang-ming Daily (Kuang-ming jih-pao), August 18, 1975. Survey of People's Republic of China Press, No. 5928 (September 4, 1975).

7. Hsia Li-chih, "Striking Contrast between Two Different Economic Systems." Red Flag, 1974, No. 11. Peking Review, 1974, No. 48. CES, IX:4 (Summer 1976).

8. Hung Yin-hang, "A Great Victory for Mao Tse-tung's Thought on the Financial and Monetary Front — China's People's Currency [jen-min pi] Has Become an Exceptionally Stable Currency of the World." People's Daily, July 6, 1969. CES, III:3 (Spring 1970).

9. Joint Investigation Group of the Kwangtung Provincial Revolutionary Committee and the Ministry of Light Industry, "Develop Production in Depth and in Breadth — Investigation Report on Multiple Utilization Conducted in Chiang-men Sugarcane Industrial Chemicals Plant, Kwangtung." Red Flag, 1970, No. 12. CES, V:2 (Winter 1971-72).

10. Kao Hsiang, "On People's Savings under Socialism." Economic Research (Ching-chi yen-chiu), 1964, No. 6. CES, I:2 (Winter 1967-68).

11. Kirin Provincial Revolutionary Committee Writing Group, "Class Struggle in the Field of Socialist Construction and Economics — Criticizing the Revisionist Economic Theory of Sun Yeh-fang." Red Flag, 1970, No. 2. CES, IV:4 (Summer 1971).

12. Ko Cheng, "Politics in Command of Economics, Revolution in Command of Production." Red Flag, 1969, Nos. 6 and 7. CES, III:3 (Spring 1970).

13. Kung Hsiao-wen, "We Must Keep Count — In Refutation of 'Statistics Is Useless.'" People's Daily, October 29, 1971. CES, VI:3 (Spring 1973).

14. Kung Hsiao-yen, "Commercial Departments Must Promote the Development of Diversified Economy." People's Daily, August 22, 1975. Survey of People's Republic of China Press, No. 5953 (October 10, 1975).

15. Ma Wen-kuei, "Discussion on the Characteristics, Objectives, and Methods of Planning Socialist Enterprises." Economic Research, 1964, No. 7. CES, I:4 (Summer 1968).

16. Ministry of Commerce Revolutionary Great Criticism Writing Small Group, "The Direction of China's Socialist Commerce." Kuang-ming Daily, November 6, 1970. CES, V:1 (Fall 1971).

17. "People's Bank Savings in China Again Increase by Big Margins." People's Daily, January 23, 1974. CES, VIII:1 (Fall 1974).

18. Revolutionary Mass Criticism Group of Workers in the Peking Knitting Works and Revolutionary Mass Criticism Writing Small Group of the Department of Textile Industries, "Criticism against Sun Yeh-fang and Struggle-Criticism-Transformation on the Economic Front." People's Daily, February 24, 1970. CES, IV:4 (Summer 1971).

19. Shen Cheng-p'ing, "Repulse the Attack of the Bourgeoisie in the Economic Field — An Important Problem in the Struggle-Criticism-Transformation of the Financial and Trade Front." Red Flag, 1969, No. 9. CES, III:3 (Spring 1970).

20. Shen Yung, "The Substance, Characteristics, and System of Socialist Public Finance." Economic Research, 1966, No. 6. CES, II:2 (Winter 1968-69).

21. Shih Ch'e, "A Preliminary Survey of Some Problems of Accumulation and Consumption in Rural Communes." Economic Research, 1965, No. 3. CES, II:1 (Fall 1968).

22. "Socialist Big Fair Is Good — An Investigation of Transformation in Rural Trade Fair in Ha-erh-t'ao Commune, Chang-wu Hsien, Liaoning Province." People's Daily, May 9, 1976. Survey of People's Republic of China Press, No. 6130 (July 7, 1976).

23. State Planning Commission Writing Group, "Launch an Intensive Campaign to Increase Production and Practice Economy on the Industrial Front." Red Flag, 1971, No. 2. CES, VI:1 (Fall 1972).

24. Su Hsing, "The Two-Line Struggle between Socialism and Capitalism in China's Rural Areas after the Land Reform." Economic Research, 1965, No. 8. CES, II:1 (Fall 1968).

25. Supply and Marketing Cooperatives of the Whole Country, Head Office, Mass Criticism Writing Group, "The Rural Economic Policy of the Party Brooks No Sabotage." People's Daily, November 30, 1976. Survey of People's Republic of China Press, No. 6340 (December 15, 1976).

26. Theory Group of the Han-ku District Office of the Tientsin Branch of the People's Bank of China, "Correctly Understand Exchange by Means of Money." People's Daily, October 22, 1975. Survey of People's Republic of China Press, No. 5991 (December 9, 1975).

27. "Two Diametrically Opposed Lines in Building the Economy." People's Daily, August 25, 1967. CES, I:2 (Winter 1967-68).

28. State Planning Commission, "Great Guiding Principle for Socialist Construction — Commemorating the First Anniversary of the Passing of the Great Leader and Teacher Chairman Mao." People's Daily, September 12, 1977. Peking Review (abridged translation), 1977, No. 39.

# About the Editor

A graduate of Pennsylvania State University, Gordon Bennett received his M.A. and Ph.D. from the University of Wisconsin. He is currently an Associate Professor of Political Science at the University of Texas at Austin.

Dr. Bennett is the author of Red Guard: The Political Biography of Dai Siao-ai (1971 with Ronald Montaperto), Yundong: Mass Campaigns in Chinese Communist Leadership (1976), and Huadong: The Story of a Chinese People's Commune (1978). In 1976 he visited the People's Republic of China with the American Hai-ch'eng Earthquake Prediction Study Delegation of the National Academy of Sciences.

For Product Safety Concerns and Information please contact our EU
representative GPSR@taylorandfrancis.com
Taylor & Francis Verlag GmbH, Kaufingerstraße 24, 80331 München, Germany

ngramcontent.com/pod-product-compliance
Content Group UK Ltd.
Milton Keynes, MK11 3LW, UK
2037061126
JK00008B/386

8 1 1 3 8 0 4 5 0 7 1 *